THE ALBERT SHAW LECTURES ON DIPLOMATIC HISTORY, 1933
THE WALTER HINES PAGE SCHOOL OF INTERNATIONAL RELATIONS

AMERICAN DIPLOMACY
DURING THE WORLD WAR

BY

CHARLES SEYMOUR

Provost and Sterling Professor of History
Yale University

BALTIMORE
THE JOHNS HOPKINS PRESS
1934

COMPOSED AND PRINTED IN THE UNITED STATES OF AMERICA
BY THE LORD BALTIMORE PRESS, BALTIMORE, MARYLAND

THE ALBERT SHAW LECTURES ON DIPLOMATIC HISTORY

Under the Auspices of the

WALTER HINES PAGE SCHOOL OF INTERNATIONAL RELATIONS

By the liberality of Albert Shaw, Ph.D., of New York City, the Johns Hopkins University has been enabled to provide an annual course of lectures on Diplomatic History. The Lectures, while continuing to be included in the regular work of the Department of History, have since the establishment of the Page School of International Relations, in 1930, been placed under its auspices.

AMERICAN DIPLOMACY
DURING THE WORLD WAR

LONDON: HUMPHREY MILFORD
OXFORD UNIVERSITY PRESS

To

EDWARD MANDELL HOUSE
Counsellor and Idealist

Wise, Courageous, Unselfish

PREFACE

The chapters which follow are not intended to constitute a comprehensive diplomatic history of the United States from 1914 to 1918. Originally composed to form a course of lectures, they are restricted to a study of the development of American policy as related to the European belligerents. Since that development was determined in all its large aspects by President Wilson, the scope of the book is even more closely restricted. It is essentially a study of the process by which Wilson, at first determined that the United States could and must stand apart from embattled Europe, was forced by the intolerable conditions of neutrality to bring America into the war and to promote a plan of international organization for peace.

I am under especial obligation to those participants in the diplomatic drama who, two decades later, have been willing to read my manuscript and to make critical comments upon the statements and conclusions contained therein: Count Bernstorff, Commander Carter, Colonel House, the Marquess of Lothian, Colonel Arthur Murray, and Sir William Wiseman. Their comments, as well as those of the anonymous German Navy archivist, are printed in the form of footnotes, with the understanding that in each case they express personal and entirely unofficial opinions. They represent varying shades of belief, not always favorable to my own conclusions. Coming from those who are entitled to speak from their own diplomatic experience their historical value is obvious.

It is with pleasure and gratitude that I acknowledge my indebtedness to those who have facilitated my studies and assisted in the preparation of the manuscript and the reading of proof: to the authorities of the Sterling Memorial Library in Yale University, especially the Librarian, Professor Andrew Keogh; to M. Pierre Renouvin of the *Musée de la Guerre* in Vincennes; to my assistant in the House Collection, Miss Helen Reynolds; and to my wife.

C. S.

Yale University,
February 8, 1934.

CONTENTS

ABBREVIATIONS

Bernstorff: Bernstorff, Count Johann Heinrich, *My Three Years in America.* New York: Scribner, 1920.

F.R.: U. S. Department of State. *Papers relating to the Foreign Relations of the United States.* Supplements. *The World War: 1914, 1915, 1916, 1917, 1918. Russia: 1918.* Edited by Tyler Dennett and Joseph V. Fuller. Washington: Government Printing Office, 1928-1933. 12 v.

G.D.: Carnegie Endowment for International Peace, Division of International Law. *Official German Documents relating to the World War.* New York: Oxford University Press, 1925. 2 v.

Grey: Grey, Edward Grey, *1st Viscount* of Fallodon. *Twenty-Five Years, 1892-1916.* New York: Stokes, 1925. 2 v.

I.P.: Seymour, Charles, *The Intimate Papers of Colonel House.* Boston: Houghton Mifflin, 1926, 1928. 4 v.

Page: Hendrick, Burton J., *Life and Letters of Walter H. Page.* New York: Doubleday, Page, 1922, 1925. 3 v.

P.H.A.: Carnegie Endowment for International Peace, Division of International Law, *Preliminary History of the Armistice. Official Documents published by the German National Chancellery by order of the Ministry of State.* Edited by James Brown Scott. New York: Oxford University Press, 1925.

Spring Rice: Gwynn, Stephen, *ed., The Letters and Friendships of Sir Cecil Spring Rice.* Boston: Houghton Mifflin, 1929. 2 v.

Ursachen: Die Ursachen des Deutschen Zusammenbruchs im Jahre 1918. [Das Werk des Untersuchungsausschusses der Deutschen Verfassunggebenden Nationalversammlung und des Deutschen Reichstages 1919-1926. Vierte Reihe. Dritter band.] Berlin: Deutsche Verlagsgesellschaft für Politik und Geschichte, 1925.

Y.H.C.: Yale House Collection. Unpublished papers of Colonel House in the Sterling Memorial Library, Yale University.

Chapter I

BACKGROUNDS

1

" Few Europeans," writes Henry Wickham Steed, " realize how extraordinary an event was the American intervention in the war." [1] The statement would doubtless apply also to most Americans. Set against the background of American ideals, traditions, and prejudices, it is astounding that the United States should have intervened in a European struggle; not merely intervened but should have poured millions of men and dollars into the trans-Atlantic stream that ran from New York to Brest. Not less astounding was the revolution in national policy, whether temporary or the authentic origin of a new world order of the future, which brought the United States into close political coöperation with the great powers of Europe and gave to an American president, for the moment at least, the dominating influence in the world. Yet, as the historian reviews the succession of determining events, step by step, the impossible becomes almost the unavoidable. So profound and far-reaching were the effects of the European war, even while the struggle was in progress, that it seemed wholly natural that this nation of the western world should intervene decisively in the affairs of the eastern. A sense of inevitableness, in which with rare exceptions all shades of American opinion were merged, made people forget how inherently improbable it all was.

[1] Henry Wickham Steed, *Through Thirty Years,* II, 161.

It is true that certain Americans, notably Richard Olney and Theodore Roosevelt, had realized and sought to make the nation realize, that the United States as a world power was bound to enter world politics. " We have no choice, we people of the United States," said Roosevelt in 1907, " as to whether or not we shall play a great part in the world. That has been determined for us by fate, by the march of events." [2] Our traditional interests in the Caribbean and in the Far East were intensified by the results of the war with Spain and the cutting of the Panama Canal. Political contacts with European rivals or partners in those regions could not be avoided. The United States arrived in the Extreme Orient as a territorial power, at a moment of crisis when, for the sake of its own material welfare as well as John Hay's Golden Rule, it was compelled to participate in the common counsel and common action evoked by the anæmia of China. In the same decade the American frontier disappeared. We entered upon a burst of intensive productive industrialism which resulted in rapid expansion of foreign trade relationships. Henceforth the rest of the world mattered a great deal to America.

The inevitable change in American policy, characteristic of a transitional period, was indicated clearly during the Roosevelt administration: by his mediation between the Russians and Japanese, by his despatch of the United States fleet on its circumnavigating cruise, most significantly by his intervention in the Algeciras Conference. Hay's coöperation with European powers in the Far East was in a

[2] Cited in Max Farrand, *The Development of the United States,* p. 332.

field long regarded as one of peculiar importance for America. But it was a new development for an American president to regard the European balance of power as his business, to utilize his position and prestige, as did Roosevelt before and during the Algeciras Conference, to assist in the maintenance of peace on the continent of Europe.[3]

How far Woodrow Wilson appreciated the change that was coming over American foreign policy when he assumed office is not clear. It is certain that he was primarily interested in domestic problems, and that he had no sympathy with the dollar diplomacy which in his opinion had motivated our Far Eastern policy. But his Mobile address indicated anxiety to coöperate with other nations, and his private negotiations with Great Britain regarding the Panama Tolls and Mexico taught him the practical value of such coöperation. Wilson was doubtless influenced by Bryan's enthusiasm for general arbitration treaties, which although conceived on a negative basis brought the United States more clearly into the center of the family of nations. From London, Ambassador Page urged the necessity of developing a feeling of close solidarity among the Anglo-Saxon peoples and argued persuasively the advantages of an understanding with the British that might have the effects if not the form of an alliance. Even more far-reaching were the ideas of Colonel House, who put before Wilson a plan providing for common action on the part of the United States, Great Britain, and Germany, calculated to provide protection for the back-

[3] For American influence at the Conference of Algeciras, see Joseph B. Bishop, *Theodore Roosevelt and His Time*, I, 467-505; Allan Nevins, *Henry White*, pp. 261-282.

ward peoples against the imperialistic rivalries of the western powers, as well as to help liquidate the growing Anglo-German hostility. Wilson took this programme so seriously that in the spring of 1914 he sent Colonel House to Germany and England, to lay the foundations of the Anglo-German *détente*. Sinister events moved too rapidly to permit its development, but the Kaiser was sufficiently impressed by the mission to write later that it " almost prevented the World War." [4]

Of such departures from American traditions, the public was no better informed at the time than of Roosevelt's intervention at Algeciras. It is unlikely that it would have approved them. The fear of entanglements with European powers remained lively. The hesitations of the Senate whenever general treaties of arbitration were presented resulted partly, perhaps, from jealousy of its control of diplomacy, but largely from popular suspicion of general agreements of any kind with foreign powers. The double principle of abstention from European politics and the exclusion of European interference from American affairs, roughly crystallized in the popular idea of the Monroe Doctrine, remained for the ordinary citizen the be-all and the end-all of foreign policy. It confirmed Washington's admonition against permanent alliances, which although delivered so long ago that its very adjectives were invariably misquoted, provided a simple chart enshrined in patriotic sanctity.

At the moment of the outbreak of the European war, there was thus little suspicion that it could ever stretch out to

[4] Charles Seymour, *The Intimate Papers of Colonel House*, I, 275 (hereafter cited as *I.P.*).

touch us. It was a tremendous, a tragic, perhaps an economically disastrous, spectacle, but it was after all something in a world different and distant from ours. American sympathies were divided, but opinion was united in the belief that the United States could never be other than a spectator. Wilson's declaration of neutrality was thus a matter of course. His injunction to be " impartial in thought as well as in action," [5] was not so generally accepted, but even those who could not share his dream of moral neutrality had at the time no idea of intervention. Theodore Roosevelt wrote to Sir Edward Grey that if he had been president he would, as the head of a signatory nation of the Hague Treaties, have protested the violation of Belgian neutrality; and Grey in reply allowed himself the luxury of dreaming that such a protest might have stopped the war and perhaps led to a league for the prevention of war. But neither the one nor the other suggested that America should intervene once the struggle had started. " The line that the present United States Government have taken," wrote Grey, " is, of course the natural and expected one." [6] Roosevelt himself, in an article for the *Outlook,* congratulated the country " that we of the western world have been free from the working of the causes which have produced the bitter and vindictive hatred among the great military Powers of the Old World. . . . It is certainly eminently desirable that we should remain entirely neutral, and nothing but urgent need would warrant breaking our neutrality and taking sides one way or the

[5] Speech of August 19, 1914, Baker and Dodd, *The Public Papers of Woodrow Wilson,* I, 158.

[6] Edward Grey, *1st Viscount* of Fallodon, *Twenty-five Years,* II, 144-145 (hereafter cited as *Grey*).

other." [7] From London Ambassador Page wrote: "What a magnificent spectacle our country presents! We escape murder, we escape brutalization. . . ." Ambassador Spring Rice in Washington insisted, on September 12, " I hope and believe that at any rate one part of the world will keep out of it." [8]

The single suggestion of intervention of any kind that Wilson considered seriously came from Dr. Charles W. Eliot of Harvard. In the first week of the war Dr. Eliot expressed a feeling which was to be characteristic of most of America three years later. Writing to Wilson on August 6, he proposed an offensive and defensive alliance between the United States and the Entente powers, including Japan,

" to rebuke and punish Austria-Hungary and Germany for the outrages they are now committing, by enforcing against those two countries non-intercourse with the rest of the world by land and sea. These two Powers have now shown that they are utterly untrustworthy neighbors and military bullies of the worst sort—Germany being far the worse of the two because she has already violated neutral territory. If they are allowed to succeed in their present enterprises, the fear of sudden invasion will constantly hang over all the other European peoples; and the increasing burdens of competitive armaments will have to be borne for another forty years. We shall inevitably share in these losses and miseries. . . . In this cause, and under the changed conditions, would not the people of the United States approve of the abandonment of Washington's advice that this country keep out of European complications? . . . This proposal would involve the taking part by our navy in the blockading process, and, therefore, might entail losses of both life and

[7] *Outlook,* September 23, 1914, p. 169.

[8] Page to House, August 28, 1914; Spring Rice to House, September 12, 1914, *I.P.,* I, 286.

treasure; but the cause is worthy of heavy sacrifices. . . . The United States is clearly the best country to initiate such a proposal. In so doing this country would be serving the general cause of peace, liberty, and goodwill among men." [9]

That Wilson did not regard the plan as entirely Utopian is indicated by the fact that he read Eliot's letter to the Cabinet. But neither the President nor public opinion were ready for it. As Eliot himself confessed in a later letter, the facts concerning the origin of the European conflict were obscure.[10] Wilson in any case would have regarded our intervention at that time, no matter what the motive, as a betrayal of trust. For him peace was an end in itself, and it was the mission of the United States to prove that greatness and peaceableness are not antithetic but complementary. " We are the champions of peace and of concord," he said, " and we should be very jealous of this distinction which we have sought to earn." The tragedy of the war ate into his soul. " I feel the burden of the thing almost intolerable from day to day," he wrote on August 25, " I think largely because there is nothing we can as yet do or even attempt. What a pathetic thing to have this come just as we were so full of hope." [11] But just because of the tragedy which had apparently sent part of the world mad, Wilson felt it all the more incumbent upon the United States to remain sane in order to offer rescue when the time should come. We

[9] Eliot to Wilson, August 6, 1914, *I.P.*, I, 287.

[10] Eliot to Wilson, August 20, 1914, *I.P.*, I, 290-291. In his final letter Eliot agreed that if seven nations by defeating Germany could demonstrate the " destructiveness of the military machine . . . the other nations had better keep out of the conflict."

[11] Wilson to House, August 25, 1914, Yale House Collection (hereafter cited as Y.H.C.).

should not be "thrown off our balance by a war with which we have nothing to do, whose causes cannot touch us, whose very existence affords us opportunities of friendship and disinterested service which should make us ashamed of any thought of hostility or fearful preparation for trouble." [12]

As Grey admitted, the neutral attitude of the United States was originally regarded in Europe as entirely natural. With the exception of Lord Kitchener, whose accurate prophecy of a four-year war seems to have been intuitive rather than rational, everyone believed that the struggle would be short. For the Germans, a lightning victory was essential, it had been promised by the Kaiser, and it was therefore inevitable. The French economist, Leroy-Beaulieu, expressed general opinion when he said that the mere cost of war on the scale waged, would end it in four months. Neither in Europe nor America did they foresee the military deadlock and the extraordinary capacity of the nations to endure it; they did not guess that it could be broken only by the injection of a new force from outside.

2

The establishment of the military deadlock in Europe had results of the first significance, not merely for the European nations, but for America. As the battle-line hardened into trench warfare, each belligerent camp sought new weapons and used them with an ingenuity and an energy that became unpleasant for the bystanders. The war was fought not merely on the battle fields. The Allies were for many months

[12] Annual Address to Congress, December 8, 1914, Baker and Dodd, *op. cit.*, I, 224, 226.

largely dependent upon munitions exported from the United States; as the war continued, American food, raw materials, and credits became of increasing importance. The Central Powers, reasonably well-equipped in the matter of munitions during the early stages of the war, were dependent upon imports for raw materials and food. Without such imports they recognized that it would be impossible for them to continue the struggle indefinitely.

The war of exhaustion thus made of the attitude of America a factor of decisive importance. Both sides looked to the United States for the aid that might lawfully be expected from a neutral, and each hoped to interfere with the aid that might be furnished to the other. They faced a delicate diplomatic problem, for it was vital to conciliate America and yet it seemed equally vital to obstruct American assistance to the enemy. The second process was likely to obscure and nullify the first. Grey stated the problem clearly from the point of view of an Allied diplomat:

" There was one mistake in diplomacy that, if it had been made, would have been fatal to the cause of the Allies. It was carefully avoided. This cardinal mistake would have been a breach with the United States, not necessarily a rupture, but a state of things that would have provoked American interference with the blockade, or led to an embargo on exports of munitions from the United States. Germany, on the other hand, did make this cardinal mistake." [13]

Ambassador von Bernstorff insisted with equal strength upon the importance of keeping the United States neutral; his protests, at least for a time, found support in the German

[13] *Grey,* II, 160. For a confirmation of Grey's opinion by a German authority, see Veit Valentin, *Deutschlands Aussenpolitik,* p. 319.

Foreign Office and exercised decisive influence on German naval policy for more than two years.

But the diplomats on each side were hard pressed by their own military and naval leaders. The Allied Admiralties urged measures that would destroy the economic vitality of the Central Powers. They disposed of the weapon of sea-power and were determined to use it; if neutral rights were touched and neutral protests resulted, it was the diplomats' business to arrange matters. "The Navy acted," wrote Grey, "and the Foreign Office had to find the argument to support the action; it was anxious work. . . . British action preceded British argument; the risk was that action might follow American argument." [14] The Allies drew the cord around the Central Powers always more tightly, as it became increasingly clear that if Germany could not be destroyed on the field of battle she could in the end be strangled. They began with extension of the contraband lists; arrested all food-stuffs and shortly afterwards all commerce whatsoever with Germany; interpreted the doctrine of continuous voyage so as to interrupt trade between neutrals on the suspicion that it was destined for transshipment to Germany; blacklisted firms suspected of trading with the Central Powers; finally rationed the neutrals adjacent to Germany, prohibiting any trade with them beyond the pre-war normal, except upon determined conditions.

The process touched the material interests of American commercials closely, and the Administration was overwhelmed with protests from irate shippers. It also touched the rights of neutrals as defined by international law on the

[14] *Grey*, II, 110.

high seas. How far the material injuries to American trade were offset and more than offset by new opportunities opened to that trade by the war; how far what the Allies called the application of old principles to new conditions was in reality a complete denaturing of international law; such questions must be settled by economic and legal historians. The fact remains that the American Government and people felt themselves attacked as to their rights and interests; attacked, furthermore, in a spot historically tender—commercial goings and comings on the high seas. The sharpness of the diplomatic controversy that followed is reflected in the published official correspondence; the danger of a definite breach with the Allies appears from the private letters and memoirs of the statesmen on each side.

Diplomacy found no solution to this controversy, beyond a *modus vivendi* unsatisfactory both to the Allies and the United States. But the rupture which Grey feared and which he believed would have been fatal to the Allies was prevented, and in large measure by the Germans themselves. The course of German policy was as obviously dictated by circumstances as that of Great Britain and France. At no time, as Bernstorff clearly shows, could the Germans reasonably expect to receive active assistance from the United States. They hoped, however, in the first place to prevent the Allies from receiving imports, especially munitions and especially from America; they also hoped to bring pressure upon the Allies indirectly or directly, so as to compel them to permit imports into Germany through neutral ports. Hence Germany's anxiety to persuade Americans to establish an embargo upon the export of munitions; hence the continual pressure upon Washington to take action against the Allies in defence of neutral rights, for such action would break the so-called blockade.

Germany had no effective means, other than the capitalization of American discontent, to persuade the United States Government to take action against the Allies. At first German opinion counted upon a voluntary embargo on the export of munitions; disappointment was keen and fury fierce over American willingness to furnish the enemies of Germany with war supplies. Organized interference with munitions industries through incitement to strikes could not be safely undertaken on a large scale and always threatened diplomatic complications. It led ultimately to the recall of the Austrian Ambassador and of the German military and naval attachés.[15] The possibility of buying up munitions firms or their products was undertaken too late and on too small a scale to be effective.[16] German propaganda designed to persuade Congress to impose an embargo upon export of munitions, proved fruitless, partly because of the methods employed, partly because of the " sales-resistance " of the Americans to German arguments, especially on the Atlantic seaboard. German historians emphasize the fact that the policy of both the military and civilian authorities of Germany during the war was such as to inhibit any efficacious propaganda.[17] Only when the Allies by their blockade of Germany interfered with American trade, did the Americans listen to German arguments. " If I am

---

[15] Constantin Dumba, *Memoirs of a Diplomat*, pp. 253 ff.

[16] Johann Heinrich von Bernstorff, *My Three Years in America*, pp. 95-97 (hereafter cited as *Bernstorff*).

[17] Hans Thimme, *Weltkrieg ohne Waffen*, *passim*.

questioned," said Bernstorff before the Reichstag investigating committee, " I shall say that if we made a mistake in the United States, it was that we dealt too much in propaganda rather than too little." [18]

If it proved impossible to interfere indirectly with the flow of American supplies to the Allies, it was equally difficult to force them to relax their control of neutral trade headed ultimately for Germany. Each time that the Berlin Government made a concession to the United States it expected that Washington would force corresponding concessions from the Allies. But the United States possessed no means of bringing effective pressure to bear upon the Allies without injuring so deeply its own commercial interests that the price seemed too high to pay. This fact was so clearly recognized by Bernstorff that he consistently urged pressure on Wilson in the direction of mediation rather than against Allied encirclement of Germany. " It would be easier to end the war," he wrote the Chancellor in May, 1916, " than to force England to lift the blockade." [19]

There remained to the Germans the weapon of direct action. The submarine warfare, if conducted without regard to the recognized rules of warning and safety of crew and passengers, would achieve Germany's double object. It would interrupt the flow of American exports to Allied countries; it would destroy the Allied blockade by a more vigorous and direct counter-blockade. In February, 1915, the

[18] Stenographic Minutes of Testimony delivered before the Reichstag investigating committee, Fifteenth Session, *German Documents relating to the World War*, II, 927 (hereafter cited as *G.D.*).

[19] Bernstorff to German Foreign Office, May 18, 1916, *G.D.*, II. 976.

campaign was started with the declaration of a war-zone around the British Isles; it resulted in the sinking of the *Lusitania.* Following American protests the unrestricted campaign was modified, and after the sinking of the *Arabic* in August the Germans promised not to sink unarmed liners without notice. Again in February, 1916, the unrestricted campaign was resumed and in March the *Sussex* was torpedoed. A note from Wilson which carried at once the form and intent of an ultimatum, resulted in a definite, although conditional, agreement upon the part of Germany to abide by the rules of cruiser warfare in the conduct of the submarine campaign.[20]

The vacillations in German policy reflected the internal struggle in Germany, parallel to that which took place in Allied countries, between the Admiralty and the Foreign Office; the former insisting upon the most effective sort of campaign regardless of neutrals, the latter insisting upon the vital necessity of conciliating the United States. In the autumn of 1916 the final issue was joined in Berlin. The military and naval chiefs declared that the blockade must be broken or the war ended. " If the war lasted," said Ludendorff, " our defeat seemed inevitable." [21] If peace could not be obtained through negotiation, and by peace the Germans meant a peace of victory, the submarine must be

[20] See *infra,* p. 123.

[21] " We were opposing the enemy in the proportion of 6 to 10, roughly estimated," Ludendorff stated in his testimony before the Reichstag investigating committee. " Our supply of war material was insufficient, and our supply of ammunition too scant, and, in cold, plain terms, this meant heavy losses of German lives which, from all points of view, simply could not be replaced," *G.D.* II, 856.

exerted to its full capacity, and without the restrictions of international law.

Thus the United States was compelled to recognize that for the innocent bystander there is no position of secure aloofness. The belligerents were reasonably and anxiously desirous of maintaining friendly relations with the United States, but for the sake of their own existence they could not help injuring American interests and rights. The United States wanted nothing more than to remain quietly apart, but found itself caught in a vise of which the jaws were made of Allied blockade and German submarine.

The problem of defense which Wilson faced was intensified because the two attacks were interdependent and he found it doubly difficult to find a solution. Germany was unwilling to give up the submarine unless Wilson by force or threats broke the Allied system of trade restrictions. This he was unable to accomplish, partly at least because German methods alienated American sympathy. " One effect of the British blockade," writes Commander Kenworthy, " was so to irritate Germany into so irritating America that the British could continually screw the vise tighter." [22] Wilson protested constantly but vainly that regard for international law must be absolute and not relative. " Each Government should understand that the rights we claim from it have no connection which we can recognize with what we claim from the other, but that we must insist on our rights from each without regard to what the other does or does not do." [23] But the connection between the two remained a

[22] Joseph W. Kenworthy and George Young, *Freedom of the Seas,* p. 73.

[23] Wilson to House, May 20, 1915, Y.H.C.

matter of fact. Neither the Allies nor Germany would accept a compromise between submarine and blockade; without a compromise the solution of neither problem was possible.

In each belligerent nation sentiment was inflamed against America and especially Wilson, by his failure to interfere successfully with the war methods of the other side. The blame was placed upon American shoulders. In Germany the anger aroused by the importation into Allied countries of American munitions, under the ægis of British control of the seas, and the development of the Allied blockade, culminated in the conviction that since Wilson did nothing effective to support the German contention he must be thoroughly anti-German. Any suggestion he made was suspect. "At present," wrote Bernstorff to House in July, 1915, " nobody in Germany believes in the impartiality of the American Government. That is the great difficulty." [24] In the Allied countries, Wilson's patience in the face of apparent German disregard of his protests against submarine warfare aroused distrust and contempt. The soldiers called the unexploded dud that fell in the trenches a " Wilson." In February, 1916, Ambassador Page wrote of the attitude of the members of the British Government towards our Government: " Not one of them has any confidence in the strength of the President for action." [25] Nothing could indicate more clearly the intensity of Wilson's efforts to maintain an exact neutrality than the abuse he received from

[24] Bernstorff to House, July 27, 1915, Y.H.C.
[25] Burton J. Hendrick, *Life and Letters of Walter Hines Page*, III, 282 (hereafter cited as *Page*).

each side.[26] The state of mind that produced the abuse effectively hindered any compromise between the methods that directly touched United States' interests.

Since he started with the principle that the peace of America must be preserved at all hazards, Wilson had to meet the double attack with whatever peaceful weapons diplomacy could supply. With the Allies he was willing to compromise and negotiate, entering protests that would safeguard the principle of the American contention, and trusting to later arbitration to secure compensation. Until his patience was stretched taut by repeated extension of Allied measures of restriction he sought to avoid open notes of protest and to bring pressure through personal negotiations. Only toward the end of the period of our neutrality did he seriously consider the advisability of utilizing economic reprisals against the Allies.

With the Germans, on the other hand, he refused to compromise, since he regarded the unrestricted submarine campaign as an attack upon humanity. Lives of non-combatants,

[26] Cf. the comment of the British Ambassador in Washington, who while he had little sympathy with either the personality or the policy of Wilson, regarded such abuse as both unjust and impolitic: " The Government shows its earnest desire to maintain absolute impartiality and to keep the peace. I see in England there is a disposition to criticize this Government and the People. It cannot be wondered at that the American People are determined to keep out of the war which is frightful in itself to those that take part in it and very profitable to those who do not. . . . It seems to be rather hard on the President and his Government that he is denounced with equal fierceness in every country in the world," Spring Rice to Grey, December 3, 1915, Stephen L. Gwynn, *The Letters and Friendships of Sir Cecil Spring Rice,* II, 300 (hereafter cited as *Spring Rice*).

even when they ventured upon the seas under a belligerent flag, he placed in a different category from American property rights. There could be no compensation for lost lives. He was willing to negotiate privately with the Germans, and in this way actually secured postponement of the unrestricted submarine campaign. He did not overstress technical rights. But he never wavered from the principle which he laid down when the first submarine war zone was declared, that the destruction of the lives of American citizens on the high seas was " an indefensible violation of neutral rights," that the American Government would hold Germany to " a strict accountability for such acts," that America would take " any steps it might be necessary to take to safeguard American lives." [27] From the beginning of the controversy Wilson met the Allied attack with protests, the German with warnings.

This difference in method led Germans at the time and some historians since to accuse Wilson of clear-cut transgression of his own adjuration to complete neutrality.[28] The general consensus of historical opinion, with which even Bernstorff and the more thoughtful Germans agree, is that while the President may not have been personally impartial, he maintained a technical neutrality in circumstances of the greatest difficulty. That Wilson inclined toward the Allied cause, except perhaps during the six months imme-

[27] Lansing to Gerard, February 10, 1915, *Papers relating to the Foreign Relations of the United States, 1915, Supplement, The World War,* 99 (hereafter cited as *F.R., Suppl.*).

[28] Notably the anonymous author of the biographical sketch of Bryan, in Samuel Flagg Bemis, *The American Secretaries of State,* X, 33, 36.

diately preceding American intervention, is reasonably clear.
Like most Americans he was appalled by the invasion of
Belgium. The stories of German atrocities, whether or not
exaggerated, affected him deeply, and seemed to be confirmed by the sinking of passenger vessels by the submarines.
At the moment of the outbreak of the war Colonel House
found him inclined to lay heavy responsibility upon Germany
and her military machine, and fearful of the consequence
of German victory. " If Germany won it would change the
course of our civilization and make the United States a military nation." [29] A year later, when a member of the cabinet
suggested pressure upon the Allies to relax the blockade,
the President, according to the Attorney-General, broke out:
" Gentlemen, the Allies are standing with their backs to the
wall fighting wild beasts. I will permit nothing to be done
by our country to hinder or embarrass them in the prosecution of the war unless admitted rights are grossly violated." [30]

More important, perhaps, and certainly more permanent,
was his inherited dislike of German political philosophy.
Wilson felt that the war was a conflict between principles.
Probably most historians of today would agree with him,
although they might not agree that the issue was one between
moral influence and material force, as it used to be phrased.
The conflict of principle had little or nothing to do with the
origins of the war, and no amount of new light on those
origins can alter the difference in political philosophy that
separated Germany and Austria-Hungary on the one side
from France and Great Britain on the other. Since the
failure of the Forty-Eighters and the triumph of Bismarck,

[29] House Diary, August 30, 1914, *I.P.*, I, 293.
[30] *I.P.*, II, 50.

Germany had accepted the Hegelian doctrine which made of the State an entity apart from and above the collective mass of individual citizens. The State as personified in the Kaiser, was entirely irresponsible to the people, promoting their welfare but not necessarily their wishes, acting for but not by the people, drawing upon the loyalty of the military caste, which stood apart, and upon that of the civil functionaries. Generals and ministers were responsible to the State, that is the Kaiser, but not to the people. This philosophy was wholly antipathetic to the French or British, who accepted the sovereignty of the people and accordingly its control of both military and civil affairs; it was repugnant to Wilson, the disciple of the Virginia Bill of Rights, as it was to most Americans.

Such a philosophy Wilson had in mind when he later spoke of the " military masters of Germany " or the " single, arbitrary power " that could disturb the peace of the world. Less instructed in political philosophy, but generally aware of the trend of government in the Central Empires, the mass of Americans talked of German " militarism." It was a fact not to be proved by the size of armies or their efficiency, or by the bad manners of German officers. It was none the less a fact, and one which alienated the sympathies of American people and American Government. No one perceived its importance more keenly than Ambassador von Bernstorff. When asked by the Reichstag investigating committee to explain the failure of German propaganda, and whether it would not have been successful if more stress had been laid upon the purity of German ideals in the war, he replied: " This brings us, of course, to the question of philosophy of life. If, in our propaganda in the United States, we had unqualifiedly found ourselves in agreement with the ideas which governed the American people, then of course we would have been much more successful with our propaganda. But since that was not the case . . . the natural result was that the propaganda fell to the ground." [31]

Wilson, perhaps unconsciously, transferred his dislike of a philosophy to those who professed it. Sir Edward Grey spoke his language. Following an interchange of letters with him he writes that Sir Edward " comprehended, as usual." The Germans he could not understand and he did not trust. " I do not feel that Bernstorff is dealing frankly with us," he wrote in July, 1915. A month later: " I am suspicious enough to think that they are merely sparring for time." Shortly afterwards, regarding Bernstorff, " You know I trust neither his accuracy nor his sincerity." [32] Such suspicion was quite unjustified so far as the German Ambassador was concerned, for no one worked more effectively to persuade his Government to accept Wilson's demands;

[31] Stenographic Minutes of Reichstag investigating committee, Fifteenth Session, *G.D.*, II, 928.

[32] Wilson to House, July 21, 29, August 25, 31, 1915, Y.H.C. Cf. a report from the British Ambassador of a conversation with Wilson during the early days of the war: " The President said in the most solemn way that if that [the German] cause succeeds in the present struggle the United States would have to give up its present ideals and devote all its energies to defence, which would mean the end of its present system of Government. . . . I said [after quoting Wordsworth], ' You and Grey are fed on the same food and I think you understand.' There were tears in his eyes, and I am sure we can, at the right moment, depend on an understanding heart here," Spring Rice to Grey, September 8, 1914, *Spring Rice*, II, 223.

3

but despite the President's determination to remain impartial it doubtless colored his attitude.

On the other hand there is no evidence to show that such a prejudice brought Wilson to adopt differing methods in protecting American rights from Allied and German attacks. He saw a sharp distinction between attacks upon property rights and attacks upon human non-combatant lives; he was not to be shaken from his conviction of this distinction by any argument that it was merely the right to travel that he was protecting, and he refused to warn American citizens off merchant ships. "What we are contending for in this matter," he wrote Senator Stone, "is of the very essence of the things that have made America a sovereign nation. She cannot yield them without conceding her own impotency as a nation, and making virtual surrender of her independent position among the nations of the world." [33] At no time were his feelings so stirred by any interference with trade.

Certain it is that the distinction Wilson thus made led him directly on to the path of American intervention. If he could not induce the Allies to mitigate the blockade, and if the German submarine was the answer to the blockade, and if Wilson refused to compromise with the submarine, diplomacy would be hard put to it to find a peaceful solution. Wilson had started with the principle of peace as an end in itself; as the war proceeded he became more thoroughly convinced of the wisdom, even the sanctity, of this policy. But directly across it cut the double attack from the belligerents, touching the core of America's national position.

[33] Wilson to Stone, February 24, 1916, *F.R., 1916, Suppl.*, 177-178.

As the war continued the situation became literally intolerable.

" I know that you are depending upon me to keep this Nation out of the war," said the President in a public address, in February, 1916: " So far I have done so, and I pledge you my word that, God helping me, I will—if it is possible. But you have laid another duty upon me. You have bidden me see to it that nothing stains or impairs the honor of the United States, and that is a matter not within my control; that depends upon what others do, not upon what the Government of the United States does. Therefore there may at any moment come a time when I cannot preserve both the honor and the peace of the United States. Do not exact of me an impossible and contradictory thing. . . ." [34]

From the threat of this dilemma Wilson constantly strove to escape, first by successive proposals of compromise between the Allied blockade and the submarine warfare, next by offers of mediation that might lead to peace. With increasing clarity he perceived that the only alternative to American intervention in the war would be the ending of the war. Belligerent attacks upon neutral rights would sooner or later make the continuance of neutrality impossible. Not so much because of an idealistic principle of serving the rest of the world as to avoid participation in the war, Wilson sought every opportunity to bring about a negotiated peace.

His efforts towards mediation were doomed to failure. The longer the war continued and the greater the desirability of peace, the more difficult it was to induce either side to consider it. The greater the sacrifices made, the greater

[34] Speech at Milwaukee, January 31, 1916, Baker and Dodd, *op. cit.*, II, 48.

must be the compensation and the less the chance of compromise. Even the promise of American assistance in the winning of moderate terms, did not persuade the Allies to renounce their determination to inflict a crushing defeat upon the Central Powers. On the other hand the German interpretation of "moderate peace terms," offended the judgment of President Wilson as it did the aspirations of the Allies. It is true that the President's policy was not entirely waste effort, since the programme of peace that Wilson developed while still neutral, became the basis of his whole purpose after America intervened actively in the war. But it did not succeed in its immediate aim. The dominance of the war machines in each belligerent camp ensured the continuance of the ever-increasing carnage.

By the end of 1916, the failure of American attempts to compromise between blockade and submarine and the failure of efforts to secure a peace conference, left the United States in a position where fresh belligerent attacks upon neutral rights must precipitate it into war. The declaration of the unrestricted submarine warfare in January, 1917, proved the last straw that broke the back of neutrality.

America entered the war on the side of the Allies, not so much because of political or even economic factors, as from sentimental reasons. The people of the United States were appalled by the submarine warfare.[35] American history and tradition, if sentiment were pushed to one side, demanded that the United States should join with Germany to combat

[35] Comment by the German Navy Archivist, September 15, 1933: " We cannot close our eyes to the fact that often in decisive hours an act of the German submarine war tore apart the threads of the diplomatic web woven between Berlin and Washington."

British command of the seas and to secure a balance of sea power. "But the American ruling class were on the whole pro-British in sentiment, and the Germans alienated the sympathies of multitudes who might have been their supporters on grounds of traditional policy."[36] Two years of acrid dispute with Germany over a mode of warfare which public opinion regarded as shocking to its moral instincts, overshadowed the traditional dispute with the Allies over the Freedom of the Seas.

Business interests were bound up with the maintenance of foreign trade which was controlled by the Allies. But this fact by no means justifies the belief that those interests forced the United States into the war. From the economic point of view continued neutrality was for them the supreme desirability, just as for Wilson it was the supreme political purpose. If conditions of neutrality had remained bearable, there would have been no intervention. That they had become actually unbearable is evident from a more detailed study, first of the effects of the so-called Allied blockade, next, of the German submarine campaign.

[36] Kenworthy and Young, *op. cit.*, p. 37.

Chapter II

ALLIED INTERFERENCE WITH NEUTRAL TRADE

1

" Command of the sea," we are told, " means the nearly complete defence of sea commerce and communications for allies and neutrals and a nearly complete denial of them to the enemy. Such a command of the sea ensures final victory." [1] Generally speaking, the Allies enjoyed this position of control during the first two and a half years of the World War, were threatened with its loss during the critical months of 1917, regained it in the final year. By sheer weight of surface shipping they maintained control against the German challenge of mines and submarines. Their command was not complete at any time. The German High Seas Fleet, unable to protect German commerce and to menace Allied communications, nevertheless as a " fleet in being " exercised a far-reaching influence on the course of the war. By its mere existence, it immobilized the British Grand Fleet, and it kept open for Germany the vital Baltic trade.[2] Furthermore the capacity of the submarine as a commerce destroyer, demonstrated by the events of 1917, provided even during the early months of the war a continual threat to Allied maritime control.

[1] Kenworthy and Young, *Freedom of the Seas,* p. 123.
[2] Montagu W. Consett, *The Triumph of Unarmed Forces,* p. 18.

But the German Naval Staff recognized too late the potentialities of the submarine and adopted it only as a measure of desperation, when its political disadvantages more than outweighed its tactical value. For thirty months, partly at least because of the American attitude, the Germans resigned to the Allies the command belonging to surface power. They could harass enemy trade but not interrupt it, nor, outside of the Baltic, could they protect their own. The Allies were further able to fortify their command of sea trade through the advantages they possessed in the control of cables and of coal, through their superiority in financial power, and through a factor not fully appreciated at the time—the all-pervasive cleverness of their Naval Intelligence.

This command of the seas the Allies were bound to capitalize to the full. In a short war it might turn the scale; if the struggle were prolonged it would be deadly. Germany was dependent upon imports both for the physical means of conducting war and for the equally vital maintenance of national morale. The problem of raw materials and foodstuffs hung its shadow over her from beginning to end. It was the business of the Allies to cut off those imports to the last ton.

The process led inevitably to conflict with the interests and the feelings of neutrals, especially of the greatest of neutrals, the United States. The belligerent in command of the seas naturally claims the utmost extension of restrictions upon the Freedom of the Seas compatible with existing circumstances. He is restrained to some extent by the recognition of neutral rights, as expressed in custom or special

conventions—so-called international law. He is restrained
much more forcibly by the necessity of conciliating the neutrals, for sea power is determined less by rules than by circumstances. " International law," says Commander Kenworthy, " whether customary or conventional, had broken
down whenever seriously contrary to the belligerent interest." [3] The commanding sea power, be it the Northern
States in the Civil War or the British in the World War,
would not permit an ill-defined " international law " to
interfere with measures apparently essential to national existence. Mr. Asquith made practical confession of such
determination. " We are not going to allow our efforts,"
he told the House of Commons on March 1, 1915, " to
be strangled in a network of juridical niceties. . . . Under
existing conditions there is no form of economic pressure
to which we do not consider ourselves entitled to resort." [4]

On the other hand concessions to neutrals, even such as
might injure the effectiveness of the blockade, might be and
were demanded by considerations of higher policy:

" Blockade of Germany," writes Sir Edward Grey, " was
essential to the victory of the Allies, but the ill-will of the
United States meant their certain defeat. After Paris had
been saved by the Battle of the Marne, the Allies could do
no more than hold their own against Germany; sometimes

[3] Kenworthy and Young, op. cit., p. 57.

[4] Hansard, Parliamentary Debates, 5th series, LXX, 600. Cf.
Queen Elizabeth's remark to the Polish Ambassador in 1597 (cited
in Kenworthy and Young, op. cit., p. 27) : " For your part you seem
indeed to us to have read many books, but yet to have little understanding of politics, for when you so often make mention of the
Law of Nations you must know that in time of war betwixt
Kings it is lawful for the one party to intercept aids and succours
to the other and to care that no damage accrue to himself."

they did not even do that. Germany and Austria were self-supporting in the huge supply of munitions. The Allies soon became dependent for an adequate supply on the United States. If we quarreled with the United States we could not get that supply. It was better therefore to carry on the war without blockade, if need be, than to incur a break with the United States about contraband and thereby deprive the Allies of the resources necessary to carry on the war at all or with any chance of success. The object of diplomacy, therefore, was to secure the maximum of blockade that could be enforced without a rupture with the United States." [5]

This is tantamount to stating that the determining factor in a blockade is neutral power. The belligerent must strike a compromise between his resolution to win the war by utilizing command of the seas and his reluctance to risk the unfriendliness of a neutral capable of harming him, through an embargo, through convoys of neutral shipping, or even through active belligerency. The Allied economic war against the Central Powers thus was forced to proceed cautiously, step by step. As the measures applied were tested and found insufficient to restrict German imports, new measures were tried out. In each case the sentiment of the neutrals was also tested, and wherever possible concessions made. For the diplomats the invariable aim was not so much to conform with international law as to retain neutral good-will. " Don't forget," wrote Ambassador Spring Rice, " that George III lost the United States through the lawyers and by pressing a legal point. . . . The vital points for us are that this country should serve as a base of supplies, and should not intervene by force, that is by convoy, to break the blockade." [6]

[5] *Grey,* II, 107.
[6] Spring Rice to Grey, October 24, 1915, *Spring Rice,* II, 282.

As against the diplomats, the Admiralties and public opinion generally in the Allied countries insisted always upon more stringent control of neutral commerce that might find its way into Germany. Internal conflict was confused by demands of commercial interests which saw in the destruction of neutral trade the chance of new markets for themselves, and of financiers who were interested in the neutral markets, wanted to maintain the commercial balance, must maintain the pound sterling, and were accordingly indulgent to exports to neutral ports, even when they guessed that those exports would later find their way into Germany.[7] Obviously the problem of maintaining good relations as well as the blockade was one to tax the capacity of the most skillful of diplomats.

2

The Allied economic campaign against the Central Powers has generally been spoken of as a "Blockade." But in the formal sense in which the word is used in the documents of maritime law, there was at no time a blockade; the measures that travelled popularly under that name were merely a sort of economic strangling through processes which, at least according to the contentions of American lawyers, were unknown, or contrary to accepted international custom. An officially declared blockade of the German North Sea coast, even if feasible on the naval side, would have produced incomplete results. The Allies did not control the Baltic and could not prevent German trade with Sweden, still less with the contiguous states, Denmark and Holland.

[7] Louis Guichard, *The Naval Blockade,* pp. 3-4; Consett, *op. cit.,* XII, 252-278.

They felt compelled therefore to substitute for an official blockade a series of processes that would have the same economic effects on Germany, by an interruption of the trade of neutral ports which might serve Germany as a base of supplies. Roughly speaking, those processes were of three kinds. In the first place the Allies extended the traditional principle of the belligerent's right to seize contraband, by adding to the list of contraband articles, by finding justification for the seizure of conditional contraband, and by the control of neutral vessels through the right of visit and search. In the second place, contending that German infractions of maritime law gave the Allies the right to reprisals, they proceeded to interrupt all commerce whatsoever with Germany (Reprisals Order of March 11, 1915). Finally they introduced a third general policy, that of rationing the neutrals of northern Europe, permitting them to import only sufficient for their normal needs and thus preventing transshipment to Germany.

At the very beginning of the war the Allies made plain that they would interpret the belligerent right to seize contraband in a sense most favorable to the belligerent that held the command of the seas. To the American suggestion that the Declaration of London be regarded as an effective code, a request which Germany and Austria had offered to accept, they replied evasively.[8] The provisions of the Declaration, which although approved by the delegates of the

[8] Bryan to Page, August 6, 1914; Gerard to Bryan, August 22; Penfield to Bryan, August 23, 1914, *F.R., 1914, Suppl.*, 216-218. For the documents connected with the Declaration of London, see J. B. Scott, *ed., The Declaration of London,* with introduction by Elihu Root.

Powers had not been ratified, would assure free passage of conditional contraband if discharged at a neutral port, and would thus make it possible for Germany to provision herself through the northern neutrals as easily as through Hamburg. The British and French agreed " to adopt generally the rules of the declaration in question, subject to certain modifications and additions which they judge indispensable to the efficient conduct of their naval operations." [9]

The first of these modifications lay in the replacement of the lists of absolute and conditional contraband, by much more inclusive lists.[10] From time to time the neutrals were notified of further extensions and revisions. Additions to the contraband lists were determined by military exigencies, since developments in modern warfare attached the highest military value to commodities which formerly had been regarded as conditional contraband or free goods. They were determined also by the probability of acceptance by the United States, the one neutral that might effectively dispute the list.

" The first step," writes Sir Edward Grey, " was to put on the list of absolute contraband all the articles that were

[9] Page to Bryan, August 26, 1914, *F.R., 1914, Suppl.,* 218. The United States Department of State regarded the modifications as so far denaturing the Declaration of London, which had been recognized as forming an " indivisible whole," that on October 22, 1914, it withdrew its proposal for the adoption of the Declaration as a code and stated that it would uphold its citizens' rights as " defined by the existing rules of international law and the treaties of the United States," *F.R., 1914, Suppl.,* 258.

[10] British Order in Council of August 20; French Decree of August 25, 1914, *F.R., 1914, Suppl.,* 219-220.

essential for armies under modern conditions; the second and more important step was to get the United States to accept that list." [11]

The Allies were careful therefore to extend the contraband lists gradually. The three most desirable additions from the Allied point of view were copper, rubber, and cotton. They decided to concentrate upon copper and rubber, lest the declaration of cotton as contraband should increase the existing economic distress of the cotton-growing states of the South. " There were already materials enough for friction," writes Grey, " between us and the United States; the fomenting of these was the trump card of German diplomacy." [12] Thus it was not until August, 1915, that cotton was placed upon the contraband list. By that time American trade had recovered and a minimum price for cotton was guaranteed; a crisis in affairs with Germany, furthermore, distracted American attention.[13] In the meantime the Allies replied to the confiscation by the German Government of all supplies of grain and flour in that country, with the declaration that the distinction between foodstuffs destined for the army and those for the civilian population was thereby abolished.

" In any country in which there exists such tremendous organization for war as now obtains in Germany there is no clear division between those whom the Government is responsible for feeding and those whom it is not. . . . However much goods may be imported for civil use it is by the

[11] *Grey,* II, 108.
[12] *Grey,* II, 115.
[13] *Page,* I, 368; Wilson to House, July 27, August 5, 1915, Y.H.C.

military that they will be consumed if military exigencies require it, especially now that the German Government have taken control of all the foodstuffs." [14]

Thus began the so-called food blockade.

The extension of the contraband lists, although so serious an infraction of the Declaration of London as practically to destroy its meaning, was not so irritating as a second modification which permitted the Allies to seize conditional contraband, even though discharged at a neutral port. " Germany could import goods," writes Grey, " as easily through Dutch, Danish, or Swedish ports as through her own, and in Sweden especially there were people disposed to make Sweden a source of supply for Germany." [15] Accordingly the British Order in Council of August 20, 1914, decreed that conditional contraband would be liable to capture, no matter what the port of destination, on the presumption of ultimate enemy destination, if consigned to or for an agent acting under the control of the enemy state. On October 30, another Order in Council made a concession in form to the United States but reserved the right to interrupt conditional

[14] Grey to Page, February 10, 1915, *F.R., 1915, Suppl.*, 324-334. Comment of German Navy Archivist, September 15, 1933: " It is not correct to picture English methods for confiscation of food imports into Germany as beginning as late as January, 1915, when the German Administration took over grain and flour. This German emergency decree gave the English the welcome grounds of argument that *now* no distinction could longer be made between the civilian population and the armed forces of the nation. In reality, however, such confiscation without distinction of all German-bound food material by England actually dates from the order of August 20, 1914."

[15] *Grey*, II, 109.

contraband if consigned " to order "; that is, in blank. The shipper must prove innocence of intent to transship to the enemy. The greater part of American shipments, because of the lack of adequate credit facilities, were in fact consigned " to order." [16]

Such invasions of neutral rights, at least as understood by the United States, became more vexatious because of the mechanism of control exercised by the British navy. Allied methods quite as much as, or more than, policy infuriated American shippers, who suspected and openly alleged British plans to kill American trade under the excuse of national self-protection. They objected particularly to the development of the belligerent right of visit and search, which the Allied navies interpreted to mean the right to bring ships into port on suspicion.

Immediately upon the declaration of war the Allies had established cruising lines, especially around Scotland, at the entrance of the Channel, and before Genoa and Barcelona. The Hague Conference had recognized the right of visit on the high seas only. Difficulties arose at once with the Dutch Government, when the *Niew Amsterdam* carrying a thousand tons of contraband and 750 mobilized German reservists, was ordered into Brest harbor, on the ground that the size of the contraband cargo prevented transfer at sea.[17] A lively dispute loomed up around the question as to whether the increased size of merchant vessels and cargoes ought to permit a change in custom.

[16] *F.R., 1914, Suppl.,* 219, 244-246.

[17] Guichard, *op. cit.,* p. 30; Consul-General Skinner to Bryan, September 25, 1914, *F.R., 1914, Suppl.,* 320.

Allied difficulties were eased by German naval intervention. On August 7 the Germans announced to neutrals their intention of sowing mines at points of embarkation and debarkation of British troops; two Danish boats were shortly thereafter blown up at the mouth of the Tyne; in the last week of October the *Berlin* sowed mines up and down the west coast of Ireland. The Allies seized the diplomatic opportunity. They warned neutral shipping that because of the danger fom German mines it was important to stop in Allied ports to pick up reliable pilots who would take the ships safely through the dangerous waters. A manifesto of November 2 directed neutral ships to certain specified ports. Thus the Allies cleverly used the danger from German mines to compel neutral ships to submit to visit and search under simpler conditions. At the same time the British Admiralty, using the excuse that German merchant vessels flying neutral flags had laid mines in the North Sea, gave notice that after November 5 the whole of the North Sea would be considered a military area. "All merchant and fishing vessels of every description are hereby warned of the dangers they encounter by entering this area except in strict accordance with Admiralty directions." [18]

The United States Government took no official notice of the declaration making of the North Sea a military area.[19]

[18] Grey to Spring Rice, November 3, 1914, *F.R., 1914, Suppl.*, 464.

[19] Comment of German Navy Archivist, September 15, 1933: " It is strange that the legal and military aspects of this English declaration of naval warfare have hardly been noticed by the American world. The American Government never protested. The brief mention of the English naval offensive as an order to neutral shipping interests to steer certain courses through the North Sea

But it protested warmly against the bringing of neutral ships into port for search, despite the plausibility of the excuse offered. " The belligerent right of visit and search requires that the search should be made on the high seas at the time of the visit and that the conclusion of the search should rest upon the evidence found on the ship under investigation, and not upon circumstances ascertained from external sources." [20] The Allies in reply cited certain precedents, and as the controversy developed especially emphasized the argument that the size of modern boats demanded a modification of old practice; they were not contending for anything more than the adaptation to new commercial conditions of an old right already existing. No final conclusion was reached in a long correspondence.[21]

During its course the Allies drafted rules for the routing of ships: in the Channel every ship must indicate its destination, and if headed for a neutral port the visit would take place in the Downs; in the Mediterranean every ship was visited in principle in Gibraltar or Alexandria, and its port of destination signaled to Toulon or Malta; a fourth harbor, Kirkwall, was used on the Scotch coast. The fineness of the sifting of neutral trade is indicated by the fact that from January to July, 1915, 2466 ships arrived in the neutral ports

---

territory as an aid in the search by English warships, overlooks the essential."

[20] Lansing to Spring Rice, November 7, 1914, *F.R., 1914, Suppl.,* 339-340.

[21] American notes of December 26, 1914, October 21, 1915; British notes of February 10, 1915, April 24, 1916, *F.R., 1914, Suppl.,* 372-374; *F.R., 1915, Suppl.,* 324, 578-601; *F.R., 1916, Suppl.,* 368-382.

4

of the North Sea, of which 2132 had been minutely studied
by the Allied authorities.[22]

With all the restrictions placed upon neutral trade designed to intercept contraband, the results did not satisfy
the Allies. Direct imports from the United States to Germany were practically stopped, but indirect trade, via the
northern neutrals, increased notably. American exports to
Sweden and Norway increased seven-fold; to Denmark, almost five-fold.[23]

At the beginning of 1915 Germany was thus only slightly
incommoded in her economic life by the Allied process of
strangulation through control of contraband. But the Allies
could pull the strings tighter. One method, hardly legal,
which the British had considered at the very beginning of
the war, in the previous August, would be to utilize Allied
command of the high seas so as to cut off Germany from all
maritime trade, contraband or free.[24] The British Admiralty
whose influence constantly increased, pressed for such a step.

[22] Guichard, op. cit., p. 34.

[23] Direct imports into Germany from the United States in
December and January, 1914-1915, amounted to 8.7 millions of
dollars as compared with 86 millions in the corresponding months
of the preceding year.

The increase in United States exports to northern neutrals is
indicated in the following table:

	Dec.-Jan. 1913-1914	Dec.-Jan. 1914-1915
	In millions of dollars	
Holland	19.3	26.8
Sweden	2.2	17.7
Norway	1.5	7.2
Denmark	3.	14.5

Ibid., p. 43.

[24] Page, III, 155-157.

The Foreign Office opposed it because of the obvious difficulty of justifying on legal grounds this departure from international custom. But in the spring of 1915, conscious of the necessity of stopping German imports from the neutrals, the British Government determined to enforce it. They presented the plan as an act of justifiable reprisals, consequent upon the illegal sowing of mines and the declaration of a war zone around the British Isles by Germany.

On March 1, 1915, Mr. Asquith explained to the House of Commons that in view of Germany's disregard of international law " her opponents are, therefore, driven to frame retaliatory measures, in order, in their turn, to prevent commodities of any kind from reaching or leaving Germany. . . . The British and French Governments will, therefore, hold themselves free to detain and take into port ships carrying goods of presumed enemy destination, ownership, or origin." [25] On March 11, the Reprisals Order in Council setting forth the measures necessary to carry this policy into effect, was promulgated.[26]

The Reprisals Order, which inaugurated what has been termed the pseudo-blockade, naturally evoked strong neutral protests. It amounted to a confession that since an official blockade of German ports was impossible, the Allies would blockade neutral ports. British naval authorities admit that it was of " a very revolutionary character," that it was a measure " outside ordinary naval law which could not have been put into force legally, at any rate, had it not been for

[25] Hansard, *Parliamentary Debates*, 5th series, LXX, 600; Spring Rice to Bryan, March 1, 1915, *F.R., 1915, Suppl.*, 127-128.

[26] Text of the Reprisals Order in Page to Bryan, March 15, 1915, *F.R., 1915, Suppl.*, 143-144.

the prior infringements of Germany." [27]   Mr. Asquith's refusal to be " strangled in a network of juridical niceties," goes far towards an admission of illegality. If the principles upon which the Order was based were juridically sound, why were they not put in force at the beginning of the war? French historians have later expressed the feeling that " although the position of the Allies was quite arguable in equity it was somewhat ambiguous in point of law, as will be perceived from the tone of Sir Edward Grey's reply." [28] The French, indeed, always more sensitive than the British to the letter of the law, and prompted by the entrance of some British submarines into the Baltic, suggested some months later that the legal aspects of the situation be cleared by the declaration of an official blockade.[29]

The British, however, perceiving the difficulties or impossibility of an official blockade, and unmoved by legal doubts, made of the Reprisals Order the second of their chief processes in the strangulation of the Central Powers. The United States protested formally and through private

[27] Consett, op. cit., p. 28; Kenworthy and Young, op. cit., p. 127. " It is hardly to be expected," writes Admiral Consett, " that America would acquiesce, to the infinite injury of her own interests, in our proposed rejection of principles to which we had agreed in peace time, because in war time we found they did not suit us," op. cit., p. 32.

[28] Guichard, op. cit., p. 51.

[29] The British raised a double objection to an official blockade at this time: first, that at the moment when the Allies were protesting that the submarine could not be used legally as a weapon of naval warfare it would be inconsistent to invoke British control of the Baltic through submarines as justification of the blockade; second, that the approach of winter would make actual control impossible, ibid., p. 52.

appeals. President Wilson declared that the proposal " seeks
to alter hitherto fixed international laws "; it should, he
believed, have been preceded by a conference. Ambassador
Page, with all his British sympathies, confessed that they
had put themselves " legally wrong." The State Department
pointed out that in refusing to declare a blockade the British
had created a curiously paradoxical situation: " The first
sentence claims a right pertaining only to a state of blockade.
The last sentence proposes a treatment of ships and cargoes
as if no blockade existed. The two together present a proposed course of action previously unknown to international
law." The Reprisals Order further seemed to contravene
directly the provisions of the Declaration of Paris, that free
ships make free goods and that the neutral flag covers enemy
goods except contraband of war.[30]

To such protests the Allies replied politely, but tardily,
and with no suggestion of yielding. The United States, on
its side, could not bring effective pressure to bear without
measures that would injure American trade much more than
would the Reprisals Order. " The attitude of the United
States," reported the British Ambassador from Washington,
" is peculiar. They cannot recognize the Order in Council,
but they are anxious to promote trade and therefore to assist
as far as they can in the private negotiations conducted by
Crawford under your direction." [31] Through these private

[30] Page to House, July 21, 1915, *I.P.,* II, 57; Wilson to House,
March 23, 1915, Y.H.C.; Bryan to Page, March 5, 30, 1915, *F. R.,
1915, Suppl.,* 133, 154-156. See also Maurice F. Parmelee, *Blockade
and Sea Power,* pp. 39 ff.

[31] Spring Rice to Grey, April 30, 1915, *Spring Rice,* II, 265.
The measures taken by American shippers to certify through the
agents of a British consulate that the manifests were genuine and

agreements the welfare of the chief American trading interests was protected. But waves of resentment against the British swept American commercial opinion, which continually threatened to force retaliatory methods upon the American government. These protests were not translated into action. From the long and inconclusive debate between the State Department and the Foreign Office, the Reprisals Order emerged essentially intact.

Partly to meet neutral protests, partly to control more effectively exports to Germany through neutral countries, the Allies put into effect a third restrictive method, that of rationing the neutrals. The principle of the rationing system was based juridically upon the case of the *Kim,* which with three other steamers, all of Norwegian or Swedish nationality, was intercepted in October, 1914, on its way to Copenhagen. The ships were laden with lard and other food products consigned " to order." The Prize Court decided against the shippers on circumstantial evidence: it was shown that during the two previous years only some million and a quarter pounds of lard were imported into Denmark from all quarters, whereas the quantity in these four ships alone amounted to more than nineteen million pounds. The lard was obviously destined for transshipment to Germany. " To hold the contrary," decided the court, " would be to allow one's eyes to be filled by the dust of theories and technicalities and to be blind to the realities of the case." [32]

the cargoes non-contraband, are described in a despatch from Spring Rice, December 11, 1914, *ibid.,* 246-247.

[32] Kenworthy and Young, *op. cit.,* p. 46 (citing Sir S. Evans, *The Kim,* 1915, Probate) ; Guichard, *op. cit.,* p. 62.

Excess over normal quantities of importation could thus be regarded as an indication of enemy destination. In October, 1915, rationing committees were created, sitting in London to determine quotas for Holland and the Scandinavian countries, in Paris for Switzerland. This new form of blockade at source was conducted by negotiations with syndicates of commercial representatives in the neutral countries. As the Americans pointed out, they were questionable in the legal sense and open to the gravest abuses in the practical. The system could be, and allegedly was, utilized by the Allies to secure a monopoly of neutral markets for their own goods.

" While we were endeavouring to stop the American part of this traffic," writes the former British Naval Attaché at Stockholm, " we learn with some surprise that the mercantile community of Great Britain were trading pretty much to the same extent as America—and to all intents and purposes with the enemy; for trade with Germany's neighbours was trade with Germany. . . . Let him [the reader] put himself in America's place . . . he may well question the soundness, or even the justice, of the law, which places the belligerent under no legal obligation to apply its principles to himself." [33]

To all this the Allies merely replied that it was obvious that the neutral ports were simply serving as the backdoors of Germany. The question of destination was one of fact and not of theory. There could be but one interpretation of the entire cargoes of meat consigned to a lighterman, to a dock laborer, to a maker of musical instruments, or to a non-existent firm. Instead of relaxing the rationing system the

[33] Consett, *op. cit.*, pp. 50, 61-62. For a description of such special agreements see *Parliamentary Papers, Misc.*, 1916, Cd. 8145.

Allies proceeded to develop it to a point that needed only American coöperation in place of protest to give perfect control. "The blockade was transformed from a cordon of warships to a system of contracts."

Such were the three main instruments by which the Allies attempted to throttle the Central Powers economically: the extension of the principle of contraband; the pseudo-blockade established by the Reprisals Order; the rationing system. There were offshoots and refinements: control and holding-up of the mails, the blacklisting of firms suspected of trading with the enemy. "When we find that the working of this system was supervised by an immense intelligence machine that checked and counter-checked it at every point, so that for a factory to be "blacklisted' by the British was even more damaging to it than to be blown up by the Germans, we recognize a new form of blockade." [34]

Most of the restrictions that appeared likely to touch American interests were gradually arranged by private negotiations. Certainly commerce and trade were never more profitable for Americans. The Allied command of the sea, on the whole, was not exercised in a way seriously to injure American pockets. But it did injure American pride. Herein, as Ambassador Spring Rice perceived, lay the chief ultimate danger:

"No one could argue for a moment that our war measures have ruined this country. Judged by figures alone,

[34] Kenworthy and Young, *op. cit.*, p. 77; Page to Lansing, January 5, 1916; Memoranda of Polk, July 20, 22, 25, 1916; Skinner to Lansing, July 21, 1916; Page to Lansing, October 11, 1916, *F.R., 1916, Suppl.*, 330, 411-412, 421-424, 455-456. See also J. B. Scott in *American Journal of International Law*, X, 832-842.

America has never been so rich. But the facts are that American trade is in a way under British control. In order to avoid the Prize Courts, everything that passes across the Atlantic goes under a pass signed by a British officer. In order to prevent Germany receiving intelligence by the mails, every letter going from America to the continent is subject to inspection. In order to prevent allied subjects trading with the enemy, the operations of American commerce are subject to a general power of control, and American citizens may be ruined at any moment by being put on a black list in Paris and London. . . . Our sea power is as 'wide and general as the casing air.' It is objectionable, not so much because it is what it is, but because it is so all-pervading." [25]

3

In meeting the issues that arose between the Allies and the United States, the diplomats on each side had a double purpose in mind: first, the preservation of friendly relations, which for all concerned was of more importance than the scoring of any detailed diplomatic or commercial success; second, the arrangement of a settlement providing for the maximum of national desires. The double purpose might be, and in many phases of the problem became, self-contradictory.

For the Allies it was vitally important to capitalize command of the seas so far as to keep supplies out of Germany, even though neutral rights were invaded and neutral trade injured; but not so far as to endanger a breach with America and a stoppage of American supplies to Great Britain and France. "We are constantly being told," said Grey to a House of Commons that insisted on increasing restrictions on trade, "that certain supplies which come from abroad are

[25] Spring Rice to Grey, July 31, 1916, *Spring Rice* II, 343.

absolutely essential for the Ministry of Munitions. . . . The business of the Foreign Office is to keep the diplomatic relations such that there is no fear of these supplies being interfered with." [36]

On the American side, while it was equally vital to protect neutral rights and American property, the cost of such protection in terms of present and future American interests must be carefully considered. Rightly or wrongly, those in charge of United States foreign policy believed that our political interests of the future were bound up with the good-will of Great Britain and France. Even more clearly, they realized that an immediate breach with the Allies, especially if it involved measures interfering with trade, would impose heavy penalties upon the economic life of the nation. " If it came to the last analysis," wrote House to Wilson, " and we placed an embargo upon munitions of war and foodstuffs to please the cotton men, our whole industrial and agricultural machinery would cry out against it." [37]

The Allied diplomats were, of course, as clearly aware of the situation as the American and did not fail to capitalize their advantage. " The brutal facts are," wrote Ambassador Spring Rice to Grey, " that this country has been saved by the war and by our war demand from a great economical crisis; that in normal times Great Britain and her colonies take forty per cent of the total export trade of the United States. We have therefore the claims of their best customer and at the present moment our orders here are absolutely essential to their commercial prosperity." [38] This realization

[36] Hansard, *Parliamentary Debates,* 5th series, LXXVIII, 1319.
[37] House to Wilson, July 22, 1915, *I.P.,* II, 58.
[38] Spring Rice to Grey, November 21, 1915, *Spring Rice,* II, 300.

permitted the British, at least in their private negotiations, to assume a reasonably firm tone. " No matter how low our fortunes run," declared the Ambassador to Colonel House, " we will go to war before we will admit the principle of blockade as your Government wishes to interpret it. If we acquiesced, it would be all to the advantage of Germany, whom you seem to favor." [39] More calmly and sadly, Grey wrote, following the American note of protest in October, 1915:

" If we admitted all its contentions, it would be tantamount to admitting that under modern conditions we could not prevent Germany from trading, at any rate through neutral ports, as freely in time of war as in time of peace . . . it looks as if the United States might now strike the weapon of sea-power out of our hands and thereby ensure a German victory." [40]

But neither a German victory nor the economic sacrifices involved in the only retaliatory measures possible against the Allies, were desired by the American Government and people. The failure to support American protests by economic pressure is to be explained not by legal niceties, but by the fact that the cost to our own commercial interests and to our sentimental sympathies would have seemed too high.

Thus, while neither the Allied nor the American diplomats were able ever to reach a settlement of the issues that divided them, they avoided the breach which would have been costly or fatal to each. The Allies escaped the mistake

[39] House Diary, October 14, 1915, *I.P.,* II, 76.
[40] Grey to House, November 11, 1915, *I.P.,* II, 79-80.

of the Germans, who over-estimated the importance of military factors at the expense of political, an error which, as Grey insists, "brought the United States into the war and ended in the defeat of Germany." [41] The United States, unable to secure any formal relaxation of the measures of restriction, set its legal case on record and in practice not merely preserved but developed its overseas trade to an unprecedented degree.[42]

President Wilson maintained his policy of the middle of the road, in the face not merely of difficulties from abroad but of constant and contradictory criticism at home. During the first year of the war, American shippers deluged the State Department with telegrams of protests against Allied interference. The chairman of the Senate Foreign Relations Committee argued vehemently that the Government was unduly favoring the Allies.[43] The Secretary of State him-

[41] *Grey*, II, 117.

[42] The chief indication of the degree to which, under the Allied system, American trade with neutrals was protected, is to be found in the vastly increased stringency of restrictive measures after the United States entered the war. During the fiscal year July 1, 1917 to July 1, 1918, as compared with the previous year, American exports to Sweden fell from 24 million dollars worth to 4; exports to Holland from 109 millions to 6. On the other hand American exports to Spain, which could not transship to Germany, fell only from 77 millions to 67 millions; and those to Norway, where transshipment was carefully guarded against, actually increased threefold. The figures indicate that the diminution in American exports to European neutrals, was thus the result not so much of American use of her own products as it was an aspect of the blockade system, Guichard, *op. cit.*, p. 132.

[43] Lansing's detailed reply to these charges is contained in the letter to Senator Stone signed by Bryan, *F.R., 1914, Suppl.*, vii-xiv.

Bryan

self, although he signed the American notes to all the belligerents, believed that Wilson's policy was not impartial, and that there was no essential difference between Allied and German infractions of American rights, the one touching rights of trade, the other merely rights of travel.[44] The Germans and their supporters insisted that the President's failure to use economic pressure against the Allies, as he used diplomatic threats against the Germans, proved him to be unneutral.[45]

On the other hand, Wilson's own Ambassador in Great Britain, Walter Hines Page, was intensely critical of the policy underlying American protests as he was of the tone of the notes. They were, he believed, needlessly obstructive, legalistic, and technical. " God deliver us, or can you deliver us," he cabled to House in October, 1914, " from library lawyers. They often lose chestnuts while they argue about burns." [46] In his opinion nothing counted so much as Anglo-American friendship. "A cargo of copper, I grant you, may be important; but it can't be as important as our

[44] For a defense of Bryan's point of view by an American historian, see the anonymous biographical sketch of William Jennings Bryan in Samuel Flagg Bemis, *Secretaries of State*, X, 30. The author believes that German submarine warfare followed naturally upon American willingness to accept Allied trade restrictions. Since America did not " vindicate its declared rights against violation from one quarter," it faced the necessity of " meeting violations from another." The American argument that it was not our business to redress German naval inferiority by an embargo on munitions, he regards as specious. Cf. Bryan to Wilson, April 23, 1915, William Jennings Bryan, *Memoirs,* pp. 396-397.

[45] For the German point of view, see the Stenographic Minutes of the Reichstag investigating committee, *G.D.,* II, 718 ff.

[46] Page to House, October 20, 1914, *I.P.,* I, 305.

friendship. It's the big and lasting things that count now. I think of the unborn generations of men to whom the close friendship of the Kingdom and of our Republic will be the most important political fact in the world. . . . It's no time, then, to quarrel or to be bumptious about a cargo of oil or of copper, or to deal with these gov'ts as if things were normal." [47]

The oil and copper men, however, felt differently, and the fact that those responsible for American policy could appreciate their point of view as Page did not, at the same time that they saw the necessity of friendly relations with the Allies, gave to the American attitude a sense of balance which, if it did not make for universal popularity, was conceived in the economic and political interest of the nation. Lansing, who was responsible for the notes of protests and who succeeded Bryan as Secretary of State in July, 1915, was insistent, as a lawyer, that every alteration in established international custom must be questioned. As a diplomat, however, he confessed that " that time-honored refuge of jurists," precedent, would have to be abandoned, and that to the novel problems raised, " natural justice and practical common-sense " would have to be applied.[48] Despite the sharp tone of his notes, he was personally convinced that America's future interests were wrapped up in Allied victory.

[47] Page to House, November 9, 1914, *I.P.,* I, 309-310.

[48] Address before Amherst alumni, February, 1915, cited by J. B. Scott, *Review of Reviews,* LI, 424. Bryan evidently played a rôle of small consequence in determining relations with the Allies, even while Secretary of State. The British Ambassador reported: " Bryan, of course, regards the war mainly as a background to his own peace treaties. It is hard to take him seriously," Spring Rice to Grey, August 25, 1914, *Spring Rice,* II, 220.

When he assumed the Secretaryship of State he made notes
of the aims that should guide him. He then expressed the
belief that " there existed a deep-seated opposition between
the German system and democracy, that America's task was
to save democracy, and that she must eventually take part in
the war if that course was necessary to prevent a German
victory." [49] At the very moment of drafting one of his
strongest notes of protest, he wrote to House: " In no event
should we take a course that would seriously endanger our
friendly relations with Great Britain, France, or Russia, for,
as you say, our friendship with Germany is a matter of the
past." [50]

For Wilson and House, a break with the Allies was
almost unthinkable, and at least until the summer of 1916
they believed that hostile economic pressure would cost
America much more than it was worth. " In regard to our
shipping troubles with Great Britain," wrote House in May,
1915, " I believe that if we press hard enough they will go
to almost any limit rather than come to the breaking point.
But, in so doing, we would gain their eternal resentment for
having taken advantage of their position, and our action
would arise to haunt us—not only at the peace conference,
but for a century to follow." [51] The President replied: " I
think of it just as you do," and urged House to make suggestions for " a line of action at once practicable and effective that would escape the consequences you (and I) would
dread and deplore." [52]

[49] Pratt's biographical sketch of Robert Lansing, Bemis, *op. cit.,*
X, 55.

[50] Lansing to House, July 30, 1915, *I.P.,* II, 70.

[51] House to Wilson, July 22, 1915, *I.P.,* II, 70.

[52] Wilson to House, July 27, 1915, Y.H.C.

The President and his chief adviser in foreign affairs, unlike Page, regarded it as important that America's case should be placed on record in public notes of protest. But they counted upon securing real concessions through personal negotiations, and were always anxious to soften to a reasonable degree the tone of the notes. A strong note provoked public opinion on the other side and made it all the more difficult for the British Foreign Office in its struggle with the British Admiralty. "It would be better," wrote Colonel House to Mr. Polk in the summer of 1916, "if we could get what we are after without taking such a positive stand publicly. It is the publicity of these things that always does the harm and to which they [the British] object. They have told me repeatedly that if we would tell them confidentially our position, they would try to meet it." [53] Wilson himself was always alive to the danger of public pressure. "I hoped to influence the matter unofficially," he cabled in the spring of 1915, "and avoid the strong note which otherwise must be sent." [54] In the same spirit House was able, without any concession of principle, to alter the form and tone of a strongly worded note of protest and thus to avoid the feeling which Spring Rice believed would have produced a "big catastrophe equal to or worse than, that brought on by Cleveland's Venezuela despatch." [55]

This determination to maintain friendly relations, matched by an equal determination on the part of the British Foreign

[53] House to Polk, July 25, 1916, *I.P.*, II, 314.

[54] Wilson to House, May 26, 1915, Y.H.C.

[55] Spring Rice to Grey, October 1, 1914, *Spring Rice*, II, 233. The incident is described by House in almost identical terms, *I.P.*, I, 307.

Office, provided the basis for practical compromise in the issue with the Allies. " I cannot see how there can be any serious trouble between England and America," wrote House to Page, " with all of us feeling as we do." [56] But this sentence, written in full confidence in the autumn of 1914, House would hardly have dared to repeat in 1916, after two years of diplomatic stress and protest. No solution of the larger issues was apparent, small incidents were magnified, the patience of responsible leaders was stretched taut. In September, 1916, the British Ambassador commented upon " the hostile disposition of people, generally very friendly, in New York. I happened to call upon a good friend of ours in the State Department. He burst out in a long and violent diatribe against all our proceedings which he said were doing us more harm than the German had ever done. He surprised me by the extraordinary violence of his language. . . . He was known as being rather violently pro-ally. . . . The case is significant." [57]

Without German interference, indeed, it is doubtful whether even the determination for good-will of Wilson and Grey could have succeeded. " The first German U-boat campaign gave us our greatest assistance," writes Churchill. " It altered the whole position of our controversies with America. A great relief became immediately apparent." [58] Had Germany held her hand and permitted America to fight for her the battle of the Freedom of the Seas against the Allied blockade, America's quarrel would have been so

[56] House to Page, October 29, 1914, *I.P.,* I, 309.
[57] Spring Rice to Grey, September 15, 1916, *Spring Rice,* II, 349.
[58] Winston Churchill, *The World Crisis,* II, 306.

definitely with the Allies that the whole character of Allied-American relations would have been different.[59] Even as it was, the nerves of President Wilson began to tighten during the summer and autumn of 1916 and it is uncertain how long they could have stood the tension. The constant ground swell of irritation with the Allies threatened always to develop into a storm. Conditions of neutrality, as the President wrote House in November, 1916, had become " intolerable." [60]

4

Even at the very beginning of the war President Wilson was not so thoroughly convinced of the security of America's aloof position as his public statements would indicate. As early as September, 1914, in one of the intimate discussions he liked to carry on in his study with Colonel House, he confided to his friend, perhaps only partially in earnest, some of the forebodings that troubled him:

" He read a page from his ' History of the American People,' " Colonel House noted in his diary, " telling how during Madison's Administration the War of 1812 was started in exactly the same way as this controversy [with the Allies] is opening up. The passage said that Madison was compelled to go to war despite the fact that he was a

[59] Comment by Colonel House, June 24, 1933: " If Germany had not alienated American sympathies by her mode of warfare, the United States would not have put up with Allied control of American trade on the high seas. I told the Allies at the Armistice Conferences that if in a future war similar control were exercised over our trade with a nation that had our sympathy, such as France, a rupture could not be avoided."

[60] Wilson to House, November 24, 1916, Y.H.C.

peace-loving man and desired to do everything in his power
to prevent it, but popular feeling made it impossible. The
President said: ' Madison and I are the only two Princeton
men that have become President. The circumstances of the
War of 1812 and now run parallel. I sincerely hope they
will not go further." [61]

The obvious desirability of avoiding the more apparent
dangers anticipated inspired the American suggestion of
August 6, 1914, that the belligerent powers adopt the Declaration of London, as a code applicable to all matters relating to naval warfare. Unsatisfactory as its provisions were
likely to prove in fixing with certainty the conditions of neutral trade, there was obvious value to the neutrals in having a
limit set upon the articles that might be declared contraband.
Although on its face the Declaration favored the Central
Powers, the Allies would later have benefited from German
acceptance of a code of naval warfare, and might, through
liberal interpretation, conceivably have exercised a real control over trade actually destined for Germany.

Disappointed by the British evasion of the request for
the acceptance of the Declaration of London, Lansing sought
a compromise that would eliminate the strongest of the

[61] House Diary, September 30, 1914, *I.P.,* I, 303-304. Roosevelt
harbored a similar thought, although he expressed it in a manner
not complimentary to the President: " President Wilson," he wrote
Grey, " is certainly not desirous of war with anybody. But he is
very obstinate, and he takes the professorial view of international
matters. I need not point out to you that it is often pacifists who,
halting and stumbling and not knowing whither they are going,
finally drift helplessly into a war, which they have rendered inevitable, without the slightest idea that they are doing so. A
century ago this was what happened to the United States under
Presidents Jefferson and Madison," Roosevelt to Grey, January 22,
1915, *Grey,* II, 151.

American objections to the Orders in Council but would also give to the Allies virtual control of cargoes destined for Germany's armed forces. If the British would accept the Declaration, an acceptance which would presumably be followed by that of the other belligerents, it would be possible for them to announce that should a port of a neutral country be used notoriously as a base for supplies to an enemy government, that port would be regarded as having acquired enemy character so far as trade in contraband was concerned, and would be subject to the rules of the Declaration of London governing trade to enemy territory.[62] The suggestion was ingenious, and had it been accepted by the British would have avoided much future friction with the United States. But it was not pressed by Ambassador Page, who apparently never attempted to understand its bearing and who refused to urge it upon Grey.[63] Nor would the British be likely to accept it in view of the possibility that later they might be compelled to cut off all trade with Germany, free as well as contraband. It resulted that the British maintained their Orders in Council, modifying them only in form, and reserving the right to stop conditional contraband consigned " to order " in a neutral country.

President Wilson was intensely troubled by the failure of the American proposal, both because of the increasing complaints of American shippers and because the attitude of the American Ambassador in London did not promise the op-

[62] Lansing to Page, October 16, 1914, *F.R., 1914, Suppl.*, 249.

[63] Page threatened to resign if the United States continued to press for the acceptance of the Declaration of London, and spoke of the Lansing proposal as unworthy of " two great, friendly, frank and truthful nations," *Page,* III, 181-189.

portunity of exercising strong diplomatic pressure in that
quarter.

" I am a little disturbed by the messages Walter Page is
sending recently," Wilson wrote to House. " It is very necessary that he should see the difficult matters between us and
the British Government in the light in which they are seen
on this side of the water, and I am sorry that he should think
the argument of them from our point of view the work of
mere 'library lawyers.' We are very much helped by his
advice, but I hope that he will not get into an unsympathetic
attitude. We are handling matters of the greatest difficulty,
because they must be handled under the influence of opinion
and it would be very unfortunate if he were to become unsympathetic or were to forget the temper of folks at home,
who are exceedingly sensitive about every kind of right." [64]

The situation was less acrid than it might have been, because of the prevailing conviction in the United States that
Germany had forced the war upon the world. " In the
glorious annals of German achievements," wrote the British
Ambassador, " nothing is so remarkable as the fact that Germany has almost made England popular in America." But
he also gave warning that the other side of the picture was
being developed:

" The American conscience is on our side, but the American pocket is being touched. Copper and oil are dear to the
American heart and the export is a matter of great importance. We are stopping this export and the consequence
is a steady howl which is increasing in volume. We should
probably do the same. But the howl may become very furious
soon." [65]

As the autumn passed, the complaints of American shippers increased in number and intensity. On December 26,

[64] Wilson to House, October 23, 1914, Y.H.C.

[65] Spring Rice to Lord Newton, October 21; to Sir Valentine
Chirol, November 3, 1914, *Spring Rice*, II, 239, 241.

the State Department despatched a formal note protesting against the harshness of Allied methods of control.[66]

The effect of the American protest, almost more than the conditions that caused it, was of significance. The note avoided taking issue with the main principle of Allied policy, the exclusion from Germany of all articles of military use; it even admitted to the British the " imperative necessity to protect their national safety ": it simply alleged unnecessary harshness of method. But it was received by the British as proof of increasing pro-German sentiment. Public opinion in England, Grey cabled on January 22, 1915, was " becoming unfavourably and deeply impressed by the trend of action taken by the United States Government and by its attitude towards Great Britain."

" What is felt here is that while Germany deliberately planned a war of pure aggression, has occupied and devastated large districts in Russia, Belgium, and France, inflicting great misery and wrong on innocent populations, the only act on record on the part of the United States is a protest singling out Great Britain as the only Power whose conduct is worthy of reproach. . . . In the struggle for existence in which this country is at stake, much store is set in England on the good-will of the United States; and people cannot believe that the United States desires to paralyze the advantage which we derive from our sea power, while leaving intact to Germany those military and scientific advantages which are special to her. . . . Should people in England come to believe that the dominant influence in United States politics is German, it would tend to create an untoward state of public opinion which we should greatly regret." [67]

[66] Bryan to Page, December 26, 1914, *F.R., 1914, Suppl.,* 372-375.

[67] Grey to Spring Rice, January 22, 1915, *I.P.,* I, 347-349; cf. Grey to Page, January 7, February 10, 1915, *F.R., 1915, Suppl.,* 299-302, 324-344.

The implication that American protests against Allied interference with neutral trade resulted from German influence, indicated a profound misapprehension of the situation in the United States and of the American official attitude. The American Government in refusing all demands for an embargo on munitions of war had not merely asserted neutral rights of export as against German hopes, and incidentally incurred German ill-will, but at the same time supplied what Grey himself termed " the need of the Allies." If these facts were not clearly appreciated by the Allied Governments, particular means must be taken to emphasize them. The President decided to send Colonel House on a special mission to Europe.

The primary purpose of the House mission was to search for an opportunity of mediation. In the circumstances no opportunity appeared, and the importance of his services lay rather in establishing a basis of trust instead of mistrust between the British and Americans, a task accomplished, according to Sir Horace Plunkett " in his own quiet, tactful, and marvellously persuasive way." As Wilson wrote, he " laid the foundations of confidence." [68]

The date of his arrival in Europe coincided with the first serious crisis in the relations of America with the belligerents, resulting from the British use of neutral flags and the German declaration of a war-zone around the British Isles within which enemy merchant ships would be destroyed. Wilson acted rapidly, in the hope of attaining a compromise between the Allied blockade and the German submarine. On

[68] Plunkett to Wilson, June 4, 1915, *I.P.*, I, 470; Wilson to House, February 13, 1915, Y.H.C.

February 20, identical notes were sent to each side, suggesting that the Germans restrict mine-laying operations and submarine attacks upon merchant vessels, in return for which the Allies would discontinue the use of neutral flags and grant the passage of foodstuffs into Germany.[69] In his private letters Wilson did not conceal his sympathies with the Allies. "I regretted the necessity of sending the note about the unauthorized use of our flag," he wrote on February 13, "but it could not be avoided, for sooner or later the use of the flag plays directly into the hands of Germany in their extraordinary threat to destroy commerce." [70] The compromise proposed on February 20 seemed to him not merely reasonable, from the varying points of view of the belligerents, but a means of escape for America from an increasingly unpleasant situation.

"Please say to Page," he cabled House, "that he cannot emphasize too much, in presenting the note to Grey, the favorable opinion which would be created in this country if the British Government could see its way clear to adopt the suggestions made there. Opinion here is still decidedly friendly, but a tone of great uneasiness is distinctly audible now, and the events and decisions of the next few days will undoubtedly make a deep impression." [71]

Neither side showed any real willingness to accept the proffered compromise. The Germans avoided a blank refusal, but insisted that not merely foodstuffs but raw materials should be allowed to pass. The British were not willing to pass even foodstuffs.[72] Three months later House

[69] Bryan to Page, February 20, 1915, *F.R., 1915, Suppl.,* 119.
[70] Wilson to House, February 13, 1915, Y.H.C.
[71] Wilson to House, February 20, 1915, Y.H.C.
[72] Gerard to Bryan, March 1, 1915; Page to Bryan, March 15, *F.R., 1915, Suppl.,* 130, 140.

returned to the proposition. During the interval, methods of warfare had become intensified: the Germans had introduced poison gas at Ypres, the danger from the submarine was more obvious; the Allies had introduced the Reprisals Order, and the effects of the food blockade were being felt.

On May 14, following the sinking of the *Lusitania,* Grey asked House what he thought Germany's reply to Wilson would be.

" I told him," reported House to the President, " that if I were writing Germany's reply I would say that if England would lift the embargo on foodstuffs, Germany would consent to discontinue her submarine policy of sinking merchantmen. Grey replied that if Germany would consent not only to discontinue that mode of warfare, but would also agree to discontinue the use of asphyxiating gases and the ruthless killing of noncombatants, England would be willing to lift the embargo on foodstuffs." [73]

The President was stirred by what seemed the first indication of willingness to make concessions on the part of a belligerent. He replied at once that he was " deeply interested " in the proposal, which " would afford a solution of a situation as trying and difficult for England as it is for us." He urged House to discover whether Grey's colleagues would support him.[74] Two days later he encouraged House to press the suggestion. He himself had just sent a strongly-worded note to Germany regarding the sinking of the *Lusitania,* and faced a rupture with Bryan, who demanded that an equally strong note be sent the Allies.

" It becomes more and more evident that it will presently become necessary for the sake of diplomatic consistency and

[73] House to Wilson, May 14, 1915, *I.P.,* I, 443.
[74] Wilson to House, May 16, 1915, Y.H.C.

to satisfy our public to address a note to Great Britain about the unnecessary and unwarranted interruption of our legitimate trade with neutral ports. It would be a great stroke on England's part if she would of her own accord relieve this situation and so put Germany wholly in the wrong and leave her without excuse that the opinion of the world could tolerate. It would be a small price to pay for cessation of submarine outrages." [75]

Negotiations with the British were the more difficult, since the Liberal Cabinet was in dissolution. But on May 21, Grey reported that he had discussed the proposal with the prospective members of the new Coalition Cabinet and from them had received the definite impression that they would favor it. [76] Wilson thereupon instructed Ambassador Gerard, in Berlin, to raise the question of compromise with the Germans. The matter was of some delicacy, since Wilson did not wish the Germans to get the impression that he was retreating from the firm stand he had taken in his *Lusitania* note. Nor did he wish the British to feel that the American right to ship non-contraband goods to neutral ports would be satisfied by the free passage merely of foodstuffs. [77] To House the proposal seemed the only practicable solution. " It will be a great diplomatic triumph for the President," he wrote, " if brought about, and it will settle our contentions with both Governments." [78]

[75] Wilson to House, May 18, 1915, Y.H.C.

[76] Mr. Lloyd George states that while Grey was prepared to consider the proposal, he did not consult the Cabinet. " Had he done so they would have turned it down emphatically. Whether he consulted the Prime Minister before expressing his readiness to enter into an arrangement on this basis I am not prepared to say," *War Memoirs of David Lloyd George,* II, 122.

[77] Wilson to House, May 23, 1915, Y.H.C.

[78] House Diary, May 21, 1915, *I.P.,* I, 450.

Hopes of a compromise between submarine and blockade were definitely dashed by Germany. When Ambassador Gerard raised the proposal in Berlin he was informed that the Germans might consider it if free passage were granted to raw materials as well as to foodstuffs. Germany, the Foreign Minister asserted, was in no need of food.[79] As House cabled to the President, " This does away with their contention that the starving of Germany justifies their submarine policy." [80] Thus passed an opportunity which, if it could have been capitalized, might have had momentous results. Its passing not merely ensured the prolongation of the food blockade but eliminated the only chance of stopping the submarine warfare which ultimately led to American intervention.

The United States had fruitlessly put forward two proposals designed to protect neutral trade rights without infringing the belligerent right to intercept contraband: the acceptance of the Declaration of London, interpreted to meet

summary

[79] Gerard to House, May 24, 1915, *I.P.,* I, 448.

[80] House to Wilson, May 29, 1915, *I.P.,* I, 452. Berlin may have felt, as Wilson feared, that American opposition to the submarine warfare was not so strong as set forth in the *Lusitania* note. Word had just been received of the conversation between Bryan and Ambassador Dumba, in which Bryan was reported as intimating that the note need not be taken too seriously. Comment of German Navy Archivist, September 15, 1933: " It is important to emphasize the German contention that not merely cutting off food but also the stopping of the import of raw materials was regarded as a serious danger in the event of a long war. It is true that the German official and unofficial reports emphasized the danger of starvation, but this was rather done with a propagandist eye to world opinion. It is hardly fair from the German point of view to picture their insertion of a demand for freedom of import of raw materials as an evasion."

new conditions; the compromise between blockade and submarine. A third proposal set forth by Colonel House before Allies and Germans in the spring of 1915 met a similar fate. This was the recognition of the doctrine of the Freedom of the Seas.

This doctrine, the main aspect of which is the exemption of all private property from capture on the high seas, had been embodied by the United States in a treaty with Prussia, in 1785, and unsuccessfully pressed upon the sea powers in 1823 and again at the Congress of Paris in 1856. At the second Hague Conference in 1907 the Americans urged its acceptance. The British again refused to support the proposal, believing that their navy was a better protection for British trade than any paper agreement. France, Russia, and Japan voted against it, while Germany, Austria-Hungary, and Italy voted for it. Unfortunately the division was on lines corresponding to the two armed and hostile camps of Europe. The proposal was thus associated in British minds with the policy of Germany in its threat to British sea power.

Colonel House could count on German support of the doctrine, whether as an immediate step towards compromise or as an ultimate condition of peace. He believed that he could show the British that conditions of naval warfare had so changed that their traditional opposition was unreasonable. It was true that the Germans would gain obvious advantages by freedom of trade in foodstuffs and raw materials through neutral ports. But House argued that the advantages that would accrue to the Allies, if less obvious, were just as great or greater. They would be estopped from directing against Germany an offensive blockade of doubtful legality; but their defensive position would be enormously strengthened. Secure from an effective blockade of their ports by reason of the superiority of their surface fleet, they would receive a guarantee against the danger of submarine interference with commerce in the ocean lanes. Their communications with the Dominions and colonies could not be severed. The powers with the most colonies and the widest overseas trade, House argued, would stand to gain most.[81]

The attitude of the British Foreign Office was not entirely unsympathetic. More clearly than the naval officers they realized that British command of the seas was threatened by modern developments. In his conversations of February, House found Grey willing to consider the immunity from capture of all private property on the seas. On February 11, Sir William Tyrrell stated that:

"Great Britain recognized that the submarine had changed the status of maritime warfare and in the future Great Britain would be better protected by such a policy [absolute freedom of merchantmen of all nations to sail the seas in time of war unmolested] than she has been in the past by maintaining an overwhelming navy." [82]

As House had anticipated, the Germans accepted the proposal with enthusiasm. Unfortunately for its success they

[81] Lord Loreburn, one of the few British leaders who at this time agreed with House, said that " if we could incorporate this idea into the peace convention it would not only be a great act of statesmanship, but it would perhaps be the greatest jest that had ever been perpetrated upon an unsuspecting nation—having, of course, Germany in mind," House to Wilson, May 3, 1915, *I.P.,* I, 424.

[82] *I.P.,* I, 370. Grey publicly intimated (*Pall Mall Gazette,* November 15, 1915), that it might be possible to accept the immunity of private property at sea as one of the conditions of peace.

immediately published their approval and in such terms that it was generally regarded as German-made.[83] It was remembered that similar proposals had been supported by the Central Powers against the Entente in 1907. The British " blue-water school " saw in it the end of British sea-power. But the vital element in British opposition to the Freedom of the Seas lay in their distrust of Germany and their unwillingness to substitute paper conventions in place of material power. The phrase " a scrap of paper " was always in their minds. Even Grey, who did not disapprove the Freedom of the Seas in principle, was unwilling to trust to an agreement with Germany. Conventions of such a type, he insisted, were worse than useless unless there were an association of nations to enforce them. " One lesson from the experience of the war," he wrote later, " is that we should not bind ourselves to observe any rules of war, unless those who sign them with us undertake to uphold them by force, if need be, against an enemy who breaks them." [84]

[83] When House talked to Bryce he found that he " did not seem in favor of it, saying he had heard that Dernburg very much desired it. I replied that I was the instigator of it in Germany, and the Germans were merely echoing the thought I had given them. He laughed and said he felt better," *I.P.,* I, 464.

[84] *Grey,* II, 106. Cf. Grey to Roosevelt, December 18, 1914, *ibid.,* II, 148. In a letter to House of August 10, 1915, Grey insisted, " International Law has hitherto had no sanction. . . . If that can be secured, freedom of the seas and many other things will become easy. But it is not a fair proposition that there should be a guaranty of freedom of the seas while Germany claims to recognize no law but her own on land, and to have the right to make war at will," *I.P.,* II, 88. At the Armistice Conference, Lloyd George expressed a similar thought speaking of the British command of the neutral goods that might enter Germany through

At the very moment that House was urging consideration of the Freedom of the Seas upon the British, point was given to British suspicion of Germany by the sinking of the *Lusitania*. The burst of emotion that followed ruined all chance of using the proposal as a method of compromise.[85]

5

The failure of the third positive attempt to find some way of regulating the control of neutral commerce, threw Wilson back upon a merely negative policy, that of protesting in public against the methods of the Allies and warning them in private that unless they were relaxed friendly relations with America could not be maintained. Wilson's warnings were conceived in the friendliest spirit, but they grew progressively sharper.

" There is something I think ought to be said to Sir Edward Grey," he cabled House on May 5, " of which I wish you would speak to Page but which I cannot convey through him but must convey through you because I wish it to be absolutely unofficial and spoken merely in personal friendship. A very serious change is coming over public sentiment in this country because of England's delays and many arbitrary interferences in dealing with our neutral cargoes. The country is listening with more and more acquiescence, just because of this unnecessary irritation, to the suggestion of an embargo upon shipments of arms and war supplies, and if this grows much more before the next session of Congress it may be very difficult if not impossible for me to prevent action to that end." [86]

---

neutral ports: " I should like to see this League of Nations established first before I let this power go," *infra,* p. 375.

[85] *I.P.,* I, 433 ff.

[86] Wilson to House, May 5, 1915, Y.H.C.

Three weeks later the President emphasized American opposition to the Reprisals Order that had inaugurated the pseudo-blockade:

" We feel that the blockade recently proclaimed has not been made in fact effective and the impression prevails here that Sir Edward Grey has not been able to fulfill his assurances given us at the time of the Order in Council that the Order would be carried out in such a way as not to affect our essential rights. There is an accumulating public opinion upon these matters of which I think the Ministers there should know, and the recent explanations do not touch the essence or meet the opinion." [87]

Members of the Cabinet, which was for the most part pro-Ally, reinforced Wilson's warnings. Secretary Bryan demanded that a note be sent the Allies at least as strong as that sent to Germany regarding the *Lusitania*. Secretary Lane complained:

" We have been very meek and mild under their use of the ocean as a toll-road. Of course, the sympathy of the greater part of the country is with the English, but it would not have been as strongly with them, not nearly so strongly, if it had not been for the persistent shortsightedness of our German friends. I cannot see what England means by her policy of delay and embarrassment and hampering. Her success manifestly depends upon the continuance of the strictest neutrality on our part, and yet she is not willing to let us have the rights of a neutral. . . . There isn't a man in the Cabinet who has a drop of German blood in his veins, I guess. Two of us were born under the British flag. I have two cousins in the British army, and Mrs. Lane has three. . . . Yet each day that we meet we boil over somewhat, at the foolish manner in which England acts. Can it be that she is trying to take advantage of the war to hamper our

[87] Wilson to House, May 23, 1915, Y.H.C.

trade? . . . If Congress were in session, we would be actively debating an embargo resolution today." [88]

So long as the submarine situation remained unsettled, Wilson, unlike Bryan, was not willing to precipitate public friction with the Allies by sending them a comprehensive note of protest. But on July 8, House, who had returned to the United States, warned Grey that " in the event our immediate differences with Germany are composed, there will at once arise a demand for an adjustment of our shipping troubles with England. There is an influential element here that persists in pressing this issue to a conclusion, and it is something of which the President must take cognizance." [89] British preparations to make cotton contraband further troubled Wilson. At the end of the month, he commented with some sympathy on Grey's plea that to abandon the blockade would prolong the war, but added: " That is perhaps true, but it will not satisfy the United States. . . . How far do you think they will yield? I should like to press for the utmost and yet I should wish to be sensible and practical." [90] A week later he wrote House: " I would deeply appreciate any suggestions you may have thought out on this infinitely difficult matter. We cannot long delay action. Our public opinion demands it." [91]

[88] Lane to House, May 5, 1915, *I.P.*, I, 458-450. Cf. Spring Rice to Grey, September 15, 1916: "There certainly seems to be an impression among our friends here that many of our measures are taken as much with the object of promoting our own trade at the expense of the trade of the neutrals as for injuring the enemy," *Spring Rice,* II, 348.

[89] House to Grey, July 8, 1915, *I.P.,* II, 57.

[90] Wilson to House, July 21, 1915, Y.H.C.

[91] Wilson to House, July 27, 1915, Y.H.C.

As had happened three months before, Germany proceeded to ease the situation by bringing on a new submarine crisis. On August 19, a German submarine sank the *Arabic,* and for the next five weeks the diplomatic situation was dominated by the resulting negotiations with Berlin. But even in the midst of that crisis Wilson worried over the dispute with the Allies. "We must write to England and in very definite terms." [92] With a good deal of skill the German Ambassador, at the moment that he intimated that Germany would yield on the submarine issue, suggested that the Allies should also make concessions.

"It certainly does look," wrote Wilson, "as if a way were opened out of our difficulties, so far as Germany is concerned. That only makes more perplexing our questions as to how to deal with England, for apparently we have no choice now but to demand that she respect our rights a good deal better than she has been doing." [93]

The President, who lacked neither astuteness nor humor, commented ruefully upon the invariable demand of Bernstorff, that Wilson adopt as strict an attitude toward Allied as toward German infractions of international law. "Germany has at last come to her senses and is playing intelligent politics. She is seeking to put us into a position where we shall have to play to some extent the rôle of catspaw for her in opening trade to her." [94]

In early October, the *Arabic* case was settled according to American demands. A period of quiet discussion set in so far as the submarine dispute was concerned. "Now that

[92] Wilson to House, August 21, 1915, Y.H.C.
[93] Wilson to House, August 31, 1915, Y.H.C.
[94] Wilson to House, August 31, 1915, Y.H.C.

the German crisis is over," wrote the British Ambassador,
" it is the turn of the Allies." [95] He further warned the
Foreign Office: " You may expect pretty strong communication. Until popular opinion is convinced of the necessity of
taking sides (which it is not) Government must be impartial." [96] The American note of October 21 bore out the
Ambassador's warning. It covered comprehensively all the
American objections to Allied restrictions and it set forth
those objections in a tone that could be moderately described
as firm. Ambassador Page characterized it as " an un-
courteous monster of 35 heads and three appendices . . .
not a courteous word, not a friendly phrase, nor a kindly
turn in it, not an allusion even to an old acquaintance, to
say nothing of an old friendship . . . there is nothing in
its tone to show that it came from an American to an Englishman." [97] Wilson, despite his anxiety to remain on cordial
terms with the Allies, believed that the time had come for
a sharp tone, in view of British disregard of private protests. " It disturbs me a little," he wrote, " that Page should
be so consistently seeking to give us the unfavorable English
view." [98] As Spring Rice himself recognized, the Allies
were using the United States as a base of supply and had
just floated a loan; in all reason they must be prepared to
give something if they were to continue to receive. [99]

[95] Spring Rice to Grey, October 7, 1915, *Spring Rice,* II, 282.
[96] *I.P.,* II, 71.
[97] Page to House, November 12, 1915, *Page,* II, 78. The text
of the American note is in Lansing to Page, October 21, 1915, *F.R.,*
1915, Suppl., 578-601.
[98] Wilson to House, October 18, 1915, Y.H.C.
[99] Spring Rice to Grey, October 7, 1915, *Spring Rice,* II, 282.

But although Page's objections did not affect Wilson's determination to issue the note, his prophecies that it would produce no results proved entirely correct.[100] Ambassador Spring Rice stated flatly that Great Britain could never accept the contentions of the American Department of State. Grey wrote to House:

" We must either continue the difference of opinion with your Government, or give up definitely and openly any attempt to stop goods going to and from Germany through neutral ports . . . that would go near abdicating all chance of preventing Germany from being successful. . . . I am convinced that the real question is not one of legal niceties about contraband and other things, but whether we are to do what we are doing, or nothing at all. The contentions of your Government would restrict our operations in such a way that Germany could evade them wholesale." [101]

An inconspicuous phrase in this letter gives the clue to the policy that the British and at least some of the Americans hoped to follow: " continue the differences of opinion with your Government." Why not? argued Ambassador Page. Was it not preferable to put up with the carrying of our cargoes into Allied ports, accepting the consequences of the pseudo-blockade, depending upon British prize courts for

[100] " It is certain that the note will receive no serious attention," Page cabled to Lansing, " until the present tension is relaxed and its presentation at this moment is likely to result in a public reception that may tend to defeat its purpose," Page to Lansing, October 15, 1915, Y.H.C.

[101] Grey to House, November 11, 1915, I.P., II, 79-80. Spring Rice, while he urged minor concessions, urged that a debate over the major points be avoided: " I think it would be a pity to take words too seriously. The Germans have not and they have not suffered. The best comment that our press can make is nothing at all," Spring Rice to Grey, October 28, 1915, Spring Rice, II, 297.

redress, than to engage in an economic conflict with the Allies that would be all to Germany's advantage?

But the President's patience was becoming exhausted. He daily encountered what he described as the " demand in the Senate for further, immediate, and imperative pressure on England and her allies." [102] The hope of settling finally a formula with Germany that would end the *Lusitania* negotiations became brighter, and affected the problem of Allied interference directly. " It now looks as if our several difficulties with Germany would be presently adjusted," he cabled to House on January 12. "As soon as they are, the demand here, especially from the Senate, will be imperative that we force England to make at least equal concessions to our unanswerable claims of right. This is just." [103]

Colonel House, who believed that there would soon be an opportunity for Wilson's putting forward a peace offer, begged for delay.

" Page had Sir Edward Grey and Lord Robert Cecil to lunch, and we discussed these matters at length. Lord Robert told me, and Sir Edward confirmed it, that if he acceded to your request his resignation would be demanded at once. Personally, he is willing to do anything. He even goes so far as to suggest that it might come to the complete abandonment of the blockade, in which case Germany would perhaps win. He does not believe there can be halfway measures. . . . It would be a calamity if anything should happen to prevent Sir Edward's continuance in the Government until peace is made. And yet if we push them too hard upon the question of neutral trade, he is likely to go. The feeling is becoming more and more set, and the country is demanding that the Government stand firm. . . ." [104]

[102] Wilson to House, December 24, 1915, Y.H.C.
[103] Wilson to House, January 12, 1916, Y.H.C.
[104] House to Wilson, January 16, 1916, *I.P.*, II, 132-133.

Once more the Germans intervened to throw the dispute with the Allies into the background. No agreement could be reached on the *Lusitania* formula; the armed merchantmen issue was handled awkwardly; and on March 24, a German submarine sank the *Sussex*. The ensuing crisis resulted in an ultimatum from Wilson to Berlin; it was concluded by the most complete assurance yet given by Germany that submarines would not be used to attack merchant vessels except according to the rules of international law.

The President turned again to the question of Allied restrictions, and this time with an attitude quite changed from the sympathy of the preceding year. The change doubtless proceeded in part from Germany's diplomatic surrender. More important was the fact that Wilson had put up to the Allies a basis for peace which he regarded as highly favorable to them, and had been snubbed. He began to ask himself whether the motives of the Allies in waging war were not, in fact, as aggressive as those of Germany.

"It seems to me," he wrote on May 16, "that we should really get down to hard pan. The at least temporary removal of the acute German question has concentrated attention here on the altogether indefensible course Great Britain is pursuing with regard to trade to and from neutral ports and her quite intolerable interception of mails on the high seas carried by neutral ships. . . . We are plainly face to face with this alternative therefore. The United States must either make a decided move for peace (upon a basis that promises to be permanent) or, if she postpones that must insist to the limit upon her rights of trade and upon such freedom of the seas as international law already justifies her in insisting on as against Great Britain, with the same plain speaking and firmness that she has used against Germany. And the choice must be made immediately. Which does Great Britain prefer? She cannot escape both. . . . Sir Edward should understand all this and that the crisis cannot be postponed; and it can be done with the most evident spirit of friendliness through you. Will you not prepare a full cable putting the whole thing plainly to him? We must act, and act at once, in the one direction or the other." [105]

The reply of Grey to House's cable was virtually a *non possumus*. The Allies could not consider peace, and could not give up the blockade. Popular feeling in England against Wilson was strongly unfriendly. Even Ambassador Page could write, " I have moods in which I lose my patience with them and I have to put on two muzzles and a tight corset to hold myself in. . . . They get more and more on edge as the strain becomes severer. There'll soon be very few sane people left in the world." In the middle of June, nevertheless, the Ambassador pleaded for continuing patience on the part of the United States Government with the Allied blockade.

" They won't relax it; they can't. Public opinion wouldn't stand it an hour. As things are now, an Admiral has said in a public speech that it is necessary to hang Grey if they're going to win the war. We've planted ourselves firmly on (1) we've stated our position on the international law involved; our record on that score stands; and (2) we've cleared the ground for claims for damages. As I see it, that's all we can do—unless we are prepared to break off relations with Great Britain and get ready for war, after arbitrators have failed." [106]

Page's prophecy again proved correct. Instead of relaxing the blockade the British published on July 7 an Order in Council setting aside what was left of the Declaration of

[105] Wilson to House, May 16, 1916, Y.H.C. House's cable of May 19 to Grey, *I.P.,* II, 286.
[106] Page to House, May 30, June 16, 1916, *I.P.,* II, 302, 311.

London.[107] The announcement came at a time when American opinion was upset by the controversy over holding-up of American mail. " This question touches the conveniences of so many people," wrote Spring Rice to Grey, " that I fear the excitement against us will prove a formidable factor. Whether we have the right or not to exercise control over the post, we are certainly invoking on our heads a great deal of indignation from many powerful people." At the same time he reported an interview " with an extremely exasperated official who hinted not obscurely that American patience was coming to an end." [108]

On July 18 the Allies published the blacklist of firms with which Allied firms were forbidden to trade. Not of great practical moment, so far as the United States was concerned, it increased resentment.[109] The effect upon Wilson was important.

" I am, I must admit," he wrote on July 23, " about at the end of my patience with Great Britain and the Allies. This blacklist business is the last straw. I have told Spring Rice so, and he sees the reasons very clearly. Both he and Jusserand think it is a stupid blunder. I am seriously considering asking Congress to authorize me to prohibit loans and

[107] For the Anglo-French negotiations leading up to the abrogation of the Declaration of London, see Guichard, *op. cit.*, pp. 75-80. Text of the British Order in Council, *F.R., 1916, Suppl.*, 413-415.

[108] Spring Rice to Grey and to de Bunsen, *Spring Rice*, II, 318, 331.

[109] " If the British Government would only keep quiet," wrote Polk to House July 22, " it could have been handled comparatively easily, but . . . they did it, of course, in a wrong way," *I.P.*, II, 312. Ambassador Page described the blacklist as " tactless and unjust," *Page*, II, 184. For the American reply of July 26, written by Polk, see *F.R., 1916, Suppl.*, 421-422.

restrict exportations to the Allies. . . . Polk and I are compounding a very sharp note. I may feel obliged to make it as sharp as the one to Germany on the submarine. . . . Can we any longer endure their intolerable course?" [110]

Thus Wilson had at last reached the point not merely of calling for authority to utilize economic pressure against the Allies, but of putting them in his own mind on the same plane with the Central Powers. When Ambassador Page returned for a brief vacation in September the President told him that " when the war began he and all the men he met were in hearty sympathy with the Allies; but that now the sentiment toward England had greatly changed. He saw no one who was not vexed and irritated by the arbitrary English course." [111]

Before adjournment in September Congress conferred on the President the authority for which he asked, to inaugurate drastic retaliatory measures. On September 8, Congress also proceeded to vote the largest naval appropriation ever passed by the legislative body of a state not at war. The bill provided for the construction of 137 new vessels of all classes, and if carried into effect would enable the United States to dispute with the British the mastery of the seas. Wilson's attention was called to the dangers inherent in future naval competition and to probable British protests. " Let us build a navy bigger than hers," he replied, " and do what we please." [112]

[110] Wilson to House, July 23, 1916, Y.H.C.
[111] Page, II, 185.
[112] House Diary, September 24, 1916, I.P., II, 316.

6

Despite the best will for cordial relations on both sides, despite political and economic factors enforcing that will, conditions resulting from the war were driving the United States Government further and further apart from the Allies. Public protests and private warnings produced no effect upon Allied restrictions. The convoying of American ships, Grey's worst nightmare, an obvious method of breaking the blockade, was discussed. An embargo, which would have equally disastrous effects upon Allied fortunes as well as upon diplomatic relations, had become a distinct possibility.[113] The British Ambassador gave clear warning to his Government.

" The reason why there has been no embargo on arms and ammunition is not sympathy with us, but the sense that the prosperity of the country on which the administration depends for its existence would be imperilled by such a measure. If there is a scarcity of material here, or any other reason why an embargo would pay, we should have an embargo. . . . Restraints on shipping may be ordered. Transport may be impeded. A loan may be made more difficult. We are not secure against such measures. . . . The object should be to ascertain when the breaking point is near and where. There may be a breaking point. Do not deceive yourself as to that." [114]

Wilson himself, for whom at first friendly relations with the Allies had been a major object of policy and to whom he secretly gave his warm personal sympathy, had begun to think of them in the same terms as he thought of the Germans; to regard both sides as equally guilty in prolonging a disastrous and indecisive conflict, both sides as equally intent

[113] *Grey,* II, 116.
[114] Spring Rice to Cecil, August 13, 1916, *Spring Rice,* II, 345.

on selfish war aims, both sides careless of neutral rights. On November 24, 1916, he wrote to House asking that he pass on to Grey, " in the strongest terms," the dissatisfied feeling of the American people,

" growing more and more impatient with the intolerable conditions of neutrality, their feeling as hot against Great Britain as it was at first against Germany and likely to grow hotter still against an indefinite continuation of the war. . . . I do not think that he ought to be left in any degree of ignorance of the real state of our opinion." [115]

As on other occasions, Germany provided the solution of an intolerable situation between America and the Allies, and this time decisively. By forcing once more the submarine issue, Germany not merely threw into the background the dispute with Great Britain and France over trade rights, but compelled the United States to enter the war on their side.

[115] Wilson to House, November 24, 1916, Y.H.C.

Chapter III

THE SUBMARINE

1

The utilization of sea-power by the Allies in the World War had enormous and far-reaching consequences. It resulted directly, as we have seen, in the controversy with the United States over interference with neutral trade. Indirectly it was the ultimate cause of Germany's adopting, in desperation, measures that brought the United States into the war, according to Grey the supreme diplomatic mistake that ensured German defeat. Following the train of consequences further, the United States was thereby led to the formulation of a new world policy, revolutionary both as regards America and the rest of the world.

Allied control of the seas first hindered and then prevented import by Germany of the materials necessary to her life and conduct of the war; it also made it possible for the Allies to draw freely upon the resources of neutral nations, especially the United States. German efforts to overcome this double disadvantage with legitimate weapons were entirely in vain. The attempts of their diplomats to persuade the United States to insist upon the right to ship goods freely to the northern neutrals were bound to be fruitless. German propaganda failed in its attempt to arouse effective American feeling against the blockade or in favor of an embargo upon American exports to the Allies. Germany must decide whether she would accept the disadvantages of inferior sea-power, which according to the military and naval chiefs meant certain defeat, or whether she would utilize the direct weapon of submarine warfare which in its only effective form was regarded by the American Government as flagrantly illegal and obviously inhuman.

The failure of the Germans to face the decision squarely at the start and to embark upon a clear-cut policy, accounts in large measure for their final defeat. The organization of the German Government, given the character of the Kaiser, was in fact and notwithstanding general opinion extremely inapt for the conduct of war.[1] Two opposing forces worked on the Kaiser, in theory the chief, and each of these forces was successful in turn. The Chancellor and the Foreign Office, keenly aware of and appalled by the political consequences of a rupture with the United States, were able to interfere with and postpone the unrestricted submarine warfare. The Supreme Command insisted that it was technically impossible to carry on an effective submarine attack on enemy commerce according to cruiser rules. " Sinking without warning, because of the enemy's method of defence [armament of merchant ships] became an absolute necessity; we had the choice of this course or completely giving up the submarine war." [2] This insistence finally triumphed. But two years of the utmost value from the point of view of the submarine commanders had been wasted.

[1] See Jean Marie Bourget, *Gouvernement et Commandement*, especially pp. 12 ff. For a German criticism see Valentin, *Deutschlands Aussenpolitik*, pp. 318-319.

[2] Andreas Michelsen, *Der Ubootskrieg*, p. 87.

During those two years Germany suffered from lack of an effective supreme control. Navy officers ignored or misunderstood orders. Diplomats were kept in the dark as to the status of internal differences of opinion in Germany. The resumption of the unrestricted campaign in February, 1916, was discussed as little with Bernstorff as with the United States Government. The Ambassador, whose professional interest in the matter was vital, was not informed of the decision of January, 1917, until ten days after it was made; in the meantime he had been compelled to negotiate in the dark.[3]

A simple chronological survey indicates the indecision of German policy. On February 4, 1915, Germany issued the declaration of a war zone around the British Isles in which commerce would be destroyed, beginning February 18. On February 12, receiving word of imminent American objections, Germany ordered submarine commanders to spare neutral ships. On May 31, despite the American *Lusitania* protest, the Council at Pless confirmed orders to sink without warning; but on June 5 the Kaiser forbade the sinking of large passenger ships. The order was kept secret, even from Ambassador von Bernstorff, so that while it destroyed naval effectiveness it brought no diplomatic advantage. After the sinking of the *Arabic* the order was published; but in February, 1916, the unrestricted campaign was resumed until the American protest that followed the torpedoing of the *Sussex*, when it was again countermanded.

[3] *Bernstorff*, p. 236. The Ambassador's testimony before the Reichstag investigating committee is printed in *G.D.*, I, 229-321; his correspondence with the Foreign Office of January, 1917, *ibid.*, II, 1043-1051.

Germany might have foregone the submarine as a weapon and utilized the opportunity to stimulate American feeling against the Allies; or she might have used the submarine ruthlessly. " Neither of these two courses was consistently followed in our policy," writes Bernstorff. " We were forever trying to square the circle, and to conduct a submarine campaign which should be from a military point of view effective, without at the same time leading to a breach with America. . . . We thus contrived at one and the same time to cripple our submarines, and yet to fail to give satisfaction to America." [4]

The attitude taken by the American Government towards submarine warfare was inspired by American interests, but incidentally it proved of the greatest assistance to the Allies, because the shadow of a breach with the United States always hung over the German diplomats. Otherwise the unrestricted campaign would have begun earlier and more effectively. The British have not always acknowledged this fact. But the German historians insist upon it. The summer of 1916, they contend, was the moment for a firm inauguration of the unrestricted campaign, and they regard the surrender of the German Government to Wilson after the *Sussex* as a disaster.[5] They are supported in this opinion by the French:

" The two years of hesitation which preceded the final adoption of the submarine war without restrictions," writes

[4] *Bernstorff,* p. 176.

[5] Michelsen, *op. cit.,* pp. 58-59. Hindenburg, however, believed that the unrestricted campaign should be postponed until the military situation was more settled, and until Germany had received fair assurance that the European neutrals would not intervene on the side of the Allies. Cf. his testimony and that of Ludendorff before the Reichstag investigating committee, *G.D.,* II, 856 ff.

Captain Laurens, "robbed the offensive of the two essential factors of success (surprise and mass). They permitted the Allies to seek and gather means of defense against this special war which would probably have proved an overwhelming success if it had been prepared in secret and put into effect suddenly and in great numbers. The same indecision prevented the Germans from establishing and realizing a programme of construction permitting them to put into continuous action a sufficient force." [6]

Germany's evaluation of the aid given involuntarily but none the less effectively to the Allies by the United States, proved to be an important factor in her final decision. As the Allies were already drawing freely upon American resources, as the United States refused to interfere with the blockade, and as Wilson's attitude prevented the Germans from using their one effective weapon on the seas, it is natural that they came to argue that conditions could not be much worse if the United States actually were in the war. At least their hands would then be free.

[6] Adolphe Laurens, *Histoire de la Guerre sous-Marine Allemande*, p. 225. "The German Naval Staff," writes Commander Kenworthy, "eventually found in its hand a weapon of greater potency than all the Big Batallions and Big Berthas and other devilments of modern war. . . . If the German Naval Staff had realized the offensive potentialities of their new weapon instead of relying on the defensive form of an out-numbered surface 'Fleet in Being,' and if the German High Command and Foreign Office had allowed the Naval Staff to concentrate from the beginning on the development of unrestricted submarine commerce destruction, supplying the necessary support and materials, Germany would have won the war either before it had provoked the United States to the point of entering it or before the United States could bring their latent strength to bear," Kenworthy and Young, *op. cit.*, pp. 83-84.

2

During the first six months of the war official relations between Germany and the United States were friendly if not cordial. Despite the instinctively pro-Ally tendency of the members of the American Administration and in the face of the strong pro-Ally enthusiasm of the Atlantic coast, the detailed problems of neutrality were handled with comparative ease. The Germans protested the sale of munitions to the Allies and feeling in Germany against America developed on this score. Ambassador Gerard accepted an irritating situation philosophically. " You never could satisfy the Germans," he insisted, " unless we joined them in war, gave them all our money and our clothes and the U. S. A. into the bargain." [7] Senators, aroused by Allied interference with our trade, protested that the Department of State was unfair to Germany. In a strongly expressed letter to Senator Stone, signed by Bryan, Lansing answered in detail and conclusively the charges of unneutrality.[8] Conscious of the fact that Germany had sold arms to Spain in 1898 and to Russia in 1905, the Berlin Government acknowledged that there was no legal ground for protests even while they insisted upon moral aspects of the situation.[9]

The proclamation of the war zone, issued by Berlin on February 4, changed the whole character of relations with

[7] Gerard to House, January 20, 1915, *I.P.,* I, 345.

[8] *F.R., 1914, Suppl.,* vi-xiv.

[9] Cf. the testimony of Helfferich, Schücking, and Bernstorff before the Reichstag investigating committee, *G.D.,* II, 717-726. Bernstorff stated, " The legal division of the Foreign Office has always been of the opinion that, formally speaking, the American Government was neutral."

Germany. This was a threat which, if carried into effect, would touch American rights much more directly and cruelly than any methods thus far attempted by the Allies. The Decree, issued by the German Admiralty, took as its justification the right to retaliate against the seizure by the Allies of foodstuffs destined for Germany's civilian population.[10] But it was recognized as primarily a method of interrupting the export of American munitions.[11] It proclaimed that from February 18, the waters around the British Isles would be

[10] Comment of German Navy Archivist, September 15, 1933: " This statement, which is not inaccurate, does not go far enough. The first impulse to the German submarine warfare was given by the English declaration of November 2, 1914, proclaiming the North Sea to be a war zone, which contrary to international law affected not merely food going to Germany but all German imports."

[11] For the origins of the Decree of February 4, see Alfred von Tirpitz, *Memoirs,* II, 390-399. The main German military effort of the spring was to be upon the eastern front; no great massing of man-power would be possible on the western front. In the latter field Germany possessed a superiority of munitions which would permit her to hold firmly unless the British, slow in their own production, could import freely from the United States. See *Grey,* II, 107. Ambassador Gerard reported in January that " a regular campaign of hate has been commenced against America and the Americans," Gerard to Wilson, January 24, 1915, *I.P.,* I, 355. The *Berliner Tageblatt* was evidently instructed to prepare the ground for the war zone Decree: " Rightly is the question put forward whether, if not the neutrality of the American Government, at least the neutrality, of the American people is broken by the unpermissible commerce of war material with France and England. It is impossible to look on permanently at this traffic and not do everything which lies in our power to divide in this commerce from abroad sun and light equally among all the warring nations. If possible airships and submarine boats can bring this about, it would be the height of misplaced consideration to forego their assistance," *Tageblatt,* January 24, 1915.

regarded as a war zone within which German submarines
would destroy every enemy merchant vessel found; the
safety of passengers or crews of destroyed vessels could not
be guaranteed; neutrals were warned of the danger of entering these waters, since it would be difficult to avoid mistakes,
especially if enemy ships continued the practice of raising
neutral flags.[12]

The implications of such a policy were at once apparent
to Wilson; it involved the possibility of the direct destruction of neutral property, whether or not contraband, and
perhaps of human non-combatant lives. Without hesitation
he made the capital distinction between such a threat and
Allied restrictions upon neutral trade. Whether he could
then perceive the consequences of this distinction is not clear.
He described the Decree as "their extraordinary threat to
destroy commerce," and, as two years later, he may have
wondered whether the Germans would actually carry it into
effect.[13] The American note of reply which, although signed
by Bryan, was written by Wilson and Lansing and sent to
Berlin on February 10, took the form of a warning; if un-
heeded it could hardly be anything but the prelude to a
rupture.

" If the commanders of German vessels should . . . destroy
on the high seas an American vessel or the lives of American
citizens, it would be difficult for the Government of the
United States to view the act in any other light than as an
indefensible violation of neutral rights. . . . The Government of the United States would be constrained to hold the
Imperial German Government to a strict accountability for

[12] Gerard to Bryan, February 4, 1915; Bernstorff to Lansing,
February 7, 1915, *F.R., 1915, Suppl.,* 94, 96-97.

[13] Wilson to House, February 13, 1915, Y.H.C.

such acts of their naval authorities and to take any steps it might be necessary to take to safeguard American lives and property and to secure to American citizens the full enjoyment of their acknowledged rights on the high seas." [14] What did strict accountability mean?

Outwardly, relations with Germany were not affected by the American note, and an immediate crisis was averted by good luck as well as by the orders from Berlin to exercise especial care not to sink neutral ships. The Germans hinted at the desirability of American mediation and invited the President to send Colonel House to Berlin. But the reports from Ambassador Gerard became more discouraging. "It is felt here," he wrote on February 15, "that we are partial to England. They are serious here about this submarine blockade . . . they say they will not stand having their civil population starved. . . . The sale of arms is at the bottom, and the fact that we stand things from England that we would not from Germany (according to the Germans) is the cause." [15] A month later House, just arrived in Berlin, reported that without war relations could not be worse. "This is almost wholly due to our selling munitions of war to the Allies. The bitterness of their resentment towards us for this is almost beyond belief. It seems that every German that is being killed or wounded is being killed or wounded by an American rifle, bullet, or shell." [16] Already House perceived the dangers that were to result from divided councils in Berlin, and reported that

[14] Lansing to Gerard, *F.R., 1915, Suppl.,* 98-100.

[15] Gerard to House, February 15, 1915, *I.P., I,* 376-377. Cf. House to Wilson, February 15, 1915, *I.P.,* I, 378: "The situation grows hourly worse because of the German manifesto."

[16] House to Wilson, March 26, 1915, *I.P.,* I, 404.

he " found a lack of harmony in governmental circles which augurs ill for the future. . . . The military and civil forces are not working in harmony." [17]

Inevitably the dreaded " incidents " began to occur. In March an American citizen was drowned when the *Falaba* was sunk by a submarine; shortly afterwards an American boat, the *Cushing,* was attacked by a low-flying German airplane; on May 1 an American oilboat, the *Gulflight,* was torpedoed with the loss of two lives. Wilson cabled for advice as to the best way of handling what was obviously a serious situation. House reported his fear that " a more serious breach may at any time occur, for they seem to have no regard for consequences." Two days later he was with King George in Buckingham Palace and fell to discussing the possibility of the sinking of an ocean liner. The King said, " Suppose they should sink the *Lusitania* with Americans aboard." [18] At two o'clock of the same day a German submarine torpedoed and sank the *Lusitania* off the southern coast of Ireland. More than eleven hundred of her passengers and crew were drowned, among them one hundred and twenty-four Americans, men, women, and children.

The sinking of the *Lusitania* had consequences from which German diplomacy never recovered. It brought the war home to a mass of Americans for whom until then it had been little more than a moving picture. It made impossible any sort of understanding between the United States and Germany as against Allied interference with neutral trade. It raised definitely and for the first time the question of

[17] House to Wilson, April 11, 1915, *I.P.,* I, 413-414.
[18] Wilson to House, May 4, 1915, Y.H.C. House to Wilson, May 5, 1915, House Diary, May 7, 1915, *I.P.,* I, 432.

American participation in the war, and it pointed unequivocally to Germany as the enemy of the future. Wilson could have broken relations with Germany on the following day; he would have received a tumult of applause from the eastern states and at least acquiescence from the rest of the country. Ambassador Page emphasized the loss of influence that would follow Wilson's failure to take strong action.[19] Colonel House, a determined pacifist, was convinced that other submarine attacks would follow and that intervention could not be avoided in the end:

" If war follows," he cabled, " it will not be a new war, but an endeavor to end more speedily an old one. Our intervention will save, rather than increase, the loss of life. America has come to the parting of the ways, when she must determine whether she stands for civilized or uncivilized warfare. We can no longer remain neutral spectators. Our action in this crisis will determine the part we will play when peace is made and how far we may influence a settlement for the lasting good of humanity. We are being weighed in the balance, and our position amongst nations is being assessed by mankind." [20]

Wilson read this cable to his Cabinet. He was clearly appreciative of the factors emphasized by House, but he was not ready to admit that it was too late to stop the ruthless submarine warfare, and he was determined that he would not permit war to come as the result of emotional disturbance caused by the sinking of the *Lusitania*. If Germany was on the road to madness she must be given the chance to retrace her steps. The United States was consecrated to ideals which could not be fulfilled by force until and unless every method

[19] *Page,* III, 239-241.
[20] House to Wilson, May 9, 1915, *I.P.,* I, 434.

dictated by supreme patience had been tried and failed. This, doubtless, he tried to express a few days later at Philadelphia, when he insisted that " the example of America must be a special example . . . of peace because peace is the healing and elevating influence of the world and strife is not," which probably gives a more accurate index to his mind than the unfortunate phrase that followed: " There is such a thing as a man being too proud to fight." [21]

With a coolness that disregarded the denunciations of cowardice levelled at him by pro-Ally elements in the United States and abroad, but with obstinate determination, Wilson set himself to extract from Germany a disavowal of the sinking of the *Lusitania* and a promise to abide by the recognized rules of warning and safety of passengers and crew. He received no support in this course from Mr. Bryan. The Secretary of State suddenly realized the implications of the note of the preceding February, when the United States had given warning that it would hold the German Government to " a strict accountability." If in an exchange of notes Germany refused to alter her position, a rupture could hardly be avoided. He desired to settle the issue with Germany in the spirit of his conciliation treaties, although Germany had refused to sign the proposed treaty. In the meantime trouble could be avoided by warning American citizens to stay off ships. He regarded neutral rights of travel as no more sacred than neutral rights of trade which had been infringed by the Allies. " Germany has a right to prevent contraband going to the Allies," he wrote to Wilson, " and a ship

[21] Baker and Dodd, *The Public Papers of Woodrow Wilson,* I, 321.

carrying contraband should not rely upon passengers to protect her from attack." [22]

Wilson was entirely unwilling to accept this argument and not inclined to submit an issue touching American lives to a board of conciliation. With a heavy heart Bryan approved the text of the note which the President read to the Cabinet on May 11.[23] It was sent on May 14. As a diplomatic document the note avoided the form of an ultimatum, but its tone was vigorous. After rehearsing the earlier attacks made by the submarines, " a series of events which the Government of the United States has observed with growing concern," Wilson demanded that the Germans

" disavow the acts of which the Government of the United States complains, that they will make reparations so far as reparation is possible for injuries which are without measure, and that they will take immediate steps to prevent the recurrence of anything so obviously subversive of the principles of warfare. . . . Expressions of regret and offers of reparation in case of the destruction of neutral ships sunk by mistake, while they may satisfy international obligations, if no loss of life results, cannot justify or excuse a practice, the natural and necessary effect of which is to subject neutral nations and neutral persons to new and unmeasurable risks." [24]

The note of May 13 solidified the distinction that Wilson had already drawn in his own mind between property rights and human lives. A British journalist, Sydney Brooks, declared that the note was " not unentitled to rank amongst

---

[22] Bryan, *Memoirs,* pp. 398-399.

[23] David Lawrence, *True Story of Woodrow Wilson,* p. 144; Bryan, *op. cit.,* pp. 399-402.

[24] Text of note, Bryan to Gerard, May 13, 1915, *F.R., 1915, Suppl.,* 393-396.

the masterpieces of diplomatic literature. Reading it one
might almost picture the President as wrestling with the
Wilhelmstrasse for the soul of Germany." William Howard
Taft described it as " admirable in tone . . . dignified in
the level that the writer takes with respect to international
obligations . . . [it] may well call for our earnest concurrence and confirmation." [25] Grey passed on the word to
Wilson that " he did not see how you could do differently
from what you have done, and he intimated that if we had
done less we would have placed ourselves in much the
same position in which England would have been placed
if she had not defended Belgian neutrality. In other words,
he thought that we would have been totally without friends
or influence in the concert of nations, either now or hereafter." [26]

But Germany showed no haste to comply with Wilson's
demands. Perhaps there was some question of American
readiness to support words with action.[27] Ambassador
Gerard was pessimistic. " I am afraid that we are in for
grave consequences. This country, I fear, will not give up
the torpedoing without notice of merchant and passenger
steamers; and their recent victories over the Russians have
given them great confidence here. . . . It is the German
hope to keep the *Lusitania* matter ' jollied along ' until the

[25] Brooks, "America at the Cross Roads," in *The English Review,*
June, 1915, 358; Address by Taft at dinner of Methodist laymen,
May 14, 1915 (*Current History,* June, 1915, 447).

[26] House to Wilson, May 14, 1915, *I.P.,* I, 442.

[27] For the story of the conversation between Bryan and Ambas-
sador Dumba, as a result of which the latter reported that the
United States was not in earnest, see Bryan, *op. cit.,* pp. 377-382;
Dumba, *op. cit.,* pp. 232-235; *I.P.,* I, 451.

American people get excited about baseball or a new scandal and forget. Meantime the hate of America grows daily." [28] In his final report on the European survey which Wilson had asked him to make, House gave it as his opinion that

" Tirpitz will continue his submarine policy, leaving the Foreign Office to make explanations for any ' unfortunate incidents ' as best they may. I think we shall find ourselves drifting into war with Germany, for there is a large element in the German naval and military factions that consider it would be a good, rather than a bad, thing for Germany." [29]

3

Few persons, whether in the United States or abroad, realized how close to a diplomatic rupture with Germany the United States came as a result of the *Lusitania* crisis. Certainly the Berlin Government was not aware of the danger. Its reply to Wilson's note led a good many others than Gerard to believe that the German intention was to " jolly us along." The German reply defended the sinking of the passenger liner on the ground that she was in reality an armed cruiser and transport, carrying munitions, and as such should be treated as a vessel of war. There was no suggestion of a disavowal.[30]

Fortunately Ambassador von Bernstorff was one of the few who did realize the danger of a rupture and the fact that a diplomatic rupture inevitably meant war. He set himself to convince the German Foreign Office of this fact, spoke of the crisis as " very serious," and urged construc-

[28] Gerard to House, June 1, 1915, *I.P.*, I, 454-455. Cf. Tirpitz, *op. cit.*, II, 405-411.

[29] House to Wilson, June 16, 1915, *I.P.*, I, 469.

[30] Gerard to Bryan, May 29, 1915, *F.R., 1915, Suppl.*, 419-421.

tive steps " in order to avoid war." " I can only hope,"
he cabled the Chancellor on May 17, " that we shall survive
it without war." [31] To him must go a large share of the
responsibility for preventing a breach at this time. The
Ambassador himself gives to Wilson the credit, and goes
so far as to insist that the President alone prevented war.[32]

Wilson refused to admit that the issue could not be
settled peaceably; he also refused to permit it to become
confused by details. Germany's allegations regarding the
status of the *Lusitania* he regarded as irrelevant. American protests were based on grounds that had nothing to do
with technicalities:

" The sinking of passenger ships," he wrote in his note
of June 9, " involves principles of humanity which throw
into the background any special circumstances of detail that
may be thought to affect the cases, principles which lift it,
as the Imperial German Government will no doubt be quick
to recognize and acknowledge, out of the class of ordinary
subjects of diplomatic discussion or of international controversy. . . . The Government of the United States is contending for something much greater than mere rights of
property or privileges of commerce. It is contending for
nothing less high and sacred than the rights of humanity,
which every Government honors itself in respecting and
which no Government is justified in resigning on behalf of
those under its care and authority."

The American Government, Wilson continued, assumed that
Germany accepted " as established beyond question the
principle that the lives of noncombatants cannot lawfully or
rightly be put in jeopardy by the capture or destruction of

---

[31] Bernstorff to German Foreign Office, May 9, May 10; Bernstorff to Bethmann, May 17, 1915, *Bernstorff*, pp. 31, 144, 145.

[32] *Bernstorff*, p. 152. See Bernstorff to Foreign Office, June 2,
1915, *ibid.*, pp. 152-154.

an unresisting merchantman," and recognized " the obligation to take sufficient precaution to ascertain whether a suspected merchantman is in fact of belligerent nationality or is in fact carrying contraband of war under a neutral flag. The Government of the United States therefore deems it reasonable to expect that the Imperial German Government will adopt the measures necessary to put these principles into practice in respect of the safeguarding of American lives and American ships, and asks for assurances that this will be done." [33]

The tone of Wilson's note was by no means belligerent, but to Mr. Bryan it had the ring of an ultimatum. He insisted that a note of protest against Allied interference with trade be sent at the same time. To this Cabinet members objected, accepting Wilson's distinction between material interests and human lives. Bryan then made an accusation of pro-Ally bias, which led to a reprimand in full Cabinet meeting by the President. Already, on June 1, Houston noted that Bryan was about ready to " fly the coop." On June 4, the Secretary of State announced that he could not sign the note as it stood, and four days later presented his resignation, which was accepted promptly although with expressions of regret. The following day the note went out over the signature of Lansing, as acting Secretary of State. [34]

Thus Wilson continued to negotiate, to the discomfort of extreme pacifists like Bryan who were troubled by the firm-

[33] Text of note in Lansing to Gerard, June 9, 1915, *F.R., 1915, Suppl.,* 436-438.

[34] David F. Houston, *Eight Years with Wilson's Cabinet,* I, 135-145; Bryan, *op. cit.,* pp. 406-408, 422-424; William C. Redfield, *With Congress and Cabinet,* p. 102.

ness of his tone, and to the exasperation of pro-Ally opinion which was aroused by his willingness to continue the debate at all. The German Government had issued orders to submarine commanders to avoid the sinking of liners without notice, but fearful of public opinion at home and of the influence of Tirpitz they kept them secret. "The Foreign Office, I am sure," wrote Mr. Gerard, "wanted to make some decent settlement, but were overruled by the navy." [35] On July 8 they replied to Wilson's second note. While expressing the utmost respect for the rights of humanity, they maintained the principle that neutral citizens travelling in the barred zone did so at their own risk; they breathed complaints against British methods of restricting trade and fighting submarines; they concluded with the suggestion that Americans might cross the seas safely upon neutral vessels which would be assured protection if they raised the American flag, or upon " four enemy passenger steamers for the passenger traffic," for the " free and safe " passage of which the German Government would give guarantees.[36]

The President's patience began to weaken. " I think we might say to them," he wrote House on July 12, " that this Government is not engaged in arranging passenger traffic, but in defending neutral and human rights." [37] On the other hand he seems to have recognized that the application of German policy had been changed although no announcement had been made. "Apparently the Germans *are* modifying their methods," he wrote on July 14. " They must be made

[35] Gerard to House, June 22, 1915, *I.P.,* II, 14.
[36] German note of July 8, 1915, in Gerard to Lansing, July 10, 1915, *F.R., 1915, Suppl.,* 463-466.
[37] Wilson to House, July 12, 1915, Y.H.C.

to feel that they must continue in their new way unless they deliberately wish to prove to us that they are unfriendly and wish war." [38]

This Wilson attempted to make plain in his note of July 21. He argued that the experience of two months showed that it was possible to use the submarine effectively without the methods that inspired the criticism of humanity; he gave definite warning that repetition of acts in contravention of American rights must be regarded as "deliberately unfriendly." He flatly refused to accept the justification of the submarine attack as a retaliatory measure consequent upon Allied restriction of trade.

"Illegal and inhuman acts, however justifiable they may be thought to be against an enemy who is believed to have acted in contravention of law and humanity, are manifestly indefensible when they deprive neutrals of their acknowledged rights, particularly when they violate the right to life itself." [39]

Meanwhile Wilson urged House to impress upon Bernstorff the need of making Berlin realize how serious the situation was: "Make him feel not only that some way out *should* be found, but that some way out *must* be found and that his Government owe to themselves and the rest of the world to help to find it." [40] Bernstorff had already been working to secure the formulation of a clear policy of concessions on the submarine issue in return for American action in behalf of the Freedom of the Seas. The President, he

[38] Wilson to House, July 14, 1915, Y.H.C.

[39] Text of note of July 21, in Lansing to Gerard, July 21, 1915, *F.R., 1915, Suppl.,* 480-482.

[40] Wilson to House, July 14, 1915, Y.H.C.

insisted in his letters to Berlin, did not want war and would act against the Allies if given a chance by Germany and public opinion. He urged that Berlin express regret, offer compensation, promise to abide by cruiser rules of maritime warfare, and agree to coöperate with Wilson in an attempt to reëstablish international law on the basis of the Declaration of London.[41] Early in August he received instructions to begin negotiations on such a basis. The Ambassador worked under difficulties, for he was likely at any moment to be disavowed in Berlin and he did not possess the confidence of the President. " I do not feel that Bernstorff is dealing frankly with us somehow," wrote Wilson to House, " and if you have the opportunity, you might see what you can do to make him feel that it is up to him to do more than he has done to make his Government realize facts as they are." [42]

On the other hand, Bernstorff felt himself crippled by American unwillingness to act against the Allies, and weakened by the public notes that irritated opinion.

" The present situation is not pleasant," he wrote to House. " In the last American note such strong language was used that I am afraid I will not be able to do much in the matter. Nevertheless I am doing my best, but my efforts will certainly fail if the expected American note to England does not use just as strong a language as that employed toward us. . . . We must *certainly* stop publishing sharp and unsatisfactory notes. I do not think that public opinion in either country can stand that much longer. If I cannot

[41] Bernstorff to Foreign Office, June 9, 12, July 2, 22, 28, 1915, *Bernstorff*, pp. 159-172. Cf. Karl Theodor Helfferich, *Der Weltkrieg*, II, 322.

[42] Wilson to House, July 29, 1915, Y.H.C.

persuade my country to give an answer, we will have to trust to our good luck and hope that no incident will occur which brings about war." [43]

From Berlin Ambassador Gerard wrote: "No great news—we are simply waiting for the inevitable accident." [44]

4

On August 19, off Fastnet, a German submarine torpedoed and sank the British liner, *Arabic*. The attack was made without warning, upon a ship westward bound for New York, carrying no contraband. Two Americans were lost. It seemed a clear contravention of the principles which Wilson had proclaimed, an act which he had declared must be regarded as " deliberately unfriendly." Was it possible to avoid an open rupture?

Colonel House thought not. " If I were in his [Wilson's] place," he wrote in his diary, " I would send Bernstorff home and recall Gerard. I would let the matter rest there for the moment, with the intimation that the next offence would bring us actively in on the side of the Allies. In the meantime, I would begin preparations for defence and for war, just as vigorously as if war had been declared." [45]

For the President the question was not so simple. A diplomatic rupture almost certainly meant war; whatever the aggravation, it must be balanced against the surrender of American peace, which for Wilson was still the core of his whole policy. " Two things are plain to me," he wrote,

---

[43] Bernstorff to House, July 27, 1915, *I.P.,* II, 27.
[44] Gerard to House, August 3, 1915, *I.P.,* II, 28.
[45] House Diary, August 21, 1915, *I.P.,* II, 31.

while still smarting under the shock of the news of the *Arabic's* sinking. " 1. The people of this country count on me to keep them out of the war; 2. It would be a calamity to the world at large if we should be drawn actively into the conflict and so deprived of all disinterested influence over the settlement." [46] But the President was equally determined to compel Germany to yield on the main issue and to permit no evasion. When Bernstorff asked that he suspend judgment until he heard the German side of the sinking of the *Arabic,* Wilson confessed: " I am suspicious enough to think that they are merely sparring for time . . . how long do you think we should wait? When we asked for their version of the sinking of the *Orduna* they pigeon-holed the request and we have not heard yet." The President's suspicion survived a suggestion of yielding made by Bernstorff and he evidently guessed that the Ambassador was going further than Berlin would approve: " You know I trust neither his accuracy nor his sincerity. But it certainly does look as if a way were opened out of our difficulties, so far as Germany is concerned." [47]

If the slight ray of hope developed into a real chance of settlement, the credit was largely due to the German Ambassador. On the day following the sinking of the *Arabic* he cabled to the Foreign Office asking for authority to negotiate the whole submarine question.[48] He then proceeded to exceed that authority in the interests of peace. Learning for the first time that orders had been given not

[46] Wilson to House, August 21, 1915, Y.H.C.
[47] Wilson to House, August 25, 31, 1915, Y.H.C.
[48] Bernstorff to Foreign Office, August 20, 1915, *Bernstorff,* p. 173.

8

to sink liners without warning, and recognizing the justice of Lansing's argument that publicity was needed in order to calm opinion, he issued a statement on September 1 to that effect: " Liners will not be sunk by our submarines without warning and without safety of the lives of non-combatants, provided that the liners do not try to escape or offer resistance." [49] The publication of the statement brought a sharp reprimand from the Foreign Office, which complained that the Ambassador had exceeded instructions. Bernstorff cabled apologies for acting on his own responsibility.[50] He thereby permitted sufficient of a diplomatic victory to Wilson to ease the situation.

But the victory was neither clean-cut nor complete. The President was still dissatisfied. No disavowal of the attack on the *Arabic* had been made. The German promise was implied rather than explicit. Whatever the Foreign Office promised, the Navy might disregard. On September 4 a submarine sank the British liner *Hesperian*. " The navy people," wrote Gerard, " frankly announce that they will not stop submarining, no matter what concessions are made by the Chancellor and Foreign Office. . . . The Chancellor still seems very much afraid of Tirpitz and his press bureau." [51] The Ambassador recognized the importance of a flat disavowal by the German Government and urged it upon Berlin, always holding out the hope of American action against the British if Germany yielded on the submarine

[49] Bernstorff to Lansing, *F.R., 1915, Suppl.*, 530-531.
[50] Foreign Office to Bernstorff, September 10, 1915; Bernstorff to Foreign Office, October 2, 1915, *Bernstorff*, pp. 179-180.
[51] Gerard to House, September 7, 1915, *I.P.*, II, 37-38. Cf. Tirpitz, *op. cit.*, II, 412-413; Laurens, *op. cit.*, p. 127.

issue. Some means, he insisted in his cables, must be found to finish once and for all with the *Lusitania* and the *Arabic;* " only then shall we be in a position to see whether President Wilson will keep his word, and take energetic measures *vis à vis* England." [52]

Bernstorff, however, found great difficulty in securing anything like a disavowal. " He said," wrote House to Wilson, " his main trouble was in getting his people to believe that this Government was in earnest. He told me in confidence that he thought the sending of Dumba home had done more to make Berlin realize the gravity of the situation than anything else. . . . He thought there would be no more objectionable acts and that if we could get over the question of the disavowal for the *Arabic* there would be smooth sailing." [53]

The President maintained steadfastly his determination not to yield.

" Bernstorff is evidently anxious," he wrote on September 20, " to get his government off from any explicit or formal disavowal of the *Arabic* offense; but I do not see how we can with self-respect do that. The country would consider us ' too easy ' for words, and any general avowal of a better purpose on their part utterly untrustworthy. . . . They are moving with intentional, and most exasperating slowness in the whole matter. I fear that when they have gained the time they need, for example in the Balkans, they will resume their reckless operations at sea, and we shall be back of where we started. The country is undoubtedly back of me in the whole matter, and I feel myself under bonds to it to

[52] Bernstorff to Foreign Office, September 14, 22, 28, 1915, *Bernstorff,* pp. 182-185.

[53] House to Wilson, September 17, 1915, *I.P.,* II, 39-40.

show patience to the utmost. My chief puzzle is to determine where patience ceases to be a virtue."

A week later the President repeated his insistence upon a formal disavowal: " We would find it difficult to get to a satisfactory understanding with Berlin without a disavowal of the act of the submarine commander in sinking the *Arabic*. I do not think that opinion in this country would sustain a settlement based on anything else." [54]

In Berlin the contest between the branches of government came to a head. " The Chancellor, of course," reported Gerard, " and the Foreign Office are against ' frightfulness ' and see how ridiculous it would be to bring us into the war; but if we are dragged in—in spite of their efforts—they will as usual be most unfairly blamed. And German ' diplomacy ' will again be ridiculed—without reason." [55] But for the moment the diplomats triumphed. On October 2 Bernstorff received authority to meet the demand for disavowal; on the 5th he sent to Lansing the necessary note. The submarine commander had believed that the *Arabic* was about to ram him; but the German Government was willing to accept the British affidavits that such was not the intention of the *Arabic*. " The attack of the submarine, therefore," ran the note, " was undertaken against the instructions issued to the commander. The Imperial Government regrets and disavows this act. . . . Under these circumstances my Government is prepared to pay an indemnity for the American lives which, to its deep regret, have been lost on the *Arabic*." [56]

[54] Wilson to House, September 20, 27, 1915, Y.H.C.
[55] Gerard to House, September 27, 1915, *I.P.*, II, 43.
[56] Bernstorff to Lansing, October 5, 1915, *F.R., 1915, Suppl.*, 560.

At the last moment Bernstorff eliminated on his own authority and upon the demand of Wilson and Lansing a request for arbitration of conflicting evidence regarding the *Arabic's* intention to ram the submarine. " Jagow told me," wrote Gerard, " that Bernstorff while not exactly exceeding his instructions in his *Arabic* note, had put the matter in a manner they did not approve." [57] The Ambassador had also inserted the phrase condemning the submarine commander. " In view of the fact," he later wrote, " that it was the only hope of avoiding a breach and further delay in the negotiations would profit us nothing . . . I acted once more on my own responsibility." The German naval officers complained bitterly, and the Foreign Office rebuked the Ambassador again. But without such action Bernstorff was convinced the United States would have been at that time drawn into the war.[58]

Colonel House was of the same conviction. " In my opinion," he wrote to Gerard, " there is no German of today who deserves better of his country than Bernstorff. I hope you will impress this upon his Government. If it had not been for his patience, good sense, and untiring effort, we would now be at war with Germany." [59]

5

Thanks to Wilson's patience and Bernstorff's determination, Germany and the United States thus passed a second crisis which had brought them near to war. How near was not generally appreciated; if public opinion had not

[57] Gerard to House, October 19, 1915, *I.P.*, II, 48.
[58] *Bernstorff*, pp. 187-188, Michelsen, *op. cit.*, p. 21.
[59] House to Gerard, October 6, 1915, *I.P.*, II, 45.

been kept in the dark it might have been impossible to avoid a rupture. On September 13, Colonel House wrote to Grey: " The situation is more tense than it has ever been, and a break may come before this reaches you." [60]

Whether the diplomatic lull that succeeded the storm in German-American relations would prove to be a genuine calm was doubtful. By her instructions not to sink liners without warning and by her disavowal of the submarine that sank the *Arabic,* Germany had yielded enough to smooth over the crisis.[61] But she had not yielded on the main issue—the recognition of the illegality of unrestricted submarine warfare. Three other points remained unsettled: the question of German responsibility for American lives lost as the result of the torpedoing of Allied ships, her responsibility for compensation, and the question as to whether her instructions not to sink liners covered all merchantmen. For the moment Wilson was willing to let these matters drag along.[62] He was more interested in assuring safety to noncombatants than in legal acknowledgments by Germany. But until they were settled no satisfactory *modus vivendi* could be arranged.

Other problems than the submarine troubled relations with the Central Powers. The Austro-Hungarian Ambassador, Dr. Constantin Dumba, a genial liberal who later devoted himself to the cause of world peace, permitted his interest in preventing Austro-Hungarian nationals from

[60] House to Grey, September 13, 1915, *I. P.,* II, 45.

[61] In his report to Berlin, Bernstorff naturally emphasizes the fact that Wilson also made concessions in not pressing the wider issues, Bernstorff to Foreign Office, October 20, 1915, *Bernstorff,* p. 192.

[62] Bernstorff to Foreign Office, October 15, 1915, *Bernstorff,* p. 191.

working in American munitions plants to become confused
with efforts to cripple those plants by strikes. He was
further indiscreet and unfortunate enough to entrust despatches referring to such plans to an American newspaper
correspondent, J. F. Archibald. The latter was taken off the
boat by the British at Plymouth and the despatches published. Wilson saw in them "the admitted purpose and
intent of Ambassador Dumba to cripple legitimate industries
of the people of the United States." "I see no escape," he
wrote privately, "from asking the Austrian Government to
replace Dumba with someone who will know better what
he is privileged and what he is not privileged to do." [63]
On September 8 the recall of the Ambassador was requested.

The Archibald pouch also carried letters from the German military attaché, Major von Papen, who spoke in un-
complimentary terms of "these idiotic Yankees," and which
indicated indiscreet activities on his part and that of the
naval attaché, Captain Boy-Ed.[64] Shortly afterwards, the
British ship *Ancona* was torpedoed by an Austrian submarine
without warning. "It looks like beginning at the beginning
with Austria," wrote Wilson. "I wonder if they have not
noticed at Vienna what is going on in the rest of the
world." [65] He contented himself with asking Lansing to
draft a sharp note to Austria, which elicited a rather un-

[63] Wilson to House, September 7, 1915, Y.H.C. For Ambassador Dumba's account of his interest in Austro-Hungarian work-
ingmen and his accidental connection with Archibald, see Dumba,
Memoirs of a Diplomat, pp. 252-270. Bernstorff believed Dumba's
position had been shaken by the publication of his conversation
with Bryan over the *Lusitania* note, *Bernstorff*, pp. 197-199.

[64] *F.R., 1915, Suppl.*, 938-941.

[65] Wilson to House, November 12, 1915, Y.H.C.

gracious disavowal and promise of reparation.[66] The recall of the offending German attachés was requested.

All this continued to vex American public feeling and had its effect upon the President. In his annual December message he spoke bitterly of "the gravest threats against our national peace and safety," and the attempts "to debase our politics to the uses of foreign intrigue."[67] But his irritation did not affect his will to peace. When Mr. Brand Whitlock, Ambassador to Belgium, saw the President in December, he promised him official neutrality, but added: "I ought to tell you that in my heart there is no such thing as neutrality. I am heart and soul for the Allies." Wilson answered: "So am I. No decent man, knowing the situation and Germany, could be anything else. But that is only my own personal opinion and there are many others in this country who do not hold that opinion."[68] In his message of December 7 to Congress he again emphasized the principle that "it was necessary, if a universal catastrophe was to be avoided, that a limit should be set to the sweep of destructive war and that some part of the great family of nations should keep the processes of peace alive."

In December, Lansing and Bernstorff resumed discussions of the yet unsettled *Lusitania* problem. As Bernstorff had warned his Government, there was no chance of American

[66] Lansing to Penfield, December 6, 1915; Penfield to Lansing, December 15, 1915, *F.R., 1915, Suppl.*, 623-625, 638-639. Lansing carried out with reasonable care the injunction to make the note sharp. It aroused resentment in the Central Powers, *Bernstorff*, p. 210.

[67] Annual Address to Congress, December 7, 1915, *Congressional Record*, 64th Congress, 1st Session, Vol. 53, part 1, pp. 95-100.

[68] Brand Whitlock to C. S., December 10, 1924, *I.P.*, II, 50.

action against the Allied blockade until this basic issue was settled. On January 12, 1916, Wilson wrote that it looked " as if our several difficulties with Germany would be presently adjusted." [69] But it proved puzzling to agree upon a formula. Lansing insisted upon an admission of illegality and argued that the German defense of submarine warfare as an act of retaliation was in itself an acknowledgment that the act was illegal.[70] Berlin refused, since an admission of illegality might have been costly in the later settlement of indemnities. Furthermore, so long as Germany reserved the question of legality she was in a position to renew the unrestricted submarine warfare at an opportune moment. " Von Jagow was very explicit," reported Ambassador Gerard, " in saying that Germany had made *no agreement* with us about submarine warfare, but had only stated that certain orders had been given to submarine commanders. He said distinctly that Germany reserved the right to change those orders at any time." [71]

The chance of reaching an agreement was minimized by the lack of control in the German government, which was especially manifest at this time, for the advocates of unrestricted submarine warfare were once more pressing the Chancellor and Foreign Office.

"A great controversy is going on in Germany," cabled House to the President on January 30, " regarding undersea warfare. The navy, backed more or less by the army, believe that Great Britain can be effectively blockaded, provided Germany can use their new and powerful submarines

[69] Wilson to House, January 12, 1916, Y.H.C.
[70] *Bernstorff*, pp. 220-221.
[71] Gerard to House, February 8, 1916, *I.P.*, II, 209.

indiscriminately and not be hampered by any laws whatsoever. They also believe failure has resulted from our interference and Germany's endeavor to conform to our demands. They think war with us would not be so disastrous as Great Britain's blockade. The civil government believe that if the blockade continues, they may be forced to yield to the navy; consequently they are unwilling to admit illegality of their undersea warfare. They will yield anything but this. If you insist upon that point, I believe war will follow." [72]

The accuracy of this estimate of German feeling was proved by their refusal to ratify the formula upon which Lansing and Bernstorff had tentatively agreed.[73]

" While we are perfectly willing," wrote the German undersecretary, Zimmermann, " to settle the incident in a way which seems acceptable to the United States Government the latest proposal contains the following two sentences to the underlined passages of which we could not possibly agree: ' Thereby the German retaliation affected neutrals which was not the intention, *as retaliation becomes an illegal act if applied to other than enemy subjects,*' and ' The Imperial Government having subsequent to the event issued to its naval officers the new instructions which are now prevailing, expressing profound regret that citizens of the United States suffered by the sinking of the *Lusitania, and recognizing the illegality of causing thereby danger, and admitting liability therefor,* offers to make reparation for the lives of the citizens of the United States who were lost by the payment of a suitable indemnity.' I am afraid that if the United States Government insists on this wording, a break will be unavoidable." [74]

[72] House to Wilson, January 30, 1916, *I.P.,* II, 145-146.

[73] *Bernstorff,* pp. 220-221. An excellent résumé of the whole course of the later *Lusitania* negotiations is given by Bernstorff in his evidence before the Reichstag investigating committee, Eleventh session, *G.D.,* II, 734-736.

[74] Zimmermann to House, January 29, 1916, *I.P.,* II, 207; *F.R., 1916, Suppl.,* 154.

The Foreign Secretary was equally explicit, according to Ambassador Gerard. Jagow agreed " to accept all Bernstorff's propositions except, as he put it, one word, viz: Germany will acknowledge liability for the loss of American lives by the sinking of the *Lusitania,* but will not acknowledge that the act of sinking was illegal." [75]

Although the illegality of submarine attacks without warning formed the crux of Wilson's contention, it might have been possible to discover a compromise which would satisfy the President without the actual use of the word " illegal." But all chance of such a compromise was destroyed by the injection of a new issue which involved the Allies and threatened to bring the President into conflict with Congressional leaders. The question raised was whether armed merchant ships did not really fall into the category of ships of war and therefore were unentitled to receive the sort of immunity granted merchant vessels. The Germans had early complained that it was clearly impossible for a submarine to conform with the established rules of visit and search in the case of armed merchantmen, since the latter could open destructive fire upon the submarine when it came to the surface to give warning. The armament of such merchantmen, they contended, made it possible for them to take the offensive and for this reason they should be regarded as auxiliary cruisers.[76]

As early as October, 1915, Secretary Lansing had taken the position privately that if the United States insisted that

[75] Gerard to House, February 1, 1916, *I.P.,* II, 208. Cf. Gerard to Lansing, February 1, 1916, *F.R., 1916, Suppl.,* 156.

[76] German Memorandum of February 10, 1916, *F.R., 1916, Suppl.,* 163-166.

submarines must give warning, we should also insist that merchantmen be not armed. " If a merchantman is armed, and we insist that submarines do not sink without warning, the advantage is all with the merchantman and against the submarine." [77] Many Americans, including the Ambassador to Germany, felt the logic of this view. " I always rather sympathized with the submarine on this," wrote Gerard. " It seems to me to be an absurd proposition that a submarine must come to the surface, give warning, offer to put passengers and crew in safety, and constitute itself a target for merchant ships, that not only make a practice of firing at submarines at sight, but have undoubtedly received orders to do so." [78]

The British did not dispute the logic of this argument. They simply stated that the Germans could not be trusted not to sink the unarmed ships mercilessly.

" When we are dealing with an enemy who knows no law," wrote Balfour, " and who not once nor twice and accidentally, but repeatedly and of set purpose, has sunk peaceful traders without notice, how is it possible for these to wait until they are summoned to surrender? No summons of surrender is ever uttered. A torpedo is discharged or guns are fired, and all is over. Cold-blooded butchery takes the place of the old procedure sanctioned and approved by International Law. I cannot help thinking that if this question is looked at in a broad spirit, it will be seen that whatever are to be the laws of maritime warfare, and however they are to be enforced, it cannot be in the interests of international morals that the Municipal Law of any great neutral should be modified in the direction favourable to the perpetrator of outrages and hostile to his victims." [79]

[77] House Diary, October 2, 1915, *I.P.,* II, 73.
[78] Gerard to House, about February 22, 1916, *I.P.,* II, 210.
[79] Balfour to House, September 12, 1915, *I.P.,* II, 213-214.

Lord Bryce struck a similar note: " The one fatal objection to our accepting any promise by the German Government as to its action by submarines if we were to undertake that our merchant vessels should be unarmed, is that we could not trust any German promise." [80] Sir Horace Plunkett pleaded earnestly that any later action by Wilson in behalf of the Freedom of the Seas would suffer tremendously from any attempt during the war to change maritime law in favor of the submarines.[81]

Wilson studied the problem carefully. " I read the letters from Plunkett and Balfour," he noted, " with the greatest interest. The matter of armed merchantmen is not so simple as Balfour would make it. It is hardly fair to ask submarine commanders to give warning by summons if, when they approach as near as they must for that purpose they are to be fired upon. It is a question of many sides and is giving Lansing and me some perplexed moments." [82] The Secretary of State waited until the beginning of the new year before formulating definite proposals. On January 18, 1916, he presented to the Allied Ambassadors in Washington an informal note suggesting the disarming of merchantmen, and on January 26 he sent to the European Embassies of the United States a circular despatch outlining the arguments upon which the suggestion rested.[83]

The Germans were naturally as pleased as the Allies were appalled by the suggestion. It would have meant, as Helfferich later pointed out to the Reichstag investigating

[80] Bryce to House, February 16, 1916, *I.P.*, II, 211.
[81] Plunkett to House, September 17, 1915, Y.H.C.
[82] Wilson to House, October 4, 1915, Y.H.C.
[83] *F.R., 1916, Suppl.*, 146-147.

committee, " that armed merchant vessels would have been subjected to all those restrictions which would apply to belligerents in the harbors of the United States, and these restrictions are so far-reaching that, by this measure alone, an effective and productive use of these ships for supplying England with food and ammunition could hardly have continued to be earnestly considered. That was the solution of the entire U-boat war question." [84] For the same reason, and entirely apart from the points raised by Balfour, the Allies could not but regard the proposal as directed against their vital interests. Nor could American trading interests remain indifferent. As Bernstorff insisted, " Lansing's note means that from that day on the Americans would have had no more merchant ships at their disposal. For the fact is there were no unarmed British ships." [85]

If Germany had held her hand it is possible that the armed merchantman question, brought into prominence by Lansing's suggestion, might have raised a new controversy with the Allies and eased relations with Germany. Bernstorff believes that he could have persuaded the American Department of State into a compromise in the *Lusitania* negotiations.[86] But Berlin, supported as the Foreign Office felt by

[84] Stenographic Minutes of Reichstag investigating committee, November 14, 1919, *G.D.*, II, 731.

[85] *G.D.*, II, p. 736. Bernstorff does not believe that even had Wilson desired he could have carried through the Lansing proposal: " Mr. Wilson did not enforce the Memorandum because he could not do so without prejudicing the interests of American commerce," *Bernstorff*, p. 228.

[86] *Bernstorff*, p. 223. This is borne out by a memorandum of Lansing of a conversation with Bernstorff, February 17, 1916, in which he told the German Ambassador that the draft *Lusitania* note would be acceptable " were it not for the fact that Germany

the Lansing proposal and misled by information from the Austrian representative regarding the American attitude, decided to take positive steps. On February 8, 1915, the German Government announced that " within a short period " armed merchant vessels would be regarded as ships of war and treated accordingly.[87] The statement was regarded in effect as a new declaration of unrestricted submarine warfare, and referred to as such even by the Germans.

Whether or not Wilson had come to a complete understanding with Lansing upon a policy of disarming merchantmen along the lines of the proposals of January 18 is uncertain.[88] He may have been annoyed by what he regarded as an attempt by Berlin to force his hand. He may have changed his mind. At all events he immediately let it be known that the Lansing proposals were purely tentative, that according to custom merchant vessels had the right to arm themselves defensively, and that if a submarine attacked without warning an unresisting merchantman, with loss of American lives, the attack would be regarded as a " breach of international law, and the formal assurances given by the German Government." [89]

---

had issued a new declaration of policy in regard to submarine warfare," *F.R., 1916, Suppl.,* 172.

[87] Gerard to Lansing, February 10, 1916, *F.R., 1916, Suppl.,* 163-165. As Valentin points out, official German circles made a distinction between " unrestricted " and " sharpened " submarine operations; not *uneingeschränkte* but *verschärfte unterseebootskrieg,* Valentin, *Deutschlands Aussenpolitik,* p. 286.

[88] *Bernstorff,* p. 225. The Ambassador states that the President " had not read, or only hastily glanced through " the memorandum of January 18. No light is thrown upon the problem by available American sources.

[89] Lansing to Diplomatic Officers in European Countries, February 16, 1916, *F.R., 1916, Suppl.,* 70.

But Congress was less determined. Its leaders had been somewhat disturbed by the speeches delivered by the President in favor of military preparedness; they were frightened by the suggestion of the imminence of war with Germany on the submarine issue. For some time the conviction voiced a year back by Bryan had been gaining ground in Congress: that individual citizens of the United States had not the right to endanger pacific relations with Germany by travelling upon belligerent vessels which might be torpedoed. Commercial rights had been sacrificed in the controversy with the Allies. Why should rights of travel be held so sacred in the controversy with Germany? America would be safe if citizens were prohibited from travelling on belligerent merchant ships passing through the danger zone. In the Senate and the House resolutions to such effect were presented by Gore and McLemore.[90] Democratic leaders warned the President that they would be passed.

Bernstorff regarded the resolutions as representing merely an aspect of domestic politics, and thus interpreted Wilson's firm stand against the Gore-McLemore proposals.[91] But the President believed that if passed they would nullify his whole stand against Germany and in behalf of " human rights." They would certainly lead to an obvious abridgment of American rights under the threat of the submarine.

" For my own part, I cannot consent to any abridgment of the rights of American citizens in any respect. The honor and self-respect of the nation is involved. We covet peace, and shall preserve it at any cost but the loss of honor. . . . Once accept a single abatement of right, and many other humiliations would certainly follow, and the whole fine

[90] *Current History,* April, 1916, 14-23.
[91] *Bernstorff,* p. 236.

fabric of international law might crumble under our hands
piece by piece. What we are contending for in this matter
is of the very essence of the things that have made America
a sovereign nation. She cannot yield them without conceding her own impotency as a nation, and making virtual
surrender of her independent position amongst the nations
of the world." [92]

The foregoing letter to Senator Stone is of primary importance. It contains the gist of Wilson's attitude toward
the belligerents. It set a limit beyond which Germany might
not encroach without expecting war. If approved by the
people it made American intervention certain should Germany renew formally the unrestricted submarine warfare
with destruction of American lives. Wilson's request for
a declaration of war a year later was to be based upon it.
Thus the vote upon the Gore-McLemore resolutions was
one of the first importance, since it would determine not
merely the character of Wilson's party leadership but the
acceptance or repudiation of Wilson's attitude towards Germany. Curiously enough the Republicans, who in the
autumn election were to accuse the President of anæmic
diplomacy, furnished the mass of voters in favor of the
resolutions, voting with the Democratic leaders. But the
rank and file of the Democratic party voted against the
resolution in the House of Representatives, tabling it, 275-
135. In the Senate the majority against the Gore resolution
was still more impressive, 68-14.

The President was thus strengthened both as to party control and as to freedom of handling foreign relations.
Furthermore Germany's haste in threatening to treat armed

92 Wilson to Stone, February 24, 1916, F.R., 1916, Suppl., 177-
178.

9

merchantmen as warships, gave the State Department an opportunity to drop the Lansing proposal that Allied merchant vessels be disarmed. " In view of new orders of Germany in regard to armed merchant ships," wrote Lansing, " and interviews given out by German officials misstating position of this Government, we will move slowly in matter even if German reply satisfactory." [93] The Allies politely declined to disarm their merchant ships, and the United States Government contented itself with taking affidavits from captains of merchant vessels that their armament was purely for defensive purposes. Nor did the Germans press the issue. On March 21 House wrote to the President: " Bernstorff was with me for an hour this morning. As usual, I found him reasonable and willing to discuss pending matters quite impartially. He thinks the best thing that can be done now is to do and say nothing further in regard to the disarming of merchantmen. He intimated that they would drop it if we would." [94]

Indeed, both this issue and the unfinished *Lusitania* negotiations were quickly forgotten in the new crisis which, in the last week of March, again endangered the pacific relations of Germany and the United States.

6

In Germany the naval leaders argued for the submarine. With the new underseas fleet and disregarding any rules that prevented sinking of all ships, enemy or neutral, at sight, they promised an effective blockade of the British

[93] Lansing to Page, February 13, 1916, *F.R., 1916, Suppl.,* 168.
[94] House to Wilson, March 12, 1916, *I.P.,* II, 224.

Isles and victory. At a grand council in Charleville in the first week of March, the issue came to a decision. Falken-hayn, Chief of Staff, supported the Navy's demands, which were vigorously opposed by the Chancellor and Foreign Secretary. The Kaiser decided against them; Tirpitz was shortly thereafter reported ill and soon resigned. Once more German policy turned against unrestricted submarine warfare.[95]

Hopes that the defeat of the arch-prophet of the submarine signified the end of the submarine problem were rudely shattered. Between March 9 and March 29 eight boats were sunk by submarines. The revived campaign sur-

---

[95] Gerard to Lansing, March 2, 3, 1916, *F.R., 1916, Suppl.*, 186; Gerard to House, March 7, 14, 20, 1916, *I.P.*, II, 221-223; Tirpitz, *Memoirs*, II, 417-422; Valentin, *Deutschlands Aussen-politik*, p. 288.

Comment by German Navy Archivist, September 15, 1933: " The rôle which Admiral von Tirpitz played in the decisions concerning the submarine war, is not pictured quite correctly. The opinion is common that it was Tirpitz who first and always stood for the sharpest use of German submarines and that he was primarily responsible for their use. Compare the memoirs of Colonel House concerning his stay in Berlin in the beginning of 1916 (*I.P.*, II, 138): ' I feel that Tirpitz is almost solely responsible for German frightfulness upon the sea.' That needs straightening out. After February, 1915, Admiral von Pohl, Chief of the Admiralty Staff, was in almost complete control. Admiral von Tirpitz' influence was slight. After the *Arabic* case in September, 1915, the influence of Tirpitz was nearly excluded. . . . The reopening of the submarine warfare in February and March, 1916, was not stimulated by Tirpitz. Moreover, he was not pulled into the decisive conferences with the Kaiser which were followed by the last, final resignation of the Admiral. The responsible leader of the German war at sea after September 15, 1915, was Admiral von Holtzendorff, Chief of the Admiralty Staff."

prised Ambassador Gerard; it seemed to be entirely contrary to the policy of the Foreign Office, and apparently indicated that regardless of higher political authority the naval commanders were simply taking matters into their own hands. On March 24 the channel steamer *Sussex,* an unarmed passenger boat, was torpedoed without warning. Part of the ship continued to float, but eighty non-combatant passengers were killed or wounded. American citizens were on board, but none of them lost their lives.[96]

The crisis in relations with Germany that followed, was the most acute of any of the three major crises (*Lusitania, Arabic, Sussex*) previous to American entrance into the war. It was brief and it was concluded with a definite American diplomatic victory because the civil Government in Germany was not yet determined that the advantages of unrestricted submarine warfare outweighed the disadvantages of American intervention on the side of the Allies.

Mr. Lansing favored an immediate rupture with Germany. It was futile and humiliating, he believed, to repeat the dragging negotiations that had characterized the *Arabic* crisis. Wilson was not inclined to act so promptly. "Whether the President . . . will shrink from war at the last moment," telegraphed Bernstorff, "it is difficult to foretell." Wilson wished to get German explanations, re-emphasized his fear that if the United States entered the war it would go on indefinitely "and there would be no

[96] Affidavits, depositions, and reports regarding the sinking of the *Sussex* were printed in *European War, No. 3: Diplomatic Correspondence with Belligerent Governments relating to Neutral Rights and Duties,* pp. 249-300.

one to lead the way out." [97] On April 4, however, Lansing was requested to prepare a memorandum for a note to Germany. House described it as "an exceedingly vigorous paper . . . [It] recalls Gerard and notifies the Imperial German Government that Count von Bernstorff will be given his passports." House himself regarded a rupture as inevitable. A joint telegram which he and Wilson prepared and which the President himself typed out, warned Grey that "it seems probable that this country must break with Germany on the submarine question unless the unexpected happens. . . ." [98]

Wilson still hesitated to take the final step and held back the Lansing note that recalled Gerard. "The President has the responsibility," wrote House in his diary, "and the welfare and happiness of a hundred million people are largely in his hands. It is easy enough for one without responsibility to sit down over a cigar and a glass of wine and decide what is to be done." [99]

As in the *Lusitania* and *Arabic* crises, Bernstorff spared no activity in his efforts to prevent a break. That war was again avoided resulted from the combination of his resolution with Wilson's patience. "Bernstorff keeps his temper and his courage," wrote House, "and it is impossible not to admire these qualities in him." The Ambassador begged for delay and especially for private negotiations without exchange of published notes, "which always causes irrita-

[97] House Diary, March 30, 1916, *I.P.*, II, 227, 228; Bernstorff to Foreign Office, April 4, 1916, *Bernstorff*, p. 242.

[98] House Diary, April 5, 1916; House to Grey, April 6, 1916, *I. P.*, II, 230, 231.

[99] House Diary, April 9, 1916, *I.P.*, II, 235.

tion." [100] He believed that an official disavowal from Berlin was the only means of avoiding war and that it "was now a question of bend or break." If the supporters of the unrestricted submarine warfare in Berlin won the day war was inevitable. He begged for instructions with which he could pacify the Washington Government.[101]

Berlin however disregarded his advice and on April 10 sent, instead of a disavowal, a note attempting to prove that the *Sussex* was not torpedoed by a submarine and probably hit a drifting mine.[102] The effect of the note in Bernstorff's opinion was disastrous. "It was probably the most unfortunate document that ever passed from Berlin to Washington. Mr. Wilson thought he detected a direct untruth, and the mixture of an uneasy conscience and clumsiness which the German Note appeared to betray prompted the sharp tone of the President's reply." [103]

Whether or not Wilson was so far affected by this German note as Bernstorff believes is a matter of doubt. It certainly did nothing to convince him that the sinking of the *Sussex* was an accident. On the other hand, he remained determined to give Germany a chance of disavowal and of a renunciation of unrestricted submarine warfare. Discarding the Lansing note which would have led to a diplomatic rupture, he summed up the whole course of the submarine

[100] House Diary, April 8, 1916; Bernstorff to House, April 14, 1916, *I.P.,* II, 234, 237.

[101] Bernstorff to Foreign Office, April 8, 1916, *Bernstorff,* pp. 243, 245.

[102] Gerard to Lansing, April 11, 1916, *F.R., 1916, Suppl.,* 227-229.

[103] *Bernstorff,* pp. 247-248.

dispute in a note the conclusion of which left no room for argument. "Unless the Imperial Government should now immediately declare and effect an abandonment of its present methods of submarine warfare against passenger and freight-carrying vessels, the Government of the United States can have no choice but to sever diplomatic relations with the German Empire altogether." The note was sent to Berlin on April 18.[104]

Thus the German Government faced a definite issue: either a disavowal of unrestricted submarine warfare or a rupture. "There was no longer any doubt in Berlin, that persistence in the point of view they had hitherto adopted would bring about a break with the United States, for I received instructions to make all preparations for German merchant ships lying in American ports to be rendered useless by the destruction of their engines." [105] On April 25, House reported to Wilson: "Bernstorff has just left me. He has a cable from his Government saying in substance, 'We wish to avoid war. Please suggest how this may be done. What is meant in the note by 'illegal submarine warfare?' If we accede to their demands, will they bring pressure upon Great Britain in regard to the blockade?' I advised his sending another despatch warning them not to suggest any compromise; that if they really desired to avoid a break, it was essential for them to discontinue their submarine warfare entirely and immediately." [106]

[104] Text of note in Lansing to Gerard, April 18, 1916, *F.R., 1916, Suppl.,* 232-234.

[105] *Bernstorff,* p. 250.

[106] House to Wilson, April 25, 1916, *I.P.,* II, 239. Cf. Bernstorff to Foreign Office, May 1, 1916, *Bernstorff,* p. 251.

For two weeks the contest in Berlin was waged between the naval and military on the one hand and the civil officials on the other. The reply to Wilson's note of April 18 reflected this division of policy, for its tone and content were quite inconsistent; nor has the suspicion been dispelled that the original draft of the German reply refused Wilson's demands, but was hastily corrected so as to accept them.[107] It reached the German Embassy in Washington piecemeal, writes Bernstorff, " and while the first part was being deciphered, its harsh tone produced in an increasing degree the impression: ' Then it is war,' which was not relieved until we came to the conclusion of the text." [108] The note complained ironically of the American attitude towards the Allied food blockade.

" The German Government cannot but reiterate its regret that the sentiments of humanity which the Government of the United States extends with such fervor to the unhappy victims of submarine warfare are not extended with the same warmth of feeling to the many millions of women and children who, according to the avowed intentions of the British Government, shall be starved. . . . The German Government, in agreement with the German people, fails to understand this discrimination."

But the note none the less accepted Wilson's demands. It stated that the Government had issued new orders to submarine commanders and " is prepared to do its utmost to confine the operations of the war for the rest of its duration to the fighting forces of the belligerents." No more mer-

---

[107] Michelsen, *op. cit.*, pp. 27-28; Tirpitz, *op. cit.*, p. 423. Jagow said to Gerard of Wilson's demand that " he thought it meant a break," Gerard to Lansing, April 20, 1916, *F.R., 1916, Suppl.*, 239.
[108] *Bernstorff*, p. 252.

chant ships would be sunk without warning and without
saving human lives, unless those ships attempted to escape
or offer resistance.[109]

Germany thus promised what the United States asked.
She tried, however, to make her promise conditional upon
the removal of Allied blockade restrictions. "Should the
steps taken by the Government of the United States not
attain the object it desires, to have the laws of humanity
followed by all belligerent nations, the German Government
would then be facing a new situation in which it must
reserve itself complete liberty of decision."

Like the German Embassy in Washington, the Department of State was impressed by the unfriendly tone of the
earlier portions of the German note and assumed at first
that a break was inevitable. Even after he had studied the
complete draft Lansing regarded it as self-contradictory and
unsatisfactory.[110] How could Germany promise to confine
operations to its fighting forces for the duration of the war
and at the same time reserve the right to resume the unrestricted submarine methods if the blockade were not given
up? The Secretary favored giving Bernstorff his passports.
But the President felt that Germany had accepted his conditions and that the American contention had triumphed.

As to Germany's final reference to the Allied blockade,
Wilson decided that he would make plain that the United
States could admit of no conditional pledge. He and Lansing
each wrote a note, the President finally accepting Lansing's

[109] Text of note in Gerard to Lansing, May 4, 1916, *F.R., 1916,
Suppl.*, 257-260. German newspaper comment on the note is summarized in Gerard to Lansing, May 6, 1916, *ibid.*, pp. 260-262.
[110] House Diary, May 4, 6, 1916, *I.P.*, II, 242, 245.

with the exception of the final paragraph. That paragraph, very Wilsonian in its force, notified Germany that the United States " cannot for a moment entertain, much less discuss, a suggestion that respect by German naval authorities for the rights of citizens of the United States upon the high seas should in any way or in the slightest degree be made contingent upon the conduct of any other Government affecting the rights of neutrals and non-combatants. Responsibility in such matters is single, not joint; absolute, not relative." [111]

7

Wilson had apparently achieved a magnificent diplomatic victory. He had avoided war with Germany, maintained American prestige, and compelled Germany in the name of his principles to sacrifice the use of a weapon which, as was later proved, could be made into a terrible menace. The surrender of the German Government was regarded as disastrous by the German naval chiefs. " This blow," writes Admiral Michelsen, " was the worse because the submarines were just beginning to operate effectively again." [112]

But the danger was merely postponed and if the war continued a new crisis was bound to arise. Public opinion in Germany accepted the Government's decision, but already regarded the United States as an enemy. " Every night," wrote Ambassador Gerard, " fifty million Germans cry themselves to sleep because all Mexico has not arisen against us." [113] The tone of the press indicated that if the civil

[111] Lansing to Gerard, May 8, 1916, *F.R., 1916, Suppl.,* 263.
[112] Michelsen, *op. cit.,* pp. 58-59.
[113] Gerard to House, April 5, 1916, *I.P.,* II, 246.

officials should be overborne by the military and naval commanders and unrestricted warfare be resumed, the German people would approve. Nor did the Germans feel that in the note of May 4 they had given a pledge that the unrestricted warfare could not at some time be resumed. They had agreed to a certain policy, but had made that policy dependent upon alleviations of the Allied blockade. They had not yielded their point that the unrestricted warfare was a justifiable retaliation for Allied blockade methods. If they found themselves pressed hard and unable to end the war by military victories, it was certain that they would return to it.

In view of the *Sussex* notes it was almost inevitable that a resumption of unrestricted submarine warfare would compel American intervention. The Wilson note of April 18 was in form an ultimatum. "It is my firm conviction," writes Bernstorff, "that had it not been for this ultimatum diplomatic relations would not have been broken off immediately, even in 1917. . . . After this exchange of Notes a challenge in the form of our formal declaration of the 31st January, 1917, could no longer be tolerated." [114] In the *Sussex* crisis and in the President's letter to Senator Stone affirming American rights of travel on the high seas must be sought the basic diplomatic explanation of American intervention a year later.

Both Bernstorff and Wilson were clear in their minds that after the *Sussex* the unrestricted submarine warfare could not be resumed without forcing American intervention. Both believed that peace negotiations offered the only alter-

[114] *Bernstorff*, p. 248. This view is shared by Valentin, *op. cit.*, p. 287. Cf. Matthias Erzberger, *Erlebnisse*, pp. 216-217.

native to disaster. In the case of Bernstorff, that disaster would take the form of German defeat following American participation. He realized that Wilson could not force the Allies to lift the blockade, he foresaw the resumption of the unrestricted submarine campaign. Hence his anxiety for peace. " I always regarded American mediation as the only possible way out of the war. I had no faith in the submarine campaign as likely to save the situation, because the entry of the United States into the war would more than outweigh all the advantages that the submarine could bring us." [115]

In the case of Wilson the disaster which he foresaw was simply American participation, resulting not from idealistic policy but from emotional resentment against Germany. He began to realize that a peace conference to end the war might be the only way to keep America at peace. Thus during the course of the year 1916 his whole foreign policy was based upon the determination to bring about such a peace conference, whether by persuasion or by threats.

[115] *Bernstorff,* p. 258.

CHAPTER IV

EFFORTS TO NEGOTIATE PEACE

1

The task of the mediator, whether in a dog-fight or a human war, is apt to prove ungrateful, especially if the contest is being waged on even terms. The emotion of each contestant has been aroused to such a pitch that little space remains for reasonable argument, and any suggested compromise seems like defeat. From such emotion proceeds an excess of confidence and determination; interference is regarded as an unfriendly act robbing the belligerent of the victory just at the moment of attainment. " The President's suggestion of summoning a peace conference," wrote Grey, " . . . would be construed as instigated by Germany to secure peace on terms unfavourable to the Allies. . . ." "As soon as Mr. Wilson's mediation plans threaten to assume a more concrete form and an inclination on the part of England to meet him begins to manifest itself," wrote Jagow to Bernstorff, " it will be the duty of your Excellency to prevent President Wilson from approaching us with a positive proposal to mediate." [1] Each side had promised itself a peace of victory. The very phrase " negotiated peace " became synonymous with treachery.

In the early days of the war, before it became apparent how closely the methods of the belligerents would touch

[1] Grey to House, May 12, 1916, *I.P.*, II, 282; Jagow to Bernstorff, June 7, 1916, *G.D.*, II, 978.

American interests and threaten American rights, offers of mediation were academic; they proceeded largely from the benevolent hope of a great neutral power that it might serve each side and the world by helping to end an exhausting and indecisive struggle. But during the course of the year 1915 it became obvious that the vital and selfish interests of the nation demanded an end to the war, simply because if it went on American participation was bound to be almost unavoidable. Wilson's policy of mediation, which at least in its details had to be carried through in the utmost privacy, was not the meddling of an interfering busybody nor the dream of an impractical visionary. It was based upon the need of escaping from the untenable position of a neutral. Ending the war by negotiation or entering the war were the only alternatives.

The policy of mediation failed. In the state of mind in which the belligerents found themselves, the most skilful diplomacy could hardly have availed to bring about peace negotiations. The policy, however, was far from fruitless. In developing his plans for mediation, President Wilson was compelled to give over the traditional principle of American isolation. Almost a year before the United States finally entered the war he recognized American interest in world affairs, and in demanding that there be a new international organization to protect the future peace of the world he promised American coöperation. In the last instance, the principles which Wilson urged as the basis for the final peace settlement can be traced back to the period when he, as chief of a neutral state, hoped to end the war by negotiation.

2

At the very start of the war President Wilson sent to
each of the belligerent Powers an offer of mediation. It
was formal and general in tone, merely an expression of
willingness to act in behalf of European peace at the moment
or " at any other time that might be thought more suitable." [2]
Wilson himself evidently expected no results from the offer;
he spoke of it as his " little attempt at mediation." "All I
wanted to do," he wrote to House, " was to let them know
that I was at their service." [3] Acknowledgments from the
belligerent Powers were equally formal. From that moment
until the day Ambassador von Bernstorff was given his passports, February 1, 1917, Wilson never ceased to seek an
opportunity to initiate peace negotiations.

For this purpose he utilized Colonel House rather than
the accredited ambassadors and the officials of the State
Department. The envoys of the belligerent Powers could
talk frankly with his personal adviser, whom they called
Père Joseph, and their conversations need not be recorded
in Government archives. Inasmuch as the great obstacle to
opening negotiations was always the fear lest willingness to
converse should indicate weakness, the chance of discover-
ing a compromise was much better in the case of an unofficial
intermediary. To House the Ambassadors of Germany,
Austria-Hungary, Great Britain, and France brought information destined ultimately for the President's ear, and

[2] F.R., 1914, Suppl., 42.
[3] Wilson to House, August 6, 1914, Y.H.C.

carried on an intimate correspondence of a less formal nature than that with officials of the State Department.[4]

Early in September, 1914, a conversation between Ambassador von Bernstorff and Colonel House brought up the possibility of an informal discussion of terms with the British Ambassador. Whether Bernstorff undertook the discussion merely as a means to develop relations that might be of serious use later, whether he believed that there was actually a chance of negotiation, or whether he hoped to strengthen Germany's diplomatic position by emphasizing her willingness to enter on negotiations which the Allies were likely to refuse, is hard to determine. The British Ambassador, Sir Cecil Spring Rice, was embarrassed. He distrusted all Germans in general and Bernstorff in particular. He was afraid of the effect of any discussions on the morale of France and Russia. Furthermore, he was not anxious to consider peace at a moment when Germany held a military advantage which, in view of the potential strength of the Allies, was likely to be impermanent. " When one has knocked the other fellow down," he wrote Roosevelt, " and he is getting up, one likes to say, ' this fight is over,' but the other fellow may take a different view." [5] Like the

[4] Cf. *Bernstorff*, p. 231: " I could call on Colonel House at his private residence in New York at any time without attracting attention. . . . As a rule, I took the night train to New York and called on Colonel House in the morning, before the Press were aware that I had left Washington." See also Dumba, *Memoirs of a Diplomat*, p. 211: " Since we diplomats enjoyed no personal intercourse with Wilson, and it was almost impossible to obtain an audience save on official business, House was the welcome ear-piece for messages and information intended for the President." See also *Spring Rice*, II, *passim*.

[5] Spring Rice to Roosevelt, September 10, 1914, *Spring Rice*, II, 228.

vast majority of his compatriots he regarded Germany as an international criminal; the peace of the world, he believed, would not be safe until she was thoroughly punished. On the other hand, it would be dangerous to reject all suggestions of peace. " Germany is doing her best," he cabled Grey, " to put England in the wrong by causing a belief that England is rejecting Germany's friendly overtures." [6]

Grey was clearly of the opinion that the whole business was a diplomatic trick designed to make trouble between England and her allies, and calculated to make England appear the great obstacle to a peace offered by Germany. Any peace suggestions must therefore be treated with respect, although he was convinced that Germany would not think of terms that would be satisfactory to the Allies. [7]

Both Bernstorff and Dumba were anxious to have the United States explore every possibility of negotiation. Direct word from Germany was less encouraging:

" It seems to me that considering the turn events have taken so far," wrote Zimmermann to House, " and the apparently unabated zeal of our opponents, the question of mediation has not yet reached the stage for action. . . . Germany has always desired to maintain peace, as she proves by a record of more than forty years. The war has been forced upon us by our enemies and they are carrying it on by summoning all the powers at their disposal, including Japanese and other colored races. This makes it impossible for us to take the first step towards making peace. The situation might be different if such overtures came from the other side. I do not know whether your efforts have been

[6] Spring Rice to Grey, September 20, 1914, *I.P.*, I, 329. For Spring Rice's account of the attempted negotiations with Bernstorff see his letter to Grey, September 22, 1914, *Spring Rice,* II, 223-226.

[7] Grey to Spring Rice, September 9, 18, 1914, *Grey,* II, 119-122.

extended in that direction and whether they have found a willing ear . . . it seems to me worth while trying to see where the land lies in the other camp." [8]

From the American Ambassadors in Europe the news was definitely discouraging. Page in London interpreted correctly the British determination to carry the war to a complete victory and sympathized with it. " You needn't fool yourself; they are going to knock Germany out, and nothing will be allowed to stand in their way. . . . Pray God, don't let Butler and the Peace Old-Women get the notion afloat that we can or ought to stop it before the Kaiser is put out of business. That would be playing directly into Bernstorff's hands. Civilization must be rescued. Well there's no chance for it till German militarism is dead." [9] From Berlin, Gerard wrote: " I had a long talk with the Chancellor to-day, who sent for me as he was here a few days from the Front. He says he sees no chance of peace now. . . . The hate here against England is phenomenal." [10]

President Wilson realized that progress was not likely to be made with the Ambassadors in Washington. Bernstorff said frankly that it would be necessary to send someone to Berlin and urged Colonel House. The British were not so eager for such a mission, but felt that no harm could come of conversations with House. " It will give me great pleasure to see him," cabled Grey, " and talk to him freely. Of course he understands that all that can be promised here is that if Germany seriously and sincerely desires peace, I will con-

[8] Zimmermann to House, December 3, 1914, *I.P.,* I, 339-340.

[9] Page to House, September 15, 1914, Y.H.C.; published in part in *I.P.,* I, 333-334.

[10] Gerard to House, November, 1915, *I.P.,* I, 336-337.

sult our friends as to what terms of peace are acceptable." [11]
From neither side had come anything like a definite intimation of possible terms, although Bernstorff had hinted that there would be no objection to an indemnity for Belgium.[12]
The mission which House undertook in the spring of 1915 was thus chiefly one of investigation. It seemed the more desirable in that it offered an opportunity for direct conversations with the British regarding restrictions on American trade.

To neutrals and to some historians, the winter of 1914-1915 seemed to offer a natural opportunity for a peace of compromise. The Germans had failed in their plan of a rapid conquest of France. The western front had settled into a state of siege. Complete German victory on the Russian front would necessitate a long war, and in such a war the chances of success against the superior strength of the Entente coalition were slim. On the other side, while the Entente might be confident of ultimate victory the cost would be appalling. If the chance of peace were lost, it might never return short of complete exhaustion on both sides. In the spring each would see the hope of military success and wish to try out new armies. The longer the war continued, the harder it would be to make peace, for the expenditure of more life and treasure would demand higher recompense in peace conditions; the stiffer conditions laid down, the less hope of agreement.

[11] Grey to Spring Rice, January 22, 1915, *I.P.,* I, 347.
[12] House Diary, December 17, 1914, *I.P.,* I, 340. This suggestion was regarded by the Allied Ambassadors as a trick, *Spring Rice,* II, 226-258.

Apart from Bernstorff and Dumba, who labored incessantly for negotiations, none of the leaders in any of the
belligerent Powers were willing to recognize such arguments.
The most pacific of British statesmen, Grey, insisted that the
only satisfactory conclusion of the war would be the complete defeat of Germany, and that the only terms that could
be considered included a German indemnity to Belgium.[13]
" But Germany," wrote Gerard, " will pay no indemnity to
Belgium or anyone else." [14] King George emphatically declared to House that it was no time to talk peace. " His
idea seemed to be," reported House, " that the best way to
obtain permanent peace was to knock all the fight out of the
Germans, and stamp on them for a while until they wanted
peace and more of it than any other nation." [15]

In France there was no hint that the war could be stopped,
and Wilson's envoy did not raise the question. The war
had offered an opportunity for expansion which must not
be lost, and which could only be secured through the complete defeat of Germany: " The French not only want
Alsace and Lorraine, but so much more that the two countries are not within sight of peace." [16] In Germany it was
clear that Bernstorff's suggestion of German evacuation of
invaded territory and indemnity for Belgium would not be
considered for a moment.

The rulers, furthermore, were helpless in the grip of
public opinion which would not consider any terms that did

---

[13] *Grey,* II, 120, 128. See also Spring Rice to Roosevelt,
September 10, 1914, *Spring Rice,* II, 229.

[14] Gerard to House, February 15, 1915, *I.P.,* I, 376.

[15] House to Wilson, March 1, 1915, *I.P.,* I, 385.

[16] House Diary, March 12, 1915, *I.P.,* I, 399.

not signify complete victory. " It is a dangerous thing to inflame a people," wrote House to Wilson, " and give them an exaggerated idea of success." [17] In the abstract all the Governments were anxious to end the war; but they were powerless, even if they had been willing, to make the necessary sacrifices. " If peace parleys were begun now," said Zimmermann on March 24, " upon any terms that would have any chance of acceptance, it would mean the overthrow of this Government and the Kaiser." [18]

As he left Berlin, House confessed sad disappointment. " Everybody seems to want peace," he wrote Bryan, " but nobody is willing to concede enough to get it. . . . Germany is not willing to evacuate Belgium at all, nor even France, without an indemnity, and Count von Bernstorff's suggestion that this could be arranged was wide afield. The Allies, of course, will not consent to anything less; and there the situation rests." [19]

3

During the first year of the war American attempts to discover a basis for peace negotiations were motivated by the natural desire of a neutral to be of service to sister nations caught in a great disaster. But as the summer of 1915 closed, much more compelling reasons for seeking to end the war

[17] House to Wilson, March 26, 1915, *I.P.*, I, 404.
[18] House Diary, March 24, 1915, *I.P.*, I, 403. The above considerations provide a reasonably complete reply to the anonymous biographer of Bryan (Samuel Flagg Bemis, *Secretaries of State*, X, 31-33) who criticizes Wilson for the failure to mediate in the autumn and winter of 1914.
[19] House to Bryan, April 15, 1915, *I.P.*, I, 417.

affected the diplomacy of Wilson. The United States although not part of the war was caught by it. She was squeezed between the Allied blockade and the German submarine. The moment comparative tranquillity seemed assured in relations with Germany, the trade controversy with the Allies presented itself. " The story of the relations between America and the belligerents," writes Mr. Lloyd George, " is that of a country driven backwards and forwards between the two sides by an alternation of incidents, any one of which might easily have tipped the scales for war, had it not been counterpoised by new troubles on the other side; and had it not also been for the stubborn determination of President Wilson to keep his country out of the fight if he possibly could." [20]

It might be possible for Wilson to worry along, bickering with Great Britain without securing any adequate relief from the restrictions on trade, threatening the Germans and extracting questionable excuses for submarine " accidents," propaganda, and plots. But in the process all the moral credit of the United States would disappear; at the end of the war America would be without a friend. Furthermore, at any moment a crisis might arise which would push the country into the war, as it had been pushed into war with Spain, on purely emotional grounds. " Shall we ever get out of this labyrinth? " Wilson wrote in despair.[21]

Until the autumn of 1915 the policy of the American Government toward the belligerents had been primarily defensive. At each invasion of neutral rights, it enunciated

[20] *War Memoirs of David Lloyd George,* II, 116-117.
[21] Wilson to House, September 7, 1915, Y.H.C.

a protest, opposed a negative to the action or projected action
that threatened neutral lives or property. But in October of
that year Wilson began to develop a positive policy that
promised an exit from the labyrinth. The effort resulted
partly from the desperately uncomfortable position in which
he found himself, and which seemed to call for bold measures. It resulted also from his realization that the United
States must either end the war or be compelled to enter it.

The President never wavered in his conviction that it
was his duty to America and the world to keep out of war,
" under bonds," as he expressed it. But in the autumn and
winter of 1915 he began to ask himself whether continued
neutrality would be actually possible. He also felt it to be
his duty to protect the honor of the country and the safety
of her citizens. A time might come when there would be a
conflict between the two loyalties, " a time when I can not
preserve both the honor and the peace of the United
States." [22] With increasing clarity he perceived that the
only certain alternative to entering the war was ending it.

If the war was to be stopped, America would have to
utilize so much pressure upon the belligerents as to involve
the risk of actually intervening actively herself. Moral
suasion would hardly suffice to bring the two groups of belligerents to compromise. American mediation could not succeed without some hint of force behind it which might
easily lead to participation. But Wilson was not far from
the belief that intervention in order to end the war was

[22] Address at Auditorium in Milwaukee, January 31, 1916, Baker
and Dodd, *The Public Papers of Woodrow Wilson*, II, 48. Cf.
Wilson's other preparedness speeches published in *House Document 803*, 64th Congress, 1st Session.

preferable to slipping into the war as a result of infringement of neutral rights. Such armed mediation would involve taking sides, presumably with the group that refused a peace conference on reasonable terms. Wilson was in no doubt which side he would support if intervention seemed necessary. " Much to my surprise," wrote House of one evening when Wilson was discussing problems of neutrality in the White House study, " he said he had never been sure that we ought not to take part in the conflict, and, if it seemed evident that Germany and her militaristic ideas were to win, the obligation upon us was greater than ever." [23]

4

The suggestion of armed mediation was first made by House to Wilson in October, 1915. It involved receiving assurance from one side or the other that at the call of the United States a peace conference would be accepted, and that if the other side refused it American intervention would follow in order to enforce peace. That it should be the Allies and not Germany with whom the United States would probably coöperate, resulted from Wilson's conviction that the future of America was bound up in friendly relations with Great Britain and France. It resulted also from his belief that they would accept terms which would facilitate a future international organization for preserving peace, whereas an undefeated Germany would always remain a menace to world peace.[24]

[23] House Diary, September 22, 1915, *I.P.*, II, 84.
[24]. Comment by the German Navy Archivist, September 15, 1933: " Was Wilson's estimate of the anti-democratic character of the German Government based upon a fair and wise evaluation of

The terms that Wilson and House had in mind would certainly not satisfy either side. They provided for the evacuation of invaded territories by the Germans, an indemnity to Belgium, the cession of Alsace-Lorraine to France, in return for which something might be found to

the historical and political circumstances from which the Reich had evolved and in which it had to conduct its life? Was the World War in fact a conflict of political ideals, waged by the Allies for the alleged benefits of democracy, so that the participation of democratic North America on their side would be entirely natural? According to the German thesis we must answer both of these questions in the negative.

" The constitutional form and structure of imperial Germany, which a hostile world has generally called militarism, can only be readily understood and judged if one keeps before his eyes the historical origins, the geographical situation of the Reich, circumscribed and threatened as it was, and, by no means of least importance, the resulting character of the German people. A German historian will not find in Wilson a correct and accurate evaluation of what nature and fate have placed upon the shoulders of the German people. Wilson, with his Anglo-Saxon background and mentality, was necessarily unappreciative of Germany's position. How can one maintain that autocratic Germany was such a danger to world peace that American interests must conclude that a German victory should be prevented? Does world history show that only autocracies have waged offensive wars, and not also democracies? Was Germany the one who disturbed the peace in 1914, who alone was responsible for a plot to bring on the war, as Wilson was so earnestly persuaded? To put the question today is to answer in the negative. Much that was broadcast and believed in the United States in 1915 and 1916, objective study after the war has shown to be mere prejudice. . . . That the statesmen in London and Paris did not conduct the war for the ideal welfare of democracy but with other aims in mind, that in this respect clever, deceptive influence proceeded from London, was made plain to President Wilson from 1916 on. Paris negotiations at the time of the Peace Conference in 1919 might have removed the last doubt from his mind."

satisfy German colonial aspirations. A victorious Germany would not consider such conditions.[25] Nor would those Allied statesmen who hoped to utilize a prospective victory as a means to extensive annexations and crushing indemnities be pleased. But if by giving up their dreams of conquest they might secure American aid, there was the possibility of their acceptance. This was especially true of Grey, who made it plain that the chief object of the war in his mind was to prevent future wars and that this could be secured only through the permanent coöperation of the United States.

" If the end of this war is arrived at through mediation," Grey wrote to House, " I believe it must be through that of the United States. All our efforts are of course concentrated on saving ourselves and our Allies by securing victory in the war. But it is in my mind continually that the awful sufferings of this war will, to a great extent, have been in vain unless at the end of it nations are set and determined together that future generations shall not fall into such a catastrophe again. . . . To me, the great object of securing the elimination of militarism and navalism is to get security for the future against aggressive war. How much are the United States prepared to do in this direction? Would the President propose that there should be a League of Nations binding themselves to side against any Power which broke a treaty? . . . I cannot say which Governments would be prepared to accept such a proposal, but I am sure that the Government of the United States is the only Government that could make it with effect." [26]

[25] Cf. the comments of Bethmann, Helfferich, and Ludendorff before the Reichstag investigating committee on satisfactory peace terms and the summary of German peace terms sent to Wilson on January 29, 1917, *G.D.*, I, 322 ff, 650 ff, II, 856 ff, 1048.

[26] Grey to House, August 26, September 22, 1915, *I.P.*, II, 88-89.

This message offered an opportunity which Wilson and House immediately seized. If Grey placed so much store by the future coöperation of the United States, he might be willing to accept American mediation at the moment. The President agreed that House should write Grey insisting that it would be a world-wide calamity if the war should continue to a point where the Allies with the help of the United States could not bring about a peace of the kind Grey had in mind. House was to suggest that if the Allies agreed, he would let Germany know of Wilson's intention to mediate " and stop this destructive war, provided the weight of the United States thrown on the side that accepted our proposal could do it." If the Central powers refused, it would " probably be necessary for us to join the Allies and force the issue." [27]

The draft of the above letter, as made by House, was immediately approved by Wilson, who changed it merely to insert the word " probably " in reference to the future action of the United States. In view of later discussion as to the significance of a similar change that was made by Wilson in the draft agreement of February, 1916, it is interesting to note that the President himself refers to this alteration as an " unimportant verbal change." He could not pledge the country unalterably to specific action in the future because, as he wrote, " the exact circumstances of such a crisis are impossible to determine." There can be no question of the President's enthusiasm for the proposal. " The letter is altogether right," he wrote to House. " I pray God it may bring results." [28]

[27] House to Grey, October 17, 1915, *I.P.,* II, 90-91.
[28] Wilson to House, October 18, 1915, Y.H.C.

On November 9 Grey cabled to ask if the proposal was to be taken in connection with his own proposal for a League of Nations, as suggested in his letter of September 22. To this the reply was in the affirmative.[29]

Wilson thus took the first step toward a thorough-going revolution in United States foreign policy. If the proposed peace negotiations did not materialize because of a German refusal, he indicated the probability of American participation in the war in order to end it. He further pledged American participation in a new international organization for preserving peace, the end of American isolation. To carry through such a revolution would tax Wilson's powers of leadership. Doubtless all the implications were not clear in the President's mind. But he had entered on the path which ultimately led Europe, if not the United States, to Geneva.

Sir Edward Grey was naturally cautious. The Allies could not " commit themselves in advance to any proposition without knowing exactly what it was and knowing that the United States of America were prepared to intervene and make it good if they accepted it." [30] Wilson determined to send House again to Europe in order to prepare the ground for mediation. Both Lansing and Polk approved the plan. Bernstorff, who of course knew nothing of the proposition made to Grey but who laboured indefatigably for peace negotiations, brought word that the German Government would like House to " come directly to Berlin to discuss peace upon the general terms of military and naval dis-

[29] Grey to House, November 9, House to Grey, November 10, 1915, *I.P.,* II, 91.

[30] Grey to House, November 11, 1915, *I.P.,* II, 98.

armament." To Bernstorff House intimated that Wilson was considering intervention. "I said I believed if they would consent to a plan which embraced general disarmament, you would be willing to throw the weight of this Government into the scales and demand that the war cease." [31]

The first inquiry made by the British was for a formal assurance of American willingness to combine with the European powers in a policy that would preserve world peace. In view of the prospective revolution in American attitude they could hardly ask less. Wilson in reply sent a cable which may fairly be regarded as a land-mark in American foreign policy. "Would be glad," he telegraphed to House, "if you would convey my assurance that I shall be willing and glad when the opportunity comes to co-operate in a policy seeking to bring about and maintain permanent peace among civilized nations." [32]

The British leaders, however, were either unappreciative of the significance in American history of this cable or they were frightened by the suggestion of early steps toward peace negotiations. All were confident of ultimate victory. The proposal of American intervention, even on the terms laid down by Wilson, they looked on rather as good-natured meddling. None of them seemed to realize clearly that what

[31] House to Wilson, December 22, 1915, *I.P.*, II, 107. See also Bernstorff to Foreign Office, November 23, 1915 ("Colonel House is at least absolutely neutral, very discreet as well as trustworthy, and stands in the very center of the political situation on this side."), and Jagow to Bernstorff, December 20, 1915 ("Colonel House welcome"), *G.D.*, II, 1278-9.

[32] Wilson to House, January 9, 1916, Y.H.C.

Wilson offered was tantamount to guaranteeing victory for the Allies, provided they would give over plans of annihilating Germany in the political sense and of embarking upon a programme of wholesale annexations. Before entering serious discussions House wished to explore the possibilities in Germany.

Long conversations with the German Chancellor and Foreign Secretary revealed no chance of a consideration of any terms except those based upon German military conquests. Such a peace Germany would be glad to have. Bethmann-Hollweg, according to House, insisted that

" he was the only one in authority among the belligerents who had spoken for peace, and he could not understand why there was no receptive echo anywhere. He deplored the war and its ghastly consequences, and declared the guilt did not lie upon his soul. I tried to make him see that his peace talk was interpreted merely as Germany's desire to ' cash in ' her victories, and that the Allies did not believe she could hold her own from now on, and that another story would be told before the end. . . . The Chancellor intimated that Germany would be willing to evacuate both France and Belgium if indemnity were paid. That, I said, the Allies would not consider for a moment." [33]

Even the most liberal Germans with whom House conferred, made it plain that the only terms that could be considered were based upon the assumption of a German victory and were far from those Wilson had in mind. The attitude of the Kaiser was discouraging.[34] Following an interview with Ambassador Gerard, House reported:

[33] House Diary, January 28, 1916, *I.P.*, II, 141.

[34] Comment by the German Navy Archivist, September 15, 1933: " Looking at it from the German point of view, we must reach the

" The Kaiser talked of peace and how it should be made and by whom, declaring that ' I and my cousins, George and Nicholas, will make peace when the time comes.' Gerard says that to hear him talk one would think that the German, English and Russian peoples were so many pawns upon a chessboard. He made it clear that mere democracies like France and the United States could never take part in such a conference. His whole attitude was that war was royal sport, to be indulged in by hereditary monarchs and concluded at their will."

House was further impressed by the degree of influence exercised by the military in political matters. " If the war goes against Germany," he wrote the President, " when the army is disbanded trouble will surely come for the masters. If victory is theirs, the war lords will reign supreme and democratic governments will be imperilled throughout the world." [35]

---

conclusion that House, in the same or even higher degree than President Wilson, inclined toward the side of the Allies. He regarded Germany, and Germanism as well, with a distinct lack of sympathy and, at bottom, with hostility. During his visits of 1915 and 1916 in England these sentiments deepened. . . . The main cause that House on two occasions quickly and without having reached an understanding turned his back on Berlin, appears to have been that, because of his Anglo-Saxon sentiments, he did not bring to Berlin that essential objectivity which is necessary to a successful negotiator, . . . notwithstanding the fact that, considering the war aims of the belligerent powers, the gulf between Washington and London-Paris was far greater than that between Washington and Berlin."

[35] House to Wilson, February 3, 1916, *I.P.,* II, 148. The opinion is general that the German Government would not in 1916 have considered for a moment the terms which Wilson was prepared to suggest as a reasonable compromise. So much was told House by Prince Bismarck in 1925 (*I.P.,* II, 273). Valentin agrees, indicating the influence of the German annexationists (*Deutschlands*

From Berlin House went to Paris hopeful that the Prime Minister, Aristide Briand, who had the reputation of conciliatory tendencies, might exercise some influence upon the British in the direction of mediation. " Up to the present," he reported to Wilson, " I have been confidential with the British Government alone, and have left to them the bringing into line of their Allies. However, I was never more impressed by their slowness and lack of initiative as upon this trip, and I concluded that we had better take the risk and talk plainly to the French." [36] Briand was not flatly discouraging, and agreed to discuss the matter with the British if they raised it. But he would not commit himself in any way.[37] If victories came to them in the spring and summer the French evidently desired no meddling. What they failed to grasp, was that the war had reached a state of deadlock that could be broken only by the injection of some new force from the outside. What no one admitted for a

---

Aussenpolitik, pp. 257-273). Clear evidence that the German Government and people would not have considered these terms is to be found in the minutes of the Reichstag investigating committee. Lloyd George says (*op. cit.*, II, 140): " Nothing is more certain than that Germany in 1916 would have insisted on terms which would have been entirely incompatible with those that the President's vicar-general in the outside world, Colonel House, had agreed upon with us." Cf. also the German terms as indicated to President Wilson in January, 1917, Bernstorff to House, January 31, 1917, *I.P.*, II, 432; *F.R., 1917, Suppl.*, 35.

[36] House to Wilson, February 9, 1916, *I.P.*, II, 163-4.

[37] Of Briand, Mr. Lloyd George writes: " He had a greater personal delight in reconciliation than in strife. But although inscrutable where his own individual opinions were concerned, there could be no doubt as to his sensitiveness to parliamentary opinion. And any suspicion of leanings toward pacifism was a crime in Paris," *op. cit.*, II, 132.

moment was that a peace of compromise in 1916 would be better for all concerned than a complete military triumph in 1918.[38]

In Great Britain the opinion of members of the Government was divided. The majority of the Cabinet were convinced of the probability of ultimate victory and unwilling to accept a compromise peace unless and until the hope of complete success disappeared. They were further doubtful of the willingness of the French to coöperate in Wilson's plan of armed mediation. They felt " that Colonel House's sanguine disposition had misled him into taking too hopeful a view of the coöperation of France in an endeavour to initiate *pourparlers* with an enemy whose arms, taking the terrain of the war as a whole, were triumphant in the East and the West." [39]

Of even greater importance was the general distrust of President Wilson. They could not bring themselves to be-

[38] Cf. speech by Lieut.-Colonel Arthur Murray, C.M.G., D.S.O., made in the House of Commons early in 1916 when on leave from the trenches: " I have just returned from the Front, where it has been my privilege to live for many months in very close proximity to the enemy. Some Hon. Members wander through realms of idealism, and refuse to face solid bedrock facts. What are those facts? They are these, namely, that any treaty concluded with Germany at the present moment would not be worth the paper it was written on. . . . I think there is no doubt whatsoever that a peace formulated now would not only be an inconclusive peace, but would stereotype the evils of militarism which are so detested, not only in this House tonight, but by all of us, and more particularly I may say, by those of us who are bearing the heat and burden of the day fighting in France and elsewhere. A peace secured by bargaining with Germany at the present moment would be no peace at all," Colonel Murray to C.S., August 30, 1933.

[39] Lloyd George, *op. cit.,* II, 133.

11

lieve that he would actually enter the war if Germany refused the proposed conference. " No member of the Government," wrote Ambassador Page in his diary, " can afford to discuss any such subject, not one of them has any confidence in the strength of the President for action." [40]

On the other hand various members of the cabinet, especially Mr. McKenna and Mr. Runciman, according to the Lloyd George account, had serious misgivings as to the economic and financial position of Great Britain, and " entertained doubts of the possibility of success, if the war were prolonged beyond this year. . . . A few more thousands of our tonnage sunk by the German swordfish that swarmed around the approaches to our harbours and we could not carry on." [41] Grey himself, while still convinced that the ultimate victory of the Allies was likely and was the only satisfactory issue of the war, was always ready to consider plans that might stop the wholesale carnage, provided they also promised an organization to prevent future wars.

On February 14, after a large number of informal discussions, Colonel House met the Prime Minister and the Foreign Secretary, Mr. Balfour, Mr. Lloyd George, and Lord Reading at a dinner given by the last named. Rather to House's surprise, Mr. Lloyd George intimated that he was willing to accept Wilson's intervention, provided there could be " some preliminary understanding with the President as to the minimum terms which the Allies were to insist

[40] Page, III, 282. Cf. also Mr. Lloyd George's later comment, op. cit., II, 141: "The President at that time was resolutely pacifist." As a matter of fact this was the one time previous to 1917 when Wilson was ready to yield his pacifism to the purpose of stopping or shortening the war.

[41] Lloyd George, op. cit., II, 133-134.

upon with his sanction and support." He then proceeded to outline those terms, which tallied very closely with those indicated by Wilson and House.[42] They were approved by the others, and it was agreed that Grey and House should draft a memorandum setting forth Wilson's offer of mediation, which would then be discussed with the other Allies. On the other hand, none of the British expressed the feeling that the time had yet come for American intervention; even House was forced to admit that a successful Allied offensive making a dent in the German lines and discouraging German opinion would facilitate the matter. It was understood that the American offer would not be made until an " opportune " moment, and it was left to the Allies to decide when that moment had arrived.[43]

[42] As stated by Mr. Lloyd George, (*op. cit.*, II, 138) his terms included " the restoration of the independence of Belgium and Serbia and the surrender of Alsace and Lorraine to France, provided that the loss of territory thus incurred by Germany would be compensated by concessions to her in other places outside Europe. There were to be adjustments of the frontiers between Italy and Austria so as to liberate Italian communities still under the Austrian yoke. Russia was to be given an outlet to the sea. There were also to be guarantees against any future recurrence of such a catastrophe as this World War." Cf. with terms suggested by Colonel House, *I.P.*, II, 170 n.

[43] In his account of this dinner and its outcome, Mr. Lloyd George, perhaps inadvertently, gives the impression (*op. cit.*, II, 138) that the Cabinet was ready at the moment to accept the proposition on the conditions he himself outlines, provided it were approved by Wilson and the Allies. This is entirely contrary to the contemporary evidence of House's diary, that of Grey's memoirs, and of the memorandum itself. So far as a conclusion was reached by the dinner conference it was simply that should Wilson approve the terms as drafted in the memorandum the British would then decide if and when the matter should be taken up with the French. See *I.P.*, II, 181-2; *Grey*, II, 128 ff.

5

On February 17 Grey and House drafted the memorandum embodying the understanding of what Wilson offered. This House took back to Washington for Wilson's consideration, and on March 6 the President approved it entirely except for the insertion of the word " probably " in reference to American action if Germany failed to agree to " reasonable terms." The document entitled " Memorandum of Sir Edward Grey " was dated at the Foreign Office, 22 February, 1916. There is a touch of irony in the date, since by the document Wilson promised to enter on a course which many would have regarded as definitely contrary to Washington's advice.

Memorandum of Sir Edward Grey.[44]

(*Confidential*)

Colonel House told me that President Wilson was ready, on hearing from France and England that the moment was opportune, to propose that a Conference should be summoned to put an end to the war. (Should the Allies accept this proposal, and should Germany refuse it, the United States would probably enter the war against Germany.)

Colonel House expressed the opinion that, if such a Conference met, it would secure peace on terms not unfavourable to the Allies; and, if it failed to secure peace, the United States would [probably] leave the Conference as a belligerent on the side of the Allies, if Germany was unreasonable. Colonel House expressed an opinion decidedly favourable to the restoration of Belgium, the transfer of Alsace and Lorraine to France, and the acquisition by Russia of an outlet to the sea, though he thought that the loss of territory incurred by Germany in one place would have to be compensated to her by concessions to her in other places outside

---

[44] Published in *I.P.*, II, 201-202; *Grey*, II, 127-128.

Europe. If the Allies delayed accepting the offer of President Wilson, and if, later on, the course of the war was so unfavourable to them that the intervention of the United States would not be effective, the United States would probably disinterest themselves in Europe and look to their own protection in their own way.

I said that I felt the statement, coming from the President of the United States, to be a matter of such importance that I must inform the Prime Minister and my colleagues; but that I could say nothing until it had received their consideration. The British Government could, under no circumstances, accept or make any proposal except in consultation and agreement with the Allies. I thought that the Cabinet would probably feel that the present situation would not justify them in approaching their Allies on this subject at the present moment; but, as Colonel House had had an intimate conversation with M. Briand and M. Jules Cambon in Paris, I should think it right to tell M. Briand privately, through the French Ambassador in London, what Colonel House had said to us; and I should, of course, whenever there was an opportunity, be ready to talk the matter over with M. Briand, if he desired it.

(Intd.) E. G.

FOREIGN OFFICE
22 February, 1916

President Wilson himself sat down at the typewriter and wrote out the cable of endorsement, although the cable was sent over the signature of House:

" I reported to the President the general conclusions of our conference of the 14th of February, and in the light of those conclusions he authorizes me to say that, so far as he can speak for the future action of the United States, he agrees to the memorandum with which you furnished me, with only this correction: that the word ' probably ' be added after the word ' would ' and before the word ' leave ' in line number nine." [45]

[45] House to Grey, March 8, 1918, *I.P.*, II, 202.

Critics have maintained that the insertion of the word
" probably " by President Wilson destroyed the entire significance of his offer, blurred the trend of his policy, and
indicated to the Allies that they could not certainly count
upon American action.[46] Mr. Lloyd George speaks of " the
insertion by President Wilson of one fatal word," and declares that " Sir Edward Grey's view was that this completely changed the character of the proposal, and, therefore, he did not think it worth while to communicate the
purport of the negotiations to the Allies." [47]

This opinion is directly contrary to the evidence in the
contemporary and the later papers published by Grey. There
is no hint, whether in the comments he wrote at the time
or eight years later, that he was in the least affected by
Wilson's insertion of this single word. In a private memorandum drafted for the War Cabinet in November, 1916,
describing the whole negotiation, he states flatly that the
offer of Colonel House was " confirmed " by President
Wilson. In his *Twenty-Five Years* he treats the offer as un-
equivocal. In his later correspondence no mention whatever
is made of Wilson's insertion of the word " probably."
For him, at least, it had no significance whatever.[48]

Careful study of the memorandum shows that the insertion of the word " probably " merely brings the sentence
into conformity with that four lines above, which already
contains the word " probably " and that eleven lines below

[46] See Walter Lippmann in *Foreign Affairs*, IV, 389-391, April,
1926; also *Page*, III, 289.

[47] Lloyd George, *op. cit.*, II, 139. Comment by Colonel Murray,
August 30, 1933: " Mr. Lloyd George has no justification for this
assertion."

[48] *Grey*, II, 124-135.

which contains the same word. As far back as the first suggestion to Grey, on October 17, 1915, the President had inserted the same word " probably." [49] He could not guarantee absolutely the future diplomatic action of the United States, for he shared with the Senate the control of foreign policy and the power to declare war resides in Congress. This must have been plain to the Allies through the phrase contained in the confirmatory cable: " so far as he can speak for the future action of the United States." He gave to the Allies an expression of absolute intention contingent upon their action.[50]

[49] See *supra,* p. 143.

[50] Lord Lothian (at that time Mr. Philip Kerr), who was working in the closest intimacy with Mr. Lloyd George, disagrees with this conclusion and, unlike Grey, stresses the importance of Wilson's insertion of another " probably ": " I think your judgment about the Wilson ' offer ' of February, 1916, quite wrong in emphasis. Wilson never undertook that the United States would enter the war as a belligerent on the side of the Allies if Germany did not accept the peace terms as outlined by him and House, *viz.,* evacuation of Serbia and Belgium, and restoration of Alsace and Lorraine in return for some colonial compensation. He clearly could not have made such an ' offer ' because the final decision rested, not with him, but with the Senate. The absolute uncertainty of the ' offer ' was specifically underlined by Wilson himself when he added the word ' probably.'

" Was there any substantial reason for thinking that the U. S. A. would have implemented the ' offer,' if a peace Conference had assembled and Germany had refused the minimum terms ? Of that you are a better judge than I am, but in my view public opinion in U. S. A. in 1916 would certainly have refused to enter the war, just because Germany refused to evacuate Belgium or Alsace-Lorraine and without their own vital interests being directly challenged as they were later on by the unrestricted submarine campaign," comment by Lord Lothian, October 27, 1933.

Other critics have insisted that the whole proposition was so contrary to Wilson's pacific policy as to make it incredible that he was serious. How could the man who was later elected to the cry of " He kept us out of war " actually have embarked upon negotiations which, if the Allies had chosen to pursue them and unless Germany made surprising concessions, would have led directly to American armed intervention? The answer is to be found in the good faith of the President of the United States. If Wilson was not serious, if he approved the memorandum in a Pickwickian sense, he was guilty of a duplicity and a stupidity wholly contradictory to his character and general policy. He laid the greatest store by the sanctity of agreements; his action in the Panama Tolls controversy proved it. He was determined to maintain the friendliest possible relations with the Allies. It would have been morally and physically impossible for him to have typed the endorsement of a memorandum containing a promise which he did not mean to keep.[51]

That Wilson was serious and acting in good faith we cannot doubt. Whether he realized the extreme probability that Germany would not accept the terms indicated in the memorandum may be questioned. It is possible that he believed that if peace negotiations were once started the war could not have gone on. But it is certain that, whereas previous to the German submarine warfare he had regarded American neutrality as an end in itself, the events of the summer of 1915 had compelled him to consider the possibility of

[51] Comment by Colonel Murray, August 30, 1933: " Those of us who remember the great-mindedness with which the President sanctioned the incorporation of American troops in the British and French Armies early in 1918 will heartily endorse this."

our entering the war. If we took up arms it should be in behalf of some higher cause, in behalf of the making and preserving of permanent peace. So much is obvious from the tone of his public speeches following the drafting of the House-Grey memorandum. Indeed it is only with that memorandum as a background that his speeches can be fully understood.

" We are holding off," he said at Omaha on October 5, " not because we do not feel concerned, but because when we exert the force of this Nation we want to know what we are exerting it for." [52]
" Define the elements, let us know that we are not fighting for the prevalence of this nation over that, for the ambitions of this group of nations as compared with that group of nations; let us once be convinced that we are called into a great combination to fight for the rights of mankind and America will unite her force and spill her blood for the great things which she has always believed in and followed." [53]

This was a public paraphrase of the House-Grey memorandum. America would intervene if the Allies were serious in their protestation that they were fighting for the peace of the world and not for the destruction of Germany. Germany must be given an opportunity to consider a reasonable settlement. If she refused America was ready to impose it. " Valor," said Wilson on February 26, " withholds itself from all small implications and entanglements and waits for the great opportunity when the sword will flash as if it carried the light of Heaven upon its blade." [54] It was a

[52] Baker and Dodd, op. cit., II, 346.
[53] Address at Shadow Lawn, October 14, 1916, N. Y. Times, October 15, 1916.
[54] Address at the Gridiron Dinner, Washington, February 26, 1916, Baker and Dodd, op. cit., II, 128.

public call to the Allies to provide the opportunity for American intervention.[55]

A third line of criticism levelled against the policy implicit in the House-Grey memorandum is weighted with more validity. Germans and Austrians, some Americans, have complained that the conversations with the Allies and the endorsed memorandum itself involved a flagrant breach of neutrality by the President of the United States, and justified the common suspicion held in Germany that there was a secret understanding between the Allies and the United States. It is impossible, certainly, to justify the method employed except upon the ground of necessity. It was obviously impracticable to initiate peace negotiations without a preliminary understanding with one or both of the belligerent groups. A public call to a peace conference, with no private preparation, would have resulted merely in a furious outcry of that public opinion which had been carefully educated to believe in no peace but a peace of victory. Wilson was ready to enter such an understanding with either side that would accept a peace of compromise. This was understood by the Allies. The President, as Grey points out,

" might invite the opinion of the Allies first, but he would explore the mind of Germany too. His whole policy was founded on the assumption that the war was a stalemate, and that the most useful rôle of the United States was to

[55] A typical example of misunderstanding of Wilson's motives is provided by the editor of Spring Rice's papers: " Neither he [House] nor Wilson wished to enter the war except on conditions which would appeal to the national pride of America—to enforce a peace whose terms America dictated," *Spring Rice*, II, 325. " National pride " had little to do with Wilson's political idealism, except the pride of service; so much is plain from his published speeches and private letters.

promote an honorable end without a crushing victory. If either side, even Germany, were to agree with him in this, he would use the influence of the United States to bring the other side into line. His suggestion of mediation could not be confined to one side." [56]

But the tentative discussions with Germany had indicated no chance of winning her acceptance to terms based on a stalemate. The professions of Count von Bernstorff had been completely disavowed in Berlin. Hence Wilson turned finally to the Allies, in whose moderation, especially in that of Grey, he rightly or wrongly placed greater confidence. That Germany missed a great chance of salvation is obvious. " If she had accepted the Wilson policy, and was ready to agree to a Conference, the Allies could not have refused." So, at least, Grey insists. " They were dependent on American supplies; they could not have risked the ill-will of the Government of the United States, still less a *rapprochement* between the United States and Germany. Germans have only to reflect upon the peace they might have had in 1916 compared with the peace of 1919." [57]

It is perfectly true that the memorandum approved by the President was favorable to the Allies. That again was understood by them, at least by Grey.

" I regarded it as such, because it seemed to me certain that Germany would refuse anything like the terms suggested. The German people had been led to expect a victorious war; they had been told, and believed, that they were winning; Berlin had been beflagged again and again in honor of victories. The American terms were, it is true, not the terms that the Allies would regard as those of victory, but for Germany they were the terms of positive defeat." [58]

[56] *Grey,* II, 133-134.
[57] *Grey,* II, 135.
[58] *Grey,* II, 134.

The explanation of Wilson's attitude is partly to be found in the fact that he, like most Americans interested in war origins at that period, shared the belief that Germany was primarily responsible for the war. Moreover, and largely because of the sinking of defenseless passenger boats, he regarded the Allies as the champions of humanity; later, but while America was still neutral, he spoke of Germany as a " madman that ought to be curbed." [59] He did not wish either side to annihilate the other, but he certainly believed that " German militarism " deserved defeat. Finally, like most American students of European problems of the period, he was convinced that a permanent peace could not be obtained without adequate reparation for the wrong done to Belgium, a warm-water port for Russia, and a settlement of the Alsace-Lorraine problem. To understand his attitude we have only to remember his academic background, for nine-tenths of American professors of the time felt the same way.

· At all events Wilson gave to the Allies an opportunity to show whether they were indeed interested in securing what from their point of view might fairly be called a " peace of justice," or whether they were embarked upon a war of conquest. He opened the road to an immediate peace, with sacrifice of only their extreme ambitions, or the alternative of armed help from America in enforcing it. The offer came at a moment when Wilson and America were being excoriated for their indifference to the moral values of the Allied cause. *Punch* published a cartoon in which Uncle Sam requested the patriarch Job to resign his crown of

[59] House Diary, February 1, 1917, *I.P.,* II, 440.

patience in favor of Wilson.[60] "The British have concluded," wrote Ambassador Page, "that our Government does not understand the moral meaning of their struggle against a destructive military autocracy. . . . They feel that the moral judgment of practically the whole civilized world is on their side except only the Government of the United States. They wonder whether our Government will show in the future a trustworthy character in world affairs." [61]

The offer of Wilson provided the most complete reply to this rather confused criticism. Certainly the Allied leaders could no longer argue that they were alone in carrying the burdens of humanity while America stood aloof. If they refused to take advantage of the offer they must either be stupid or else subject to the suspicion that, like Germany, they were fighting for a peace of conquest.

6

America's offer of intervention to end the war was never taken up by the Allies. Despite frequent suggestions from Colonel House that the "opportune moment" had arrived the British steadfastly evaded committing themselves to the proposal for a conference.

"Why," asks Mr. Lloyd George, "was this conference never summoned? Who was responsible? Had it come off either Germany would have accepted the terms as soon as she realized that President Wilson was committed to their enforcement, or, in the event of their rejection, America would have come into the war in the spring of 1916, instead of twelve months later. The world would have been saved a

[60] *Punch,* February 16, 1916.
[61] Notes toward an Explanation of the British Feeling toward the U. S., September 15, 1916, Y.H.C.

whole year of ruin, havoc and devastation. What a difference it would have made!" [62]

Of the six persons who dined at Lord Reading's house on February 14, 1916, to discuss Wilson's offer—Asquith, Grey, Balfour, Lloyd George, House, and Reading himself— only three, House, Grey, and Lloyd George, have published comments upon the discussion and the resulting memorandum. Those of Lloyd George, apart from the expression of his own opinion, are of less historical value, for they are summary in nature and not based upon any evidence not already published by House and Grey. He bewails the failure of the Allies to take up the American offer and is lavish in his distribution of blame, concentrating chiefly upon Wilson for his failure to give a firmer endorsement and upon Grey for his failure to push the matter with the French.[63] He evades the obvious suggestion that he himself was in a position of such influence in the Government that he might, of his own initiative, at least have raised the matter again with the Cabinet and insisted that it be taken up with the French.[64] The truth is that Lloyd George was

[62] Lloyd George, op. cit., II, 139.

[63] "President Wilson," he hazards, "was afraid of public opinion in the U. S. A. and Sir Edward Grey was frightened of our Allies." For a thoughtful opinion on the significance of Wilson's offer see Wickham Steed, "The Man from Texas," in The Saturday Review of Literature, March 20, 1926, p. 643. For a critical treatment of the Allied refusal see T. P. Conwell-Evans' study based on the papers of Lord Noel-Buxton, Foreign Policy from a Back Bench, 1904-1918, pp. 129-134. No mention is made of the Wilson proposal in John Alfred Spender and Cyril Asquith, Life of Lord Oxford and Asquith.

[64] Comment by Colonel Murray, August 30, 1933: " It is notorious that Mr. Lloyd George has never—during his political career—

so nearly committed to the " knock-out blow " policy, that he took far less interest in what he now terms " this great and at one time promising plan " than his memoirs would indicate. " The world," he says, " was once more sacrificed to the timidity of statesmanship." But there is no evidence that he raised his finger to forward the plan, the failure of which he now laments.

To Colonel House the plan seemed then, as it does now, to provide a clear opportunity for cutting short the war, either by negotiation or by American intervention. Then and later he believed that the Allies lost a magnificent chance to save millions from the horrors of war and achieve a settlement at least as satisfactory as that of Versailles. That they should pass by the chance in the hope of completely crushing Germany and run the risk of bankruptcy themselves in the process seemed to him incredibly short-sighted.[65]

---

been slow to raise and to pursue, in or out of Cabinet, any matter upon which he has felt deeply."

[65] Comment by Colonel House, July 20, 1933: " It is futile to speculate now on where the blame lay for not acting upon this offer, but that it was not accepted constitutes one of the monumental blunders of the war."

Comment by Lord Lothian, October 27, 1933: " I think that your diagnosis implies a misreading of the realities of the position, and that the possibility of peace in 1916 really depended, not upon the Allies agreeing to a conference upon a conditional hope of American intervention if Germany proved recalcitrant, but upon Wilson having obtained from Congress authority to enter the war if Germany did not accept his minimum terms. If that had been the offer the Allies would almost certainly have acted on it and it might have ended the war on fair terms in 1916. Nothing less could have done so. . . . I think that the Allies should have pressed home the House-Wilson suggestion vigorously instead of just allowing it to lapse. But the pressing home would have been

Lord Grey is more cautious in his comments. That he regarded the offer as of the first importance is evident from his tone and from the fact that the memorandum was one of the only two papers, private or official, that he deliberately took home with him when he left the Foreign Office and London at the end of the year. Grey did not differ from House in his ultimate aim; he was not merely personally intimate with him but he esteemed his judgment. House's mind, Grey writes, " was always practical. He was not less studious of the means by which an end was to be accomplished than he was of the end itself. In this awful calamity of war the end to be sought and worked for was a just, fair, and reasonable peace." [66]

Grey and House differed primarily as to the time when Wilson's intervention should be publicly proffered. The latter believed the sooner the better. The former was convinced that the only satisfactory termination of the war was the complete defeat of Germany, and if this could be achieved by Allied arms without American intervention he was content to wait. "At present," writes Grey in reference to the memorandum, " there was no use to be made of it. We believed and the French believed, that defeat of the German armies was the only sure overthrow of Prussian militarism. . . . Both France and Russia had up to this time suffered more heavily in the war than we had. We could never be the first to recommend peace to them." In a memo-

---

to find out, in the long run publicly, exactly what the U. S. A. views as to the ultimate peace were, and whether, if Germany rejected them and the Allies accepted them, the U. S. A. would have entered the war on the Allied side."

[66] *Grey*, II, 124-125.

randum drafted for the Cabinet's information in November, 1916, Grey states that " the War Committee were informed of what had passed with Colonel House, and we were unanimously of opinion that the time had not come to discuss peace." [67]

Grey was further embarrassed by the difficulty of discussing the matter with the French, to say nothing of the Russians. The Allies were suspicious of each other and any suggestion of peace before victory was won might lead to a moral debâcle. As Page suggests, any talk of peace even among members of the same Cabinet was in the nature of something indecent. " To recommend the memorandum to the French," says Grey, " was to suggest that we were weakening and to undermine their confidence in our determination." Therefore although the matter was regarded by Grey as of the greatest importance, although it might lead to America joining the Allies, although Grey knew that House had discussed it with Briand and Briand knew that Grey knew, Grey and Briand never discussed it. A copy of the memorandum was sent through the French Ambassador to Briand with the intimation that Grey did not propose to raise the question with Briand unless he wished to discuss it with him. The latter never mentioned the matter to him.[68]

Both Wilson and House evidently underestimated the effect of what Americans would call British inertia—a tendency to let things take their course rather than embark upon a strong initiative which would certainly raise difficulties even though it accomplished results. They underestimated British unwillingness to urge any consideration of peace upon the French. " No Englishman," as Grey wrote to House on June 28, 1916, " would at this moment say to France after Poincaré's and Briand's speeches made in the face of the Verdun struggle, ' Hasn't the time come to make peace? ' " [69]

They could not understand why Grey did not emphasize the second half of the American offer; namely, that the United States was prepared to help if Germany refused terms that were certainly favorable to France. Finally they underestimated the extent of French aspirations and their unwillingness to accept any conditions.[70]

[69] Cf. memorandum of Ambassador Page of conversation with Grey, July 27, 1916 (*F.R., 1916, Suppl.,* 42): " He (Grey) said that none of the Allies could mention peace or discuss peace till France should express such a wish; for it is the very vitals of France that have received and are receiving the shock of such an assault as was never before launched against any nation. Unless France was ready to quit, none of France's allies could mention peace, and France showed no mood to quit. Least of all could the English make or receive any such suggestion, at least till her new great army had done its best; for until lately the severest fighting had not been done by the British, whose army had practically been held in reserve."

[70] Comment by Colonel Murray, August 30, 1933, in reference to Wilson's attempts to end the war by negotiation: " Everyone who was close to the heart of the stupendous struggle felt that those attempts were doomed to failure—whatever their ultimate results. The Allies were convinced—not only those in high places, but the man-in-the-street elsewhere—that if peace were made before the Military Party in Germany became discredited, that party would consolidate its position and in due course embark again on its scheme of world domination. It is no answer (on the part of those who suggest that the Allies ought to have accepted Wilson's offers) to say that the Allies, in attempting to bring

On the other hand, it is quite possible that the French and British underestimated the importance of American armed assistance. Grey speaks conservatively of American intervention as a " gain " to the Allies.[71] Writing nine years after these events House says:

" I have no doubt that when we sent the last word to Grey concerning intervention, the Allies came to much the same opinion as the Germans had come to; that is, we were totally unprepared to help or hurt further than we were doing. The Allies were getting money, foodstuffs, and arms and keeping our ships from going into neutral ports. They probably concluded, as Germany concluded, that we were doing about as much as we would do if in the war. In addition they probably considered that they would rather have this condition continue than to have our intervention and interference with the terms of peace. I do not believe the Allies thought we would make any such effort as we later did, and I believe they were as much surprised as the Germans. . . . I believe our big mistake was that we were not in a position to intervene in spite of Allied or German protests." [72]

During the four months following the drafting of the House-Grey memorandum Wilson waited for some indica-

---

about the downfall of the German military system, ran the risk of being themselves defeated, and that this was a risk they were unwise—in their own cause and that of civilization—to take. A man with a wild beast at his throat does not think of risks. For him it is a matter of life or death; and he knows that the beast, if not killed or crippled, will spring at him again. If Great Britain felt this, how much stronger were the feelings of France, upon whom, for the second time within fifty years, Germany had sprung. Never again could she hope to have such a supreme opportunity of defeating German aims. No one who fought on the battlefields of France at that time could do other than share her feelings. Thus, on the Allied side, Wilson's suggestions fell on ears untuned to grasp them."

[71] *Grey,* II, 136.

[72] House to C. S., April 6, 1925.

tion of Allied interest. They were months, curiously enough, when Wilson and the United States were intensely unpopular in England. A former Governor-General of Canada announced for publication in an American newspaper, " In this supreme crisis in which the best hopes of humanity are involved, it appears to me you have failed. . . . Belgium has lost everything but her soul. What shall be said of America? " " Confidence in President Wilson's statesmanship," said Lord Cromer, " has been rudely shaken." [73] They forgot that by a slightly stricter interpretation of the duty of a neutral Wilson could have prevented the enormous loans and, through an embargo, the export of precious munitions to the Allies; they forgot that he had forced the Berlin Government to accept his point of view on the submarine and thereby incidently protected Allied shipping. They abused him for his " spineless " policy. But when he offered to help win a moderate peace, their Governments made no response.

As the delay stretched into May and June, President Wilson sent to Grey, through House, frequent reminders that the situation might at any time be altered and the offer no longer hold good. A hint from the British Foreign Office that direct conversations between the United States and France might save the British embarrassment, had no results; Ambassador Jusserand proved definitely unwilling to take up in Paris any sort of American mediation.[74] On May 11 House wrote to Grey pleading that the complete

---

[73] *Current History,* July, 1916, p. 739. Cf. *Page,* II, 129; III, 290.

[74] Grey to House, March 24, 1916, *I.P.,* II, 274, 275.

crushing of Germany was dangerous to the future of world peace and not in England's interest:

" Italy and France would then be more concerned as to the division of the spoils than they would for any far-reaching agreement that might be brought about looking to the maintenance of peace in the future and the amelioration of the horrors of war. . . . England should be immediately responsive to our call. Her statesmen will take a great responsibility upon themselves if they hesitate or delay; and in the event of failure because they refuse to act quickly, history will bring a grave indictment against them." [75]

At the same time Wilson authorized House to cable Grey that the President was willing publicly to commit the United States to joining with other Powers in a convention looking to the maintenance of peace after war; that he wished to couple with it his purpose of calling a conference to discuss peace. " There is an increasingly insistent demand here that the President take some action toward bringing the war to a close. The impression grows that the Allies are more determined upon the punishment of Germany than upon exacting terms that neutral opinion would consider just." [76] Grey's replies were all to the effect that the situation was not ripe for intervention.

Another interview with Jusserand gave convincing evidence that the French would not listen to any proposition that contained the word peace. House reported to the President what he believed to be the real feeling of France, " that is, she had best stick to this war until Germany is crushed, for she could never again hope to have Great Britain, Russia, Italy, and Belgium fighting by her side." [77]

[75] House to Grey, May 11, 1916, I.P., II. 279-280.
[76] House to Grey, May 10, 1916, I.P., II, 278.
[77] House Diary, May 24, 1916, I.P., II, 290.

On May 19 Wilson drafted with House what was intended to be a final warning to the British: " If England is indeed fighting for the emancipation of Europe we are ready to join her in order that the nations of the earth, be they large or small, may live their lives as they may order them and be free from the shadow of autocracy and the spectre of war. If we are to link shields in this mighty cause, then England must recognize the conditions under which alone this can become possible." [78] Three weeks later it is clear that Wilson understood that the Allies did not intend to take up his proposals except as a last resort in case they faced definite defeat. House's letter of June 8 to Grey breathed acute regret and something of prophetic accuracy:

" I am afraid another year will go by leaving the lines much as they are today. . . . Unless you have better means of knowing the situation than we have, there does not seem to be much reason for the optimism of the Allies. . . . Looking at the situation from this distance it seems that England might easily be in a worse position later, even though the fortunes of Germany recede. . . . In getting rid of the German peril, another might easily be created. . . . There is nothing to add or to do for the moment; and if the Allies are willing to take the gamble which the future may hold, we must rest content." [79]

[78] House to Grey, May 19, 1916, *I.P.*, II, 287.

[79] House to Grey, June 8, 1916, *I.P.*, II, 291-292. Those who were close to Grey still feel that, considering the attitude of the German Government in 1916, a negotiated peace would have left the world continually threatened by the aspirations of the German military group. Cf. the comment of Colonel Murray, August 30, 1933: " The state of mind of the German Military Party indeed forms the crux of the situation, and unless it could be proved that Party had either relinquished its original war aims, or had become so discredited as to be likely to fall from power, the historian, in my judgment, would not be justified in attaching blame to the Allies for rejecting the President's proposals."

7

Thus ended Wilson's attempt, through a positive policy, to escape from the untenable position in which the United States was caught, to provide an opportunity of ending the war, and to define the issue upon which America would enter the war if intervention became necessary. He had tried to escape from a negative, a passive position, and had failed. Henceforward, during the succeeding nine months, as he confessed, American policy was determined not by what America wanted but by what others did.[80] Unless one is caught by what Lowes Dickinson calls the hypnosis of established facts, the historian must regret the failure. As Lord Grey says, " So disappointing have events been since 1919, so dark are the troubles still, that we are tempted to find some relief in building castles in the air; and, if the future is too clouded for this, we build them in the past." [81]

If, as a result of prosecuting the proposals of Wilson, the Allies had ended the war with a peace of understanding or even had shortened it through American help, the world would have escaped the most disastrous period, when because of complete exhaustion the cost mounted appallingly. The war had entered the stage of deadlock. It had passed beyond control.

" Governments and individuals conformed to the rhythm of the tragedy," writes Winston Churchill, " and swayed and

[80] " That [the defence of the honor of the United States] is a matter not within my control; that depends upon what others do, not upon what the Government of the United States does," Milwaukee Speech, January 31, 1916, Baker and Dodd, *op. cit.,* II, 48.

[81] *Grey,* II, 137.

staggered forward in helpless violence, slaughtering and squandering on ever-increasing scales, till injuries were wrought to the structure of human society which a century will not efface, and which may conceivably prove fatal to the present civilization. . . . Victory was to be bought so dear as to be almost indistinguishable from defeat. It was not to give even security to the victors. . . . The most complete victory ever gained in arms has failed to solve the European problem or remove the dangers which produced the war." [82]

If such is the considered judgment of a statesman never suspected of mawkish pacifism, one may well ask whether the Allies were not guilty of an awful error in refusing the opportunity opened by Wilson. What might not the world have gained if the war of exhaustion had been stopped in 1916, or shortened by American help? The Allies would have sacrificed the right to dictate a peace based upon complete military victory. But what is the value of victory when it is bought so dear as to be " almost indistinguishable from defeat "?

[82] Churchill, *World Crisis,* II, 1-2.

CHAPTER V

AMERICA ENTERS THE WAR

1

The House-Grey negotiations, based upon Wilson's suggestion of American intervention, are generally regarded as entirely fruitless. It is true that they failed to achieve their immediate purpose, the calling of a peace conference. But they were far from fruitless and can even be reasonably regarded as marking the first positive steps taken by Wilson in the development of his policy of international organization. The prospect of a conference in which America would play the rôle of mediator forced Wilson to consider seriously what should be the bases of permanent peace. The essential condition he found in Grey's suggestion of an international organization by which states could be brought easily into conference when a crisis arose.[1] He also accepted Grey's con-

[1] The most influential letter, from Grey to House, was probably that of August 10, 1915: "My own mind revolves more and more about the point that the refusal of a conference was the fatal step that decided peace or war last year, and about the moral to be drawn from it: which is that the pearl of great price, if it can be found, would be some League of Nations that could be relied on to insist that disputes between any two nations must be settled by the arbitration, mediation, or conference of others. International Law has hitherto had no sanction. The lesson of this war is that Powers must bind themselves to give it a sanction. If that can be secured, freedom of the seas and many other things will become easy," *I.P.*, II, 87. Cf. also the correspondence between Grey and

dition that to be successful the organization must include the United States.

As early as January, Wilson gave private assurance to the British, through House, of his readiness to engage the United States in so revolutionary a policy.[2] In his speech of May 27, 1916, before the League to Enforce Peace, he made public announcement that the time had come for America to coöperate to end the war and keep the peace.[3] Because of the discouraging attitude of the Allies, he decided only three days before he gave the speech to make it include merely the fundamentals of ultimate peace. Originally designed to be the occasion by which America would intervene to stop the war, it remained the basis of Wilson's policy after America had been forced into the war and contained almost every principle which he advanced during the Peace Conference.

The speech was not merely occasioned by the House-Grey negotiations, but was constructed on the main lines sketched by Grey in his letters to House. In a letter of May 18 the President suggested that he would use the understanding with Grey as to future guarantees of peace

---

Roosevelt (*Grey,* II, 146-8) which indicates the effect upon Grey of Roosevelt's idea of an international *posse comitatus.* Quite unconsciously, by a route oblique but direct, Wilson's propositions of May 27 go back to Roosevelt.

[2] Wilson to House, January 9, 1916, *supra,* p. 145.

[3] Wilson regarded the moment, as he wrote to House, as a " turning point. . . . It seems to me that we should really get down to hard pan." The United States must either, he insisted, make a decided move for peace or else take steps to protect herself from Allied attacks on trade. " We must act, and act at once, in the one direction or the other," Wilson to House, May 16, 1916, Y.H.C.

as its groundwork, and asked House to send him a copy of a letter Wilson had written regarding these guarantees.[4] But the phraseology of the chief sentence of the speech goes back to the draft Pan-American Pact, as it points forward to Article X of the League of Nations Covenant. It was characteristically Wilsonian:

"An universal association of the nations to maintain inviolate security of the highway of the seas for the common and unhindered use of all the nations of the world, and to prevent any war begun either contrary to treaty covenants or without warning and full submission of the causes to the opinion of the world—a virtual guarantee of territorial integrity and political independence."[5]

The President threw completely to one side the doctrine of isolation. "We are participants, whether we would or not, in the life of the world.[6] The interests of all nations are our own also. We are partners with the rest. What affects mankind is inevitably our affair as well as the affair of the nations of Europe and of Asia." He underlined the principles of the new organization for the creation of which the United States would coöperate with the rest of the world:

[4] Wilson to House, May 18, 1916, Y.H.C. Wilson's request is interesting, for it indicates that he did not keep copies of his more intimate correspondence even when of the first importance.

[5] Wilson sketched his first ideas of the speech in a letter to House, of May 16, 1916. In that letter the above sentence was less involved: "An universal alliance to maintain freedom of the seas and to prevent any war begun either (a) contrary to treaty covenants or (b) without full warning and full inquiry—a virtual guarantee of territorial integrity and political independence."

[6] Cf. Roosevelt's "We have no choice . . . as to whether or not we shall play a great part in the affairs of the world," *supra*, p. 2.

" First, that every people has a right to choose the sovereignty under which they shall live. . . .

" Second, that the small states of the world have a right to enjoy the same respect for their sovereignty and for their territorial integrity that great and powerful nations expect and insist upon.

"And, third, that the world has a right to be free from every disturbance of its peace that has its origin in aggression and disregard of the rights of peoples and nations."

These principles echo distinctly the tone of the Mobile address of 1913, but Wilson carried his ideas now to a positive and concrete development, for he indicated a definite mechanism, " an universal association of the nations," to enforce them. He concluded with the demand for the covenant which then and all through the Peace Conference and the struggle with the Senate seemed to him the heart of the matter—the guarantee of territorial integrity and political independence.[7]

It is an interesting illustration of the extent to which the mind of the world was caught by military events, that the revolutionary significance of the speech passed almost unnoticed. A few liberals abroad responded enthusiastically.[8] But Allied opinion in general passed over the important passages to complain of an unnecessary and unfortunate

[7] Text of speech in Baker and Dodd, *Public Papers of Woodrow Wilson,* II, 184-188.

[8] Loreburn and Bryce, for example. For attitude of Lord Bryce, see memorandum of Page of a conversation with Lord Bryce, July 31, 1916, *F.R., 1916, Suppl.,* 43. Brand Whitlock called the speech " the most important announcement concerning our foreign policy since the announcement of the Monroe Doctrine, although it will take many years before this fact is brought into relief and fully understood," Whitlock to House, 1916, *I.P.,* II, 299.

phrase referring to the present war: "With its causes and objects we are not concerned." Sir Horace Plunkett, a fervent admirer of Wilson, wrote that "unquestionably the misunderstanding of the President's Peace League speech has done immense harm to the popular feeling in England." Page reported that the speech had "created confusion. Some things in it were so admirably said that the British see that he does understand, and some things in it seem to them to imply that he doesn't in the least understand the war and show, as they think, that he was speaking only to the gallery filled with peace cranks." [9] The British Ambassador was sarcastic: "The Good Samaritan did not pass by on the other side, and then propose to the authorities at Jericho a bill for the better security of the high roads." [10]

But although contemporaries failed to grasp the importance of the speech, historians must emphasize it. Designed as an introduction to peace parleys, it was destined to become the basis of American armed intervention. When, as a result of the German submarine campaign, Wilson finally decided that the United States could no longer remain neutral, he went back to the principles of this speech as providing the framework of a new international order for which America would fight.

[9] Plunkett to House, June 7, 1916, Page to House, May 30, 1916, *I.P.*, II, 301-302. Cf. reports of Ambassador Page to the State Department; *F.R., 1916, Suppl.*, 40 ff.

[10] Spring Rice to Drummond, *Spring Rice*, II, 347. Cf. his report to Grey of May 30: "The President's speech is, of course, pure politics," *ibid.*, 334.

2

The results of the speech of May 27, 1916, were thus ultimate rather than immediate. It charted the course of later policy, but it did not affect the diplomacy of the moment. Although it pointed the way towards an essentially positive policy, the American attitude for the time became again negative and defensive. From June until December the attitude of the belligerents prevented anything else. It was, furthermore, the year of a presidential election, and as the autumn approached the possibility of a new administration loomed upon the political horizon.

The period was one of many irritations. Interchanges with the Allies regarding the blockade, the seizure and holding of mails, the blacklist, approached the acrid. Wilson confessed the end of his patience with them. He was unquestionably affected by their refusal to accept a peace conference. Allied insistence upon pushing the war to the complete military defeat of Germany raised in his mind the suspicion that they were impelled by selfish greed as much as by the desire for permanent peace. Whether the suspicion was justified is beside the point. All that he saw was, that when he offered the coöperation of America to effect what he regarded as a just settlement, they preferred to settle matters on their own terms. Wilson's feeling was reflected in Colonel House, who noted on May 13:

" a distinct feeling of cock-sureness in the Allies since Verdun. This will grow in the event they have any success themselves. . . . A situation may arise, if the Allies defeat Germany, where they may attempt to be dictatorial in Europe and elsewhere. I can see quite clearly where they might change their views on militarism and navalism. It depends entirely upon what nation uses it, whether it is considered good or bad." [11]

The summer of 1916 produced increased friction with the British. The President asked and received power to undertake retaliatory measures against the Allies if they continued interference with American trade. Congress voted the naval appropriation calculated to make the American fleet the strongest in the world. Wilson sent for Ambassador Page, "to get some American atmosphere into him." [12] Page complained that the officials of the United States failed to make any reasonable effort to maintain cordial relations with the British. "I ventured the opinion," wrote House, "if we sent Bernstorff home and entered the war, we would be applauded for a few weeks and then they would demand money. If the money was forthcoming, they would be satisfied for a period, but later would demand an unlimited number of men. If we did it all, they would finally accuse us of trying to force them to give better terms to Germany than were warranted." [13]

On their side the British expressed dissatisfaction with American policy. "We are not favourably impressed," wrote Grey to House, "by the action of the Senate in having passed a resolution about the Irish prisoners, though they have taken no notice of outrages in Belgium and massacres of Armenians." [14] An emotional crisis with the Allies threatened early in October when a German submarine, U-53, entered Newport Harbor and after remaining a few

[11] House Diary, May 13, 1916, *I.P.*, II, 284.
[12] Wilson to House, May 17, 1916, July 22, 1916, Y.H.C.
[13] House Diary, September 25, 1916, *I.P.*, II, 319-320.
[14] Grey to House, August 28, 1916, *I.P.*, II, 318.

hours put to sea and proceeded to sink a number of ships, outside territorial waters, it is true, but close to Nantucket. The British were irritated by the daring and success of the exploit and vented their annoyance upon the Americans. Feeling was not lessened by the fact that the submarine conformed with the rules of warning and that no principle of neutrality had been infringed by the United States. Page cabled describing the " fierce public feeling here against our Government," which Grey himself confessed to sharing.[15] The British Naval Attaché, Captain Gaunt, reported that the " feeling in Great Britain against the United States grows apace. The working people feel it, and in the trenches every shell that goes over and does not explode is called a ' Wilson.' " Mr. Polk felt that " we are in deep and troublous waters." [16]

In the meantime relations with Germany had been comparatively smooth. The Germans, following the advice of Bernstorff, had made no further demands that the United States end the Allied blockade. " I myself am doing everything to be forgotten," wrote Bernstorff on June 16.[17] Reports to the State Department indicated that the submarine campaign was being conducted according to cruiser rules.

But Washington received constant reminders that unless the military deadlock in Europe could be broken the danger of a resumption of illegal submarine warfare was always imminent. "Although Jagow is a Junker of the Junkers," reported Ambassador Gerard, " the Junkers are against him and claim he is too weak. He may be bounced." " The

15 Page to Lansing, October 18, 1916, I.P., II, 323.
16 House Diary, November 17, 1916, I.P., II, 327.
17 Bernstorff to House, June 16, 1916, I.P., II, 328.

U-boat question may break loose again any day." "Much underground work for a resumption of reckless submarine war going on, all part of a campaign to upset the Chancellor." [18] Bernstorff confirmed the reports:

"My Government is having a hard time and has been strongly attacked for having given up the U-boat war at the request of the United States. . . . There seems to be danger of the Chancellor being forced to retire on account of these attacks. That would, of course, mean the resumption of the U-boat war and the renewal of all our troubles. The chief argument which is being brought to bear against the Chancellor is that he gave in to the United States Government, although he knew that this Government was not neutral and was bringing pressure on Germany only, whilst it willingly permitted violations of International Law by England. There is certainly some truth in these attacks, as the British violations of International Law are increasing daily." [19]

On August 30 a radical change was made in German army control. Hindenburg became Chief of the General Staff and his all-powerful adviser, Ludendorff, Quartermaster General. The former Chief of Staff, Falkenhayn, scapegoat of the Verdun failure, was, as Gerard reported, "bounced without even the excuse of a diplomatic illness." [20] The political significance of the change was not immediately apparent. Not until the middle of October were signs forthcoming that the new masters of Germany were determined to bring decisive action in Berlin and end the contest between the Foreign Office and the advocates of unlimited submarine warfare. If peace negotiations could

[18] Gerard to House, June 7, July 12, 1916, I.P., II, 329.

[19] Bernstorff to House, July 14, 1916, I.P., II, 329.

[20] Gerard to House, August 30, 1916, I.P., II, 330; Erich von Falkenhayn, The German General Staff, pp. 284-5.

be started on the basis of the existing war map, giving Germany the advantage, they would accept mediation. Otherwise they would break the deadlock by a resumption of the submarine warfare without restrictions and without regard for the diplomatic consequences. They counted upon it to bring England to her knees and end the war victoriously.[21]

3

In the previous April Ambassador Gerard had given to the Kaiser some intimation of Wilson's intention to propose peace negotiations. He received no encouragement. The Verdun offensive was still in full swing and Germany looked for military success; Bernstorff was instructed to see that if Wilson's intervention appeared likely steps should be taken to hinder a proposal of mediation.[22] But in the autumn the new régime in Germany decided upon the desirability of a public call to negotiations. The Rumanian threat was obviously being parried; if the attack on Verdun had failed, the Allied offensive on the Somme was no more

[21] Paul von Hindenburg, *Out of my Life,* pp. 253-255; Erich Ludendorff, *Ludendorff's Own Story,* I, 365-370. Hindenburg and Ludendorff were opposed to any peace overture until after the fall campaign against Rumania. They were sceptical of the success of Wilson's mediation. Once that failed, as Ludendorff wrote, "unrestricted submarine warfare was now the only means left to secure in any reasonable time a victorious end to the war." In October, 1918, reviewing the military events that led to the German appeal for an armistice, Ludendorff told the civil Government that at the end of 1916 the "sole means of holding the western front was the U-boat war," *Preliminary History of the Armistice,* No. 38, p. 53 (hereafter cited as P.H.A.).

[22] Jagow to Bernstorff, June 7, 1916, *G.D.,* II, 978.

successful. Germany was in a strong military position. Should the Allies, contrary to expectation, agree to negotiate, Germany had all the advantage that comes from occupation of enemy territory. Should they refuse, Germany might insist before her own people and the world that the responsibility for the continuation of the war did not rest upon her shoulders and that she was compelled to launch the unrestricted submarine warfare in order to save Germany from the starvation blockade.[23]

The Germans decided that it would be preferable that the call to negotiations should come from Washington rather than Berlin. They would drop a hint to Wilson, enforcing it with a reference to the danger of renewed submarine warfare. This was done by addressing a memorandum to Ambassador Gerard, who in October had returned for a short visit to the United States. The communication was kept upon an informal basis by sending the memorandum to Bernstorff and instructing him to use his own judgment whether or when the memorandum should be delivered. Bernstorff, in turn, preserved the informality of the proceeding by requesting House to pass it on to Gerard or speak to him about it, before the Ambassador saw the President. " This way I am sure that the matter will be dealt with quite confidentially and in accord with the wishes

---

[23] Bethmann to Bernstorff, August 18, September 2, 25, *G.D.*, II, 981 ff.; Ludendorff, *The General Staff*, pp. 279 ff.; Hindenburg, *op. cit.*, pp. 231 ff.; Valentin, *Deutschlands Aussenpolitik*, pp. 294 ff. On October 7, the main committee of the Reichstag voted to approve the unrestricted submarine campaign if ordered by the Supreme Command. Friedrich Payer regards this date as that which "determined Germany's doom," *Von Bethmann bis Ebert*, p. 219.

of my Government." Bernstorff insisted that it was not intended "as a threat of more drastic U-boat warfare on our part."

Despite this disclaimer it was difficult for Wilson to interpret it otherwise.

"Your Excellency hinted to His Majesty," so ran the memorandum, "in your last conversation at Charleville, in April, that President Wilson possibly would try towards the end of the summer to offer his good services to the belligerents for the promotion of peace. The German Government has no information as to whether the President adheres to this idea and as to the eventual date at which this step would take place. Meanwhile the constellation of war has taken such a form that the German Government foresees the time at which it will be forced to regain the freedom of action that it has reserved to itself in the note of May 4th last and thus the President's steps may be jeopardized. The German Government thinks it its duty to communicate this fact to Your Excellency in case you should find that the date of the intended action of the President should be far advanced towards the end of this year." [24]

The memorandum was an obvious invitation to early action by Wilson; otherwise he must expect a resumption of submarine warfare. The warning was emphasized by despatches from Mr. Grew, American chargé in Berlin.[25]

[24] *I.P.,* II, 335-336.

[25] Comment by Count von Bernstorff, May 11, 1933: "Chapter V does not quite bring our point of view to light. I quite agree and have often said it publicly, that our civil Government did not do all they could have done, but on the other hand the American Government might have helped us more. The Memorandum . . . was written by the Emperor himself; it was not a menace but a cry for help. Gerard was distinctly unfriendly, so that I was the only link, and I was not quite trusted, as you say youself. If Wilson had sent his peace note in November, '16, it would probably have

The Presidential election fell on November 7, and until
it was settled there was nothing to be done. The moment
his reëlection was certain Wilson's mind turned again to foreign affairs. All through the election campaign he dreaded
a fresh submarine crisis; his fear of war was quickened by
the sinking of the *Marina* on October 28, under conditions
that suggested the possibility of disregard of the *Sussex*
pledge. On October 14 he told House that unless he took
action of some sort the United States would inevitably drift
into war with Germany. "He believes Germany has already
violated her promise of May 4, and that in order to maintain
our position we must break off diplomatic relations. Before
doing this he would like to make a move for peace, hoping
there is sufficient peace sentiment in the Allied countries to
make them consent." [26]

Wilson still hesitated however, and in the opinion of
Bernstorff thereby lost his opportunity.[27] On the 21st of

prevented your war and brought general peace after the Russian
revolution. A 'Peace without Victory' would have made the
'World safe for Democracy' instead of all the nationalism
created by the Versailles Treaty."

[26] House Diary, November 14, 1916, *I.P.,* II, 390-391.

[27] Comment by Count von Bernstorff, June 12, 1933: "The
situation was as follows: Our navy demanded submarine warfare.
Hindenburg and Ludendorff gave the decision for it, believing
that they could this way bring about a victorious peace. The
Emperor, Bethmann, Jagow and myself were against submarine
warfare—because of U. S. A. That is why the Emperor wrote and
sent me the 'Memorandum' you have quoted and called a 'Menace,'
and which I call 'a cry for help.' In those days Dr. Wilson was
for the first time during the war really neutral, having discovered,
that both belligerents were equally bad or equally good (as you
prefer expressing Wilson's opinion, and as the Treaty of Versailles
and subsequent events have amply proved). Therefore, after his

November he completed his message to Congress and sat down, as he wrote to House, " to sketch the paper I spoke of when you were here. Just so soon as I can give it enough elaboration to make it a real proposal and programme I am going to beg you to come down and we will get at the business in real earnest. I will make the best haste I can consistent with my desire to make it the strongest and most convincing thing I ever penned." The draft of the note was delayed by " a really overwhelming cold during nearly the whole of the week." The President wrote that " it has sadly thrown my plans out. The paper I had intended to write needed the clearest thinking I could do, and not until tonight have I ventured to begin it. Even now I have gone no further than a skeleton outline." On the following day the President reported that he had completed the first draft of the note, and asked House to come down and discuss it. " I think things are thickening and we should choose our

---

reëlection, Wilson should have come out immediately with his Peace Move (in the interest of U. S. A. and all the world, especially of his own fame). In those days he sent for Gerard and Page, but in my opinion he waited too long, and during this time Jagow was turned out of office. Bethmann was too weak to oppose the Army and Navy. The Inevitable therefore had to happen. I have always blamed *our Government,* but Wilson might have done more to strengthen Bethmann's hand and keep Jagow in office, which he (Wilson) would certainly have done, if Gerard had had a friendly understanding for the Berlin situation and reported accordingly.

" I do not believe, that the Peace Conference would have come right away, but it would have come directly after the Russian revolution. We would have had no Bolshevism and no Treaty of Versailles with all its terrible consequences—crisis, dictatorships and so on. The World might have become ' safe for Democracy,' if the ' Peace without Victory ' had been realised."

course at once, if we have data enough to form a judgment on. I am better. I hope that I had a clear head enough for the draft." [28]

The call to peace negotiations was perhaps the only possible chance of avoiding war with Germany, but it was bound to fall upon deaf ears. The Germans themselves, although they wished the President to make it, had terms in mind which the Allies would not accept unless completely defeated, and which were far from those suggested by House to Grey. Furthermore, while they were anxious that Wilson take the lead in starting negotiations, they by no means desired him as mediator.

" We entertain but little hope for the result of the exercise of good offices by one whose instincts are all in favor of the English point of view, and who, in addition to this, is so naïve a statesman as President Wilson. . . . The President would from the outset exert himself to bring about a peace based in the main on the *status quo ante,* particularly with regard to Belgium. . . . A peace founded on the absolute *status quo ante* would be unacceptable to us." [29]

The Allies, following success at Verdun and indulging in high hopes for the spring, were ready to resent any move that might seem to rescue Germany from defeat. In England the Asquith cabinet fell early in December, Grey retired, and Lloyd George based his policy upon the " knock-out blow " principle which excluded the possibility of negotiations with Germany.

While the President hesitated, the Germans took the peace offensive into their own hands. They had no indication as to

[28] Wilson to House, November 21, 24, 25, 1916, Y.H.C.
[29] Jagow to Bernstorff, June 7, 1916, *G.D.,* II, 977-978. Cf. also telegrams from Bethmann and Jagow of October 14 and November 20, 1916, *ibid.,* 989, 992.

Wilson's intentions, they were tired of waiting, and the strategy of the whole situation, political, economic, and naval demanded a decision. On December 12 they published a note of their own, expressing their willingness to enter peace negotiations. There was no indication of terms which the Germans might have in mind and the tone of the note was not conciliatory, for it sounded a *timbre* of triumph and of threats.[30]

The German peace offer, of which Bernstorff had received a hint but no definite information beforehand,[31] necessarily would ruin any effect that might have proceeded from Wilson's note. If following the Germans he issued his own invitation to peace, he would be accused of acting in collusion with them and against Allied interests. Nevertheless he decided not to hold back. The occasion was most unpropitious, but he feared that the Allies by a brusque reply to the German note might definitely ruin all chance of negotiations. He rewrote his earlier draft hastily and sent it off to the European Embassies within a few hours, hoping that it would come to the Allies before they had so finally committed themselves against peace as to make the situation worse than it had been.[32]

In his rewriting of the draft of his note, the President was careful to exclude a formal demand for peace negotia-

[30] Text of note in *F.R., 1916, Suppl.,* 94.

[31] On November 22, Jagow suggested that "provided the favorable military situation justifies it, it is our purpose, acting in conjunction with our Allies, to announce forthwith our willingness to enter upon peace negotiations," Jagow to Bernstorff, November 22, 1916, *G.D.,* II, 992.

[32] Wilson to House, December 19, 1916, Y.H.C.

tions. It was merely an appeal to the belligerents to describe
explicitly their war aims, with emphasis upon the danger of
irreparable injury to civilization if peace were long delayed,
and upon American willingness to coöperate in the maintenance of peace. "An interchange of views would clear the
way at least for conference and make the permanent concord of the nations a hope of the immediate future, a concert of nations immediately practicable." [33] As a manifesto
of Wilson's international ideas it was an admirable paper.
As a diplomatic document it was bound to be ineffective.
The President pleaded with the belligerents when nothing
except the threat of armed mediation (which the United
States could not enforce) would have been appropriate to
their temper. Wilson seemed to realize the difficulty. " I
have seldom seen anything he has written," observed House,
comparing the final draft with the original, " with so many
changes." [34]

Neither the German nor Wilson's peace note produced
any effect that gave promise of negotiations. The Allies
replied on December 30 to the former that it could not be
dealt with because after distorting plain truths it contained
no specific proposals. As Ambassador Page suggested, it was
from the Allied point of view an offer to " buy a pig in a
poke." [35]

To the Wilson note the Germans returned a reply which
although courteous was quite evasive. They were by no

[33] Text of note in *F.R., 1916, Suppl.,* 98-99.

[34] House Diary, December 20, 1916, *I.P.,* II, 405.

[35] Lord Robert Cecil to Spring Rice, December 19, 1916, *I.P.,*
II, 403. Text of Allied reply in *F.R., 1916, Suppl.,* 124-125.

means ready to disclose their war aims. They stated that a direct exchange of views appeared to them the most suitable means of arriving at peace, and repeated their suggestion of a conference for the purpose of negotiating. Obviously if they were to negotiate they wished to use the territories they had conquered as pawns in the process.[36] Ambassador Gerard suspected them of hoping to break up the Entente alliance. "Germany wants a peace conference in order to make a separate peace, on good terms to them, with France and Russia. Then she hopes to finish England by submarines, then later take the scalps of Japan, Russia, and France separately." [37]

In Allied countries, especially England, the Wilson note, coming on the heels of the German, aroused resentment. As in almost all of Wilson's speeches, a single sentence provoked bitter criticism. In this case it was the statement that the objects on both sides " are virtually the same, as stated in general terms to their own people and to the world." This was certainly not an inaccurate phrase, wherever one's sympathies lay, but to the Allies it seemed to put them on the same plane morally as the Germans and they objected. Page reported from London, " the dominant tone in public and private comment on the President's suggestion is surprise and sorrowful consternation." Sir Horace Plunkett was " terribly exercised over the President's note. He is sorry he sent it." Lord Bryce wrote with emphasis upon the unfortunate effect of Wilson's phrase and went on to give five reasons why general feeling was against opening negotia-

[36] Text of German reply in *F.R., 1916, Suppl.*, 118.
[37] Gerard to House, January 9, 1917, *I.P.*, II, 406.

tions with the Central Powers, the feeling, he said, not of jingoes but of peace-lovers like himself.[38]

As for the Allied Governments, their reply to Wilson was a courteous refusal to enter negotiations, on the ground that a durable peace presupposed a satisfactory settlement of the conflict and that at the moment it was hopeless to expect from the Central Powers the reparation, restitution and guarantees necessary to such a peace. They challenged Wilson's analogy between the war aims of the two groups. Their restatement of their own war aims, while not sufficiently candid to give any hint of the provisions of the secret treaties, made plain that they were too far from even the mildest supposition of German terms to permit the possibility of negotiations.[39]

4

As the historian looks back it is not difficult to see that the peace notes of December mark the final decisive stage in American neutrality. The President's appeal was not so much an attempt to win peace for Europe as a desperate effort to stave off war from America. The German note was the immediate prelude to the unrestricted submarine war that was bound to involve the United States. The danger of the situation was not unsuspected. Lansing gave a public and definite intimation of his fears. The British Ambassador reported: " War has gradually drawn nearer and nearer to the United States in spite of all their efforts. . . .

[38] Page to Lansing, December 22, 1916, Bryce to House, December 27, 1916, *I.P.,* II, 406-407.

[39] Text of Allied reply in *F.R., 1917, Suppl. 1,* 6-9.

Relations with Germany are becoming daily more dangerous, and with England, daily more disagreeable." As far back as November House said, " we are on the verge of war." [40]

President Wilson refused to believe it. His determination to preserve American neutrality was at its strongest during the weeks that immediately preceded the rupture with Germany. It was not weakened by the failure of the December peace notes. The events of the summer and autumn of 1916 had intensified his pacifism. The refusal of the Allies to accept his proffered intervention led him to distrust Allied motives, whatever their avowed war aims. He had been willing to intervene only if they were aiming at a peace of conciliation; such terms apparently did not suit them. He was also affected by the course of the electoral campaign, which had seemed to demonstrate that he owed his election to the votes of those who were grateful because he had kept them out of war and counted on his continuing to do so.

As he approached the crisis, he could not persuade himself that Germany would actually force America in by a withdrawal of the *Sussex* pledge. On January 4, 1917, he let fall a remark of extraordinary interest in view of the situation. House was urging the need of military preparation " in the event of war." To which Wilson replied, " There will be no war. This country does not intend to become involved in this war. We are the only one of the

[40] Spring Rice to Grey, December 15, 1916, *Spring Rice,* II, 360; *I.P.,* II, 412. Statement by Lansing, December 20, 1916: " We are drawing nearer the verge of war ourselves, and therefore we are entitled to know exactly what each belligerent seeks," *Current History,* February, 1917, 777.

great white nations that is free from war today, and it would be a crime against civilization for us to go in." [41]

Thus determined, Wilson meditated plans by which he might again develop a positive policy, freeing himself from the control of external events. The Allied refusal to the German note had been based ostensibly upon the absence of any indication of terms. He commissioned House to see whether Ambassador von Bernstorff could not secure terms from his Government as a start toward negotiations.

Bernstorff knew how tenuous was the line that still maintained relations between Germany and the United States. He knew that the renewal of submarine warfare was under consideration and constantly warned Berlin that it would bring the United States into the war. He was sincere and active in his efforts to prevent it, for like Grey he believed that to lose the neutrality of America would be the supreme diplomatic mistake. The sole means of averting hasty action by Berlin and avoiding the rupture was the actual initiation of peace negotiations. [42]

The Ambassador understood that his Government would not make any terms public. He was doubtful whether they would send them through the State Department. He promised, however, to attempt to secure them for the confidential information of Wilson. During the next three weeks he pleaded constantly with the Wilhelmstrasse for help in preserving the possibility of negotiations and for delay of the submarine decision. [43]

[41] House Diary, January 4, 1917, *I.P.*, II, 412.

[42] *I.P.*, II, 422 ff.

[43] Bernstorff to Bethmann and German Foreign Office, December 29, 1916, January 9, 16, 19, 27, 1917, *G.D.*, II, 1010 ff.

Wilson also discussed with Colonel House the advisability of another appeal to the belligerents. He felt that it was of vital moment to keep alive the public discussion of peace. It might be possible for him to set forth the principles which he himself believed should govern a reasonable settlement. Such a statement would give to Germany an opportunity to announce to the world and her own people that in view of the security which the prospective organization offered, she could afford to renounce the territorial guarantees which appeared to her enemies as a cloak for aggressive annexations. It would test the sincerity of Allied demands for a permanent settlement secure against militarism. If the United States remained neutral it would provide a basis upon which the belligerents might rely if they desired American mediation. If the United States entered the war against Germany on account of the submarine, it would serve as a platform of American war aims and a warning to the Allies that the United States was fighting primarily for the security and tranquillity of the world.

The projected speech was first planned by Wilson on January 3. By the 11th he had completed a first draft. On the 16th he wrote, " The thing is in course." He had discussed it with the Secretary of State and the chairman of the Senate Foreign Relations Committee, William J. Stone. " Neither Lansing nor Stone is very *expressive,* but both have acquiesced very generously (Stone, I thought, a little wonderingly, as if the idea stunned him a bit) ." Wilson was encouraged in his plan to prosecute peace negotiations by the evident anxiety of Bernstorff to secure definite peace terms from his own Government. He felt that there was " a very

striking and significant change of attitude on the part of the
German authorities since the old confident days before the
war. . . . It carries great encouragement with it." He also
felt that " it is most difficult to see now what our next move
should be with regard to the German proposals—how we
should handle the changed case which Bernstorff has put
in our hands." [44] Evidently he hoped that the speech he
planned would force each side to set forth its attitude with
some definiteness and that a compromise might be found.

Wilson's speech, delivered before the Senate on January
22, marks a crisis in the history of American foreign relations. As later British writers insist, it opened the " last
opportunity of ending the war with a real peace. For
America was still pacific and impartial; besides being more
powerful than ever as against war-wasted, war-wearied,
and war-weakened Europe. But unhappily for mankind, the
British and Prussian war machines had by then taken
charge." [45]

As a basis for the ultimate settlement, the address of
January 22 takes rank with that of May 27, 1916, and with
the Fourteen Points. Lowes Dickinson described it as " perhaps the most important international document of all history." [46] In his speech of May 27 the President had sketched
a new policy for the United States. In that of January 22
he proposed a new policy for the world. Courageously (and
undiplomatically so far as the belligerents were concerned)
he insisted that no security for the future could be expected

[44] Wilson to House, January 16, 17, 19, 1917. Y.H.C.
[45] Kenworthy and Young, *op. cit.*, pp. 78-79.
[46] G. Lowes Dickinson, *The Choice before Us,* p. 270.

from a settlement that left one side or the other crushed and revengeful: " It must be a peace without victory." The basis of the peace must be the right of each individual nation to decide its own destiny for itself, without interference from a stronger alien nation. " I am proposing, as it were, that the nations should with one accord adopt the doctrine of President Monroe as the doctrine of the world." The European system of alliances had proved quite inadequate to provide security; in its place he insisted that there must be a general " concert of power." [47]

But the diplomatic effect of the document, which set forth doctrines later agreed to by all the victorious Powers, at least in principle, was nil. British liberals hailed it as expressing splendid ideals but they failed, as Lord Bryce phrased it, to see how these were to be attained with the existing German Government, " a Government which goes on showing its utter disregard of justice and humanity, by its slave-raiding and other cruelties in Belgium, and by its entire contempt for the faith of treaties." [48]

Wilson himself was discouraged by the reception of the speech. He wrote that he " felt very lonely and very low in his mind." [49] Sir William Wiseman, Chief of British Intelligence, who had established intimate and confidential relations with the President and House, reported that although the Allies accepted the speech with outward cordiality, " underneath there was a deep feeling of resentment." The

[47] Text of the address of January 22, in *F.R., 1917, Suppl. 1*, 24-29.

[48] Bryce to House, January 24, 1917, *I.P.*, II, 419.

[49] Wilson to House, January 24, 1917, Y.H.C.

attitude taken was that Wilson " was making a proposal to
enforce arbitration in the future while the Allies were giving
up both blood and treasure now for the same purpose. If
Germany had arbitrated as Grey demanded, this war could
not have happened. Germany refused, and the Allies are
doing exactly " what Wilson suggested should be done in
the future. Wiseman's own view was that in pressing the
Allies too hard for peace at the moment, Wilson would harm
the cause of democracy.[50]

5

While the Allies thus felt that they were dying for ideals
about which Wilson merely talked, the Germans hardly
bothered to read the President's speech. For them the die
was already cast. On January 9, at Spa, the German Crown
Council had decided upon the unrestricted submarine warfare. Jagow, warned by Bernstorff of the certainty of American intervention in such event, had resigned. The Kaiser,
overborne by the insistence of Hindenburg and Ludendorff
that the war must be brought to a close and by the promise
of Holtzendorff that England could be isolated, approved
the decision. Bethmann yielded, still retaining the Chancellorship. The entrance of America was discounted; after all,
she would be helpless to affect the military and naval course
of the war before the Allies were crushed.[51]

[50] House to Wilson, January 25, 1917, *I.P.*, II, 420-421.
[51] Valentin, *op. cit.*, pp. 317-318. Bethmann after receiving
Bernstorff's telegram of January 27 was in a state of uncertainty
that was overborne by the insistence of the others that " victory
beckoned." See the notes of the conference of January 1, of
Bethmann, Hindenburg, Ludendorff, in Ludendorff, *General Staff,*

Ambassador von Bernstorff was not informed of the decision until January 19. He did his best to alter it. He telegraphed repeatedly to Berlin, begging for a postponement of the submarine blockade and for a specific statement of terms that might give Wilson confidence in German good faith; he warned the Government of the danger of bringing America in. The determination of the military and naval chiefs ruined his policy, which was always to keep the United States neutral and secure a peace through Wilson's mediation. The Ambassador frankly and immediately let House know that there was little hope of getting Berlin to state terms and hinting at something worse:

"I am afraid the situation in Berlin is getting out of our hands. . . . They seem to believe that the answer of our enemies to the President has finished the whole peace movement for a long time to come, and I am, therefore, afraid that my Government may be forced to act accordingly in a very short time. . . . As far as I can see, every question leads us to the same problem, viz., which methods my Government will be obliged by public opinion to use against the English starvation policy. . . ." [52]

Six days later House reported to the President: "Bernstorff has just left. He said the military have complete control in Germany, with Hindenburg and Ludendorff at the head." [53]

 On January 31 the Germans revealed their hand. Bernstorff informed Lansing that on and after February 1 the

---

I, 304-306. For Helfferich's shift of attitude to support of unrestricted submarine warfare, see his *Der Weltkrieg*, II, 379 ff. and his testimony before the Reichstag investigating committee, in *G.D.*, I, 650 ff.

[52] Bernstorff to House, January 20, 1917, *I.P.*, II, 428-9.
[53] House to Wilson, January 26, 1917, *I.P.*, II, 429.

engagements of the *Sussex* pledge would no longer be observed. German submarines would sink on sight all ships met within a delimited zone around the British Isles and in the Mediterranean. They would permit the sailing of certain American steamships, one a week in each direction from and to Falmouth, following a defined route. The ships must be marked " on ships' hull and superstructure three vertical stripes one meter wide each to be painted alternately white and red. Each mast should show a large flag checkered white and red, and the stern the American national flag. Care should be taken that, during dark, national flag and painted marks are easily recognizable from a distance, and that the boats are well lighted throughout." [54]

On the same day that this note was delivered, House received for transmission to the President a letter from Bernstorff, doubtless conceived as a gesture of courtesy but in the circumstances not devoid of irony. The Ambassador reported that the Imperial Government placed complete confidence in the President and hoped that he reciprocated. As a mark of such confidence it would inform him " *personally* " of Germany's terms of peace, which it could not publish, since the Allies had put forth terms that aimed " at the dishonor and destruction of Germany and her allies." The terms as given provided for evacuation of France and Belgium in return for an indemnity in the case of the former and a special régime protecting German interests in that of the latter; restoration of conquered German territory, and an agreement giving Germany colonies " adequate to her population and economic interests "; " strategical and eco-

[54] Text of German note, *F.R., 1917, Suppl. 1,* 97-102.

nomic " changes in the Franco-German frontier; compensation for German firms and individuals that had suffered by the war; economic and financial compensation " on the basis of territories conquered."

The letter concluded with the assurance that Germany

" would have been glad to postpone the submarine blockade, if they had been able to do so. This, however, was quite impossible on account of the preparations, which could not be cancelled. My Government believes that the submarine blockade will terminate the war very quickly. In the meantime my Government will do everything possible to safeguard American interests and begs the President to continue his efforts to bring about peace, and my Government will terminate the submarine blockade as soon as it is evident that the efforts of the President will lead to a peace acceptable to Germany." [55]

Bernstorff put the best face possible on the matter. He knew that a rupture with the United States could not be avoided and yet he could speak of safeguarding American interests and urge the President to continue efforts for peace negotiations. His letter, in the circumstances, seemed a mockery. Germany, wrote House, " desires some justification for her submarine warfare and thought she could get it by declaring her willingness to make peace." [56]

House took the Bernstorff letter to Wilson on the morning of February 1. The President had already instructed the Secretary of State to draft a note citing the history of the submarine controversy and ending with the decision to hand Bernstorff his passports. The long feared and expected diplomatic rupture had come. Wilson believed that an im-

---

[55] Bernstorff to House, January 31, 1917, *I.P.*, II, 431-433; *F.R., 1917, Suppl. 1*, 34-36.

[56] House Diary, January 31, 1917, *I.P.*, II, 434.

mediate breaking of diplomatic relations was preferable to
awaiting an attack by a German submarine, since definite
American action might " bring the Germans to their senses."
The note which had been drafted by Lansing was discussed
in a brief conference *à trois,* consisting of the President,
Lansing, and House. It was approved without change.
Wilson spent most of the morning killing time, " nervously "
arranging his books, walking up and down, trying to play
billiards. He was " sad and depressed," reports House; said
" he felt as if the world had suddenly reversed itself; that
after going from east to west, it had begun to go from west
to east, and that he could not get his balance."

Although determined that diplomatic rupture with Germany was the only possible step, the President refused to
admit that it meant the end of neutrality. He was

" insistent that he would not allow it to lead to war if it
could possibly be avoided. He reiterated his belief that it
would be a crime for this Government to involve itself in
the war to such an extent as to make it impossible to save
Europe afterward. He spoke of Germany as a ' madman that
should be curbed.' I asked," said House, " if he thought it
fair to the Allies to ask them to do the curbing without doing
our share. He noticeably winced at this, but still held to his
determination not to become involved if it were humanly
possible to do otherwise." [57]

This determination was publicly expressed by Wilson in
the address to Congress on February 3, when he announced
the dismissal of Ambassador von Bernstorff and the recall
of Ambassador Gerard:

" I refuse to believe that it is the intention of the German
authorities to do in fact what they have warned us they will

[57] House Diary, January 31, 1917, *I.P.,* II, 439-441.

feel at liberty to do. . . . Only actual overt acts on their part can make me believe it even now. . . . We wish to serve no selfish ends. We seek merely to stand true alike in thought and in action to the immemorial principles of our people. . . . These are the bases of peace, and not war. God grant we may not be challenged to defend them by acts of wilful injustice on the part of the Government of Germany."

At the same time, however, the President announced that

"if American ships and American lives should in fact be sacrificed by their naval commanders . . . I shall take the liberty of coming again before the Congress, to ask that authority be given me to use any means that may be necessary for the protection of our seamen and our people in the prosecution of their peaceful and legitimate errands on the high seas. I can do nothing less." [58]

6

Thus Wilson's hope of avoiding war did not touch his resolve to permit no compromise with Germany on the submarine issue. Suggestions of mediation or negotiation that came from the Dutch and the Swiss Ministers left him cold. He insisted that the Germans must renew and carry out their pledge of the previous April if they wanted to talk to him, or else propose peace on terms they knew he could act upon. [59] For a moment it was thought that the new Austrian Ambassador might be of service as a means of opening peace negotiations. But in view of the Austrian warning that all neutrals sailing on belligerent ships in the barred zone did so at their own risk, the President decided

[58] Text of address, *F.R., 1917, Suppl. 1,* 109-112.
[59] House to Wilson, February 10, 1917, *I.P.,* II, 445; Wilson to House, February 12, 1917, Y.H.C.

that relations with the Hapsburg Monarchy must be severed.[60]

The decision of the President to await what he called the "overt act" of Germany was based upon his remnant of hope that peace might be saved. Politically it proved sagacious. During the eight weeks that followed the dismissal of Bernstorff public opinion crystallized in the conviction that war was unavoidable. Any attempt on the part of the President to hurry the country into hostilities would have marred the almost universal appreciation of the fact that he had done everything in his power to avoid war and only accepted it as a final means of protecting the security of the United States. The prolonged reluctance of a pacifist President to depart from peace persuaded the most pacifist regions of the peremptory necessity of war.

Mistaken German diplomacy did a good deal to strengthen the feeling that war was inevitable. Zimmermann, who succeeded Jagow as Foreign Secretary, addressed a telegram on January 16 to the German Minister in Mexico, advising him

---

[60] On February 22, Ambassador Penfield was instructed to offer to Austria-Hungary limited assurances against dismemberment in the event of a request for an early peace, but he received no encouragement, Lansing to Penfield, February 22, 1917, Penfield to Lansing, February 27, 1917, *F.R., 1917, Suppl. 1,* 57, 62. The Germans evidently believed that Wilson's determination was weakening and that he would avoid war if the submarine attack "overlooked" American boats. Admiral von Holtzendorff explained to the Kaiser that this was technically impossible. The Kaiser wrote on the margin of the memorandum: "Agreed, reject . . . Now, once and for all, an *end* to negotiations with America. If Wilson wants war, let him make it, and let him then have it," Memorandum of Austro-Hungarian Embassy in Berlin, March 14, 1917, Holtzendorff to the Kaiser, March 18, 1917, *G.D.,* II, 1334-1336.

of the imminence of unrestricted submarine warfare and instructing him in case of war with the United States to attempt a German-Mexican alliance, on the understanding that Mexico would be assisted to reconquer Texas, Arizona, and New Mexico; he also instructed him to attempt an understanding between Mexico and Japan. The message was picked up by the British Naval Intelligence and handed over to the American Government on February 26. It was published immediately; nothing could have brought the war and the unfriendliness of Germany closer to the American public.[61]

In the meantime a virtual blockade of American shipping resulted from the unwillingness of American exporters to brave the submarine threat. The State Department informed the American Line that the rights of American vessels " to traverse all parts of the high seas are the same now as they were prior to the issuance of the German declaration, and that a neutral merchant vessel may, if its owners believe that it is liable to be unlawfully attacked, take any measures to prevent or resist such attacks." [62] But the Government did not provide convoys.

On February 26 the President appeared before Congress asking for powers enabling him to arm merchant vessels. The evil as yet was one of apprehension rather than fact; the " overt act " had not yet been committed. But it involved a humiliation and a material loss that could not be

[61] Page to Lansing, February 24, 1917, *F.R., 1917, Suppl. 1*, 147-148.

[62] *Current History*, March, 1917, 980.

tolerated.[63] The protection of American citizens and property on the high seas must be provided for:

" It would be foolish to deny that the situation is fraught with the gravest possibilities and dangers. No thoughtful man can fail to see that the necessity for definite action may come at any time, if we are in fact, and not in word merely, to defend our elementary rights as a neutral nation." [64]

The House of Representatives, in answer to the appeal, passed a bill conferring the necessary powers by a vote of 403 to 13. The Senate Foreign Relations Committee approved it, despite the protests of the chairman. A filibuster of twelve Senators, described by the President as " a group of wilful men," prevented it from coming to a vote. But a manifesto signed by seventy-five Senators desirous of voting for it made plain that Congressional support of Wilson's policy was all but unanimous. He proceeded of his own executive authority, and on March 12 Secretary Lansing announced that the Government would " place upon all American merchant vessels sailing through the barred areas an armed guard for the protection of the vessels and the lives of the persons on board." [65] The country was at the gates of war.

Wilson did not escape criticism for his delay or his patience in awaiting the overt act. Ambassador Page cabled

[63] " The situation," reported the British Ambassador, " is much that of a soda water bottle with the wires cut but the cork unexploded. The President appears to be watching. . . . The German threat appears to have been entirely effective. She has not committed murder but the threat of murder has kept America off the seas," Spring Rice to Balfour, February 23, 1917, *Spring Rice*, II, 381.

[64] Text of address in *Baker and Dodd*, II, 428-432.

[65] *F.R., 1917, Suppl. 1,* 171.

from London of the unfavorable impression created by the holding of American ships in port.

" Delay is taken to mean the submission of our Government to the German blockade. . . . British opinion . . . seems to be reaching the conclusion that our Government will not be able to take positive action under any provocation . . . that our Government is holding back our people until the blockade of our ships, the Zimmermann telegram, and the *Laconia* shall be forgotten and until the British navy shall overcome the German submarines. . . . So friendly a man as Viscount Grey of Fallodon writes me . . .: ' I do not see how the United States can sit still while neutral shipping is swept off the sea. If no action is taken, it will be like a great blot in history or a failure that must grievously depress the future history of America.' " [66]

In Washington, officials of the State Department and members of the Cabinet apparently had no inkling of the President's purpose.[67] The step upon which he was about to embark was a violation of everything most sacred in his political faith. He would decide for himself and he wanted no counsel based upon emotion: " we must put excited feeling away," he said a few days later. A man of strong emotions, he fought them with his Calvinist conscience. By March 27, the struggle was settled and the President's mind made up. He could not escape the fact that Germany was making war on American ships and citizens. On March 5, the Cunarder *Laconia* was sunk without warning, and of the twelve persons who perished two were American women. On March 12, the American steamer *Algonquin* was sunk without warning. On March 19, news came that within twenty-four hours three American ships had been sunk,

[66] Page to House, March 9, 1917, *I.P.*, II, 459.
[67] House Diary, March 19, 20, 22, 24, *I.P.*, II, 460-462.

in the case of one of them, the *Vigilancia,* fifteen members
of the crew had been lost. Wilson's only doubt was whether
he should ask Congress to declare war or declare that a
state of war already existed. He decided upon the latter
course, and on March 28 began to sketch the address to
Congress which he delivered five days later, on April 2.

It has sometimes been asserted that the entrance of the
United States into the World War was the result of the
influence of certain " interests," which for one reason or
another desired American participation on the side of the
Allies; that Wilson himself was caught in this influence,
thoroughly impregnated as he was supposed to be with pro-
Ally sentiment; that the declaration of the unrestricted submarine campaign was merely a pretext for belligerency
which on one score or another would have been declared
in any case.[68]

There is no scrap of valid evidence supporting this thesis,
and all that is available directly controverts it. At the
beginning of the war Wilson declared and believed that it

[68] See H. E. Barnes, *Genesis of the World War,* pp. 605 ff.
Ludendorff says (*The General Staff,* I, 337 n.), " If the submarine
campaign had really been the direct cause of the participation of
the United States in the war, she must have declared war at the
beginning of February. . . . She did not actually enter the war
until the military situation of the Entente had become worse."
Admiral Andreas Michelsen declares (*Der U-bootskrieg,* p. 163),
" Wilson's determination to help England if she needed it dates not
from the sinking of the *Lusitania* nor from the unrestricted submarine warfare, but from the moment he saw that England could
not count on a speedy victory." He adds that for a year Wilson
had been secretly gathering war materials.

could not touch us, that if we kept clean neutral hands we were fulfilling our duty and preserving our security. He was speedily disabused. The dispute with the Allies indicated that belligerent action could touch American interests and rights very closely. The German submarine attacks shocked him, and for the first time he perceived that it might not be possible to carry through two purposes that might conflict—the preservation of the honor of the country and the preservation of its peace. The problems of neutrality were intolerable; they could be ended only if the war ended. Thus he planned to intervene with a threat of armed mediation, and made his offer to the Allies to support them if they would agree to a peace conference and Germany refused. He was willing to take the chance of entering the war if it meant that the war could be stopped.

The Allies refused American coöperation in securing what they regarded as a "stalemate peace." Thereafter Wilson fell back into distrust of both sides and a fervid determination to maintain American neutrality. Nothing could shake him from this except the withdrawal of Germany's *Sussex* pledge, which, as Bernstorff says, he regarded as proof of Germany's bad faith. The most definite warnings from the American Embassy in Berlin did not shake him. "There will be no war," he insisted upon January 4.[69] Even the published declaration of the German Government did not entirely destroy his hopes of peace. He openly declared his disbelief that they would actually give effect to the policy which they knew would force the United States into the war.

[69] *Supra*, p. 192.

The British and the German Ambassadors in Washington, agreeing as to little else, are at one in describing the effect of the German submarine declaration:

" Germany misunderstood the President's mind," wrote Spring Rice. " He was bent on peace; he was determined to give Germany her chance; his great ambition was to be the mediator in a peace without victory which would give the world a permanent guarantee of international law and mutual confidence. But he did not propose to pay the price for peace which Germany thought he was willing to pay. . . . The fact that the insult was resented evidently created the deepest astonishment, and the most bitter disappointment in Berlin."

The testimony of Ambassador von Bernstorff leads to a similar conclusion:

" From that time henceforward—there can be no question of any earlier period, because up to that time he had been in constant negotiation with us—he regarded the Imperial Government as morally condemned. . . . After January 31st, 1917, Wilson himself was a different man. Our rejection of his proposal to mediate, by our announcement of the unrestricted U-boat war, which was to him utterly incomprehensible, turned him into an embittered enemy of the Imperial Government." [70]

As to the influence of " interests " whether pro-Ally or financial, if such influence existed, it did not touch Wilson, and Wilson alone determined the issue of peace or war. The Allies were in despair because of his delay and the friend of the Allies, Ambassador Page, could give them no comfort until Wilson made up his mind. There is no evidence that any financial " influence " at any time touched

[70] Spring Rice to Cecil, November 17, 1917, *Spring Rice,* II, 353; *Bernstorff,* pp. 385-386.

the President, but it is certain that none came near him in those weeks of March, 1917, when he faced his decision. Not even the Secertary of State nor the Cabinet knew how his mind was tending until the decision had been made.

Of his own conscience he made it because in no other way could he see how to protect American lives and property. It was the German submarine warfare and nothing else that forced him to lead America into war. " There is one choice we cannot make," he said to Congress, " we are incapable of making: we will not choose the path of submission."

But although it was the protection of American rights and lives that forced the issue, once Wilson had taken the decision he based our intervention upon broader principles than the defense of national interest. He had said to Congress on February 26, when he asked for authority to arm merchantmen:

" I am thinking, not only of the rights of Americans to go and come about their proper business by way of the sea, but also of something much deeper, much more fundamental than that. I am thinking of those rights of humanity without which there is no civilization."

So in his address of April 2, he insisted, " The present German submarine warfare against commerce is a warfare against mankind. It is a war against all nations." [71]

Thus the war waged by the United States was to be a war in behalf of all nations, a crusade in behalf of mankind, and it must end in a new international order which would make impossible a repetition of the catastrophe. The ideals which he had formulated while the country was still neutral must

[71] Text of the address of April 2, *F.R., 1917, Suppl. 1*, 195-203.

not be forgotten in the heat of belligerency. To the ultimate peace implicit in those ideals America must consecrate herself even at the moment of making war.

"We shall fight for the things which we have always carried nearest our hearts—for democracy, for the right of those who submit to authority to have a voice in their own governments, for the rights and liberties of small nations, for a universal dominion of right by such a concert of free peoples as shall bring peace and safety to all nations and make the world itself at last free. To such a task we can dedicate our lives and our fortunes, everything that we are and everything that we have, with the pride of those who know that the day has come when America is privileged to spend her blood and her might for the principles that gave her birth and happiness and the peace which she has treasured. God helping her, she can do no other." [72]

[72] Congress declared a state of war with Germany April 6, 1917. It passed the resolution declaring a state of war with Austria-Hungary on December 7, 1917. Turkey broke diplomatic relations with the United States April 20, 1917. Diplomatic relations with Bulgaria were not broken, *F.R., 1917, Suppl. 2,* II, 35, 459.

CHAPTER VI

DIPLOMATIC ASPECTS OF COÖRDINATION

1

Upon the coördination of the American effort in the war with that of the Allies depended the defeat of Germany. It is easy for the historian to see this, but it required some time for either Allies or Americans to appreciate the critical importance of coördination and to take adequate steps to secure it. One of the few persons who not merely saw the difficulties involved in the problem but exercised decisive influence in solving it, was Sir William Wiseman, Chief of the British Military Intelligence in the United States.

" I believe the greatest asset Germany has today," he wrote on September 26, 1917, " is the 3000 miles that separates London from Washington, and the most urgent problem we have to solve is how our two Governments, set at opposite ends of the world, can effect the close coöperation which is undoubtedly necessary if the war is to be quickly and successfully ended." [1]

At the moment the United States entered the war it is not likely that the Allies evaluated with any exactitude the rôle that America would play in the defeat of Germany, nor how sadly the Allies would need American help. There was some suggestion, previous to April, 1917, that the United States could add little to what she had already contributed.[2]

[1] Wiseman to House, September 26, 1917, *I.P.,* III, 184.
[2] Wiseman makes the comment, May 23, 1933, that in December, 1916, he could get no definite official opinion as to whether it

212

By the early summer the British appreciated the grim fact that they were scraping the bottom of their money chest and that the Americans would have to replace them as paymaster of the Allies. They began to realize that the output of American shipbuilding yards would be essential in the replacement of the ravages of the submarine. The French early perceived the need of raw materials, machinery, food, gasoline. They rather vaguely foresaw that American man-power would be important. But it was some time before British and French alike grasped the fact that the productive powers of America were not adequate to meet the demands of the Allies unless those demands were presented systematically with due regard to essential priorities. American help might be worse than useless, might clog the flow of supplies, unless it were directed to the spot where help was most needed, unless there were real coördination between the necessity of the Allies and the ability of America to satisfy it.

The Americans entered the war without clear appreciation of the desperate straits of the Allies. From the President down they were determined to put all their force and efficiency into the military effort, but they were unprepared for it. The task before them was gargantuan, perhaps the most gigantic transformation of history: the transformation of a peace-loving and unmilitary nation of one hundred million souls into a belligerent machine every motion of which must be designed for war. It took time for America to realize that unless this machine were accurately geared to the Allied

would be to the advantage of the Allies to have the United States actively intervene.

15

machine of war, most of its power would be expended in useless motion. There was real danger that in the process of developing its own military effort the United States should fail to appreciate the plight of the Allies, and Germany might win the war. "Considerations of politics and finance," wrote Lord Reading in October, 1917, "combine to enforce the view that America will put her own needs first." [3]

The situation was clearly expressed in a memorandum drafted for the British Cabinet in the summer of 1917 by Sir William Wiseman. He emphasized the fact that the sentiment of the country would be strongly against joining the Allies by any formal treaty. The Americans were determined to defeat Germany, but they did not regard themselves as in any danger; they were very remote from the war. There was some mistrust of the British:

"Our diplomatic task is to get enormous quantities of supplies from the United States while we have no means of bringing pressure to bear upon them to this end. We have to obtain vast loans, tonnage, supplies and munitions, food, oil, and other raw materials. And the quantities which we demand, while not remarkable in relation to the output of other belligerents, are far beyond the figures understood by the American public today. The Administration are ready to assist us to the limit of the resources of their country; but it is necessary for them to educate Congress and the Nation to appreciate the actual meaning of these gigantic figures. It is not enough for us to assure them that without these supplies the war will be lost. For the public ear we must translate dollars and tonnage into the efforts and achievements of the fleets and the armies. We must impress upon them the fighting value of their money. The [American] Administration are too far from the war, and have not sufficient information, to judge the merits of these

[3] Reading Memorandum on Supplies, October, 1917, *I.P.*, III, 182.

demands. The Allies will have to use patience, skill, and ingenuity in assisting the American authorities to arrive at a solution of this one grave difficulty, which is in a phrase, ' The coördination of Allied requirements.' " [4]

The problem thus had several sides. The Americans must provide an adequate organization capable of producing supplies. The Allies, who did not put forward their demands as a unit but separately, must organize these demands so as to indicate priority of Allied as distinguished from national needs. Finally, some machinery of coördination must be worked out between Allied demands and American supplies. It was first of all a task of diplomacy, although it was frequently not carried through by the conventional diplomatic process. After its importance was fully appreciated, months passed before the agencies of international coördination were able to operate effectively. But in the final months of the war a vast interallied machine controlled the economic, financial, and to a large degree the military resources of the greatest coalition in history.

"Astounding figures," writes André Tardieu, himself one of the chief agents in the process, " tell of the effort made, the help mutually furnished. In less than eighteen months the United States armed itself to the teeth. . . . An almost unbelievable achievement if one remembers the past, the existing circumstances (both material and moral), the absence of military preparedness, the total ignorance of things European. During all this time, France and Great Britain held the front waiting for the arrival of American reënforcements, the one providing transport, the other arms for the United States Army. . . . The splendor of this achievement led people to believe that it had been spontaneous. None had been more difficult." [5]

[4] Wiseman Memorandum, August, 1917, *I.P.*, III, 31-32.
[5] André Tardieu, *France and America*, p. 216.

In the final instance, the work was accomplished by skilled executives and technical experts in the various essential fields: finance, shipbuilding, transportation, manufacturing, agriculture, industrial administration. As the machinery of coördination was set up to meet each problem, operating functions were taken over by carefully selected experts. The story of their successful operation forms one of the great pages of war history. But before the machinery could be assembled and operated it was necessary to smooth away the obstructions which were inherent in any international undertaking: misunderstandings, jealousies, suspicions. This was the function of the diplomats. Preparing the way for the machine of interallied coördination was, in fact, one of the most important contributions of diplomacy and one of the least heralded. No disparagement of the accomplishment of the administrators is implied by insisting that it would have been impossible without diplomatic preparation.[6]

2

Theoretically, the Allies recognized the necessity of working as closely as possible with the Americans. Even before the United States entered the war, immediately after the

[6] Comment by Sir William Wiseman, May 23, 1933: "The chief factor facilitating coördination of effort between American and British agencies was the intimate and mutual confidence of Colonel House, Wilson's trusted adviser, and Mr. Balfour, British Foreign Secretary. If a misunderstanding arose between American and British agencies House and Balfour, who were in constant contact through my office, could agree quickly upon a solution; orders were given to put it into effect, by Balfour on his own authority, by Wilson on the advice of House. The agents who had been in disagreement found the matter settled for them frequently without knowing anything about the process of settlement."

diplomatic rupture with Germany, the British Foreign Office sent out instructions to British representatives emphasizing the fact that " full and frank coöperation between British and United States diplomatists and agents is one of the most important factors in the war." [7] The moment that Wilson asked Congress for a declaration of war, the British suggested that a " commission, technically expert," visit America " to place at the disposal of the United States Government the experience gained in this country." [8] The importance of the proposed mission was emphasized by the fact that it was to be led by the Foreign Secretary himself. At the same time the French suggested a mission under the leadership of Viviani and Joffre.

The President indicated some fear lest opinion should regard the mission as an attempt by the Allies to control the American war effort. He intended that the attitude of the United States should be one of coöperation but also of independence.

" The plan has its manifest dangers," he wrote. " I do not think that all of the country will understand or relish. A great many will look upon the mission as an attempt to in some degree take charge of us as an assistant to Great Britain, particularly if the Secretary of State for Foreign Affairs heads the commission. But, on the other hand, it will serve a great many useful purposes and perhaps save a good deal of time in getting together." [9]

Wilson did not seem to take the missions very seriously and spoke of the French as " apparently only of compliment."

[7] Drummond to House, February 9, 1917, *I.P.,* III, 32.
[8] Drummond to House, April 5, 1917, *I.P.,* III, 33.
[9] Wilson to House, April 9, 1917, Y.H.C.

The British and French envoys arrived toward the end of April and were shortly followed by Italian and Belgian missions.

The visit of the Allied missions unquestionably had the favorable effect of evoking popular enthusiasm and impressing upon the American public the fact that the war was a coöperative venture. The personality of Balfour, especially, broke down any mistrust of British motives, alike in the public mind and that of the President.[10] The missions created a background of mutual good-will which was of much political importance. The insistence of Joffre that American soldiers should be sent to France at once, determined the question, until then unsettled, as to whether American contributions should be merely economic and financial or whether a large expeditionary force should be despatched. A memorandum was drafted and approved by Wilson and Balfour which called for a million and a half American soldiers on the Western front before the end of 1918.[11] The technical members of the missions had an opportunity to explain the situation in Europe to their " opposites."

More important in its ultimate effects, was the fact that the British and Americans were able to set up a direct method of informal and constant communication. It was arranged,

[10] Comment by Colonel House, June 23, 1933: " Mr. Balfour possessed an extraordinary understanding of the mind of the American people and his public utterances all evoked a desire for cordial Anglo-American coöperation. President Wilson immediately was caught by his charm of conversation and his intellectual interests."

[11] May 23, 1917, *I.P.*, III, 58.

writes Wiseman, in order to obviate delays and to facilitate delicate negotiations,

" that Balfour should cable in a special British Government code direct to me in New York, and that I should make it my chief duty to attend to these cables and bring them immediately to Colonel House, who could telephone them over a private wire to the State Department or to President Wilson. In this way Balfour, speaking for the British Government, could get an answer from President Wilson, if necessary, within a few hours. This would have been utterly impossible had the communications gone through ordinary diplomatic channels." [12]

The importance of the first Allied missions thus should not be minimized. But they established no adequate machinery of technical coördination and were not equipped to study and settle the vital problems of finance and supply. Referring to the Balfour Mission, the British Ambassador reported on its results: " It is more in the nature of a new light and a new atmosphere. It is rather rain and sunshine than seed, although good seed has been sown." [13] The French Government appreciated the fact early in April and appointed André Tardieu as chief of a permanent commission of coördination. He arrived on May 17. Early in June the British Government sent over a similar mission under Lord Northcliffe. It was understood in each case that the new commissions would have no diplomatic duties, which would be left to the Ambassadors.

In the case of Northcliffe his functions were outlined by a cable to the British Ambassador of May 30:

---

[12] Comment by Sir William Wiseman on Anglo-American relations, February 17, 1928, *I.P.*, III, 65.

[13] Spring Rice probably to Cecil, May 18, 1917, *Spring Rice*, II, 400.

" The War Cabinet think it desirable to have some system of generally supervising and coördinating the work of the representatives of the various British departments in the United States who are employed there on matters connected with shipping, food supply, munitions, and War Office and Admiralty business. If there is no such coördination, the representatives of these departments would waste much valuable time and power, and especially would interfere with each other by mutual competition. . . . They consider it essential that . . . they should have in the United States an energetic and influential man of good business capacity and wide knowledge for purposes of general supervision and coördination . . . should have a representative in the United States charged with the duty of ensuring to the best of his ability that all possible measures are taken in order to render America's resources available in the most effective manner and with the least possible delay." [14]

The task was not simple. The United States, unaccustomed to centralized control and unprepared for the contingencies of war, could not suddenly attempt to place itself upon a war footing without confusion of effort. The eagerness of Allied agencies to stimulate more rapid production intensified the confusion. The Commissioners must persuade the United States to provide all the supplies possible and also to lend them the money to pay for them. The Allies found themselves competing with each other, for their own demands were uncoördinated, and frequently with the United States Government itself, which requisitioned ships, raw materials and manufactured products upon which the Allied agents had counted. They faced the danger of increased American prices, for there was as yet no centralized control over industry. They must avoid friction, since they were dependent upon the good temper of the United States

[14] War Cabinet to Spring Rice, May 30, 1917, Y.H.C.

Treasury. " The task is immense," cabled Northcliffe, " and ever growing. I have never worked so hard before." And on July 27: " I have long believed war can only be won from here. The position is most difficult and delicate." [15]

At the very beginning of the summer the Allied commissioners were compelled to meet a trying financial crisis:

" We seem on the verge of a financial disaster," cabled Balfour, " which would be worse than defeat in the field. If we cannot keep up exchange neither we nor our Allies can pay our dollar debts. We should be driven off the gold basis, and purchases from the U. S. A. would immediately cease and the Allies' credit would be shattered. . . . You know I am not an alarmist, but this is really serious." [16]

The crisis illustrates the value of informal diplomatic contacts between the two nations. A loan of four hundred million dollars, placed by Morgan and Company for the British, fell due on July 6. It was only immediately preceding the Independence Day holiday that the British realized that funds upon which they had counted were not to be forthcoming and they feared the possibility of a sale of collateral. The American Treasury officials had dispersed for the holiday and there was no formal machinery ready

[15] Northcliffe to the Prime Minister, September 27; to Churchill, July 27, 1917, *I.P.*, III, 86.

[16] Balfour to House, June 29, 1917, *I.P.*, III, 101. " The situation here," wrote the British Ambassador in Washington, " is much as it was in London in Canning's time when the Russian Ambassador used to call at the Foreign Office, being ignorant of French, and slap his pockets and say, ' aurum, aurum.' As England was the sole financial resource of the Allies in the war against Napoleon, so the United States are our sole resource from the financial point of view at the present moment," Spring Rice to Balfour, July 5, 1917, *Spring Rice,* II, 405.

to meet the crisis. Upon the receipt of Balfour's cable Colonel House immediately communicated with Secretary McAdoo and Governor Strong of the New York Federal Reserve Bank and brought them into touch with the British representatives.[17]

But although this immediate crisis was safely passed, the need of something better than a hand to mouth process was apparent. In a period of fourteen weeks the United States had advanced something over a billion dollars. The British insisted that the advances must continue. For three years Great Britain had supported the burden of Allied expenditure. America must now step into the breach. " Our resources available for payments in America are exhausted. Unless the United States Government can meet in full our expenses in America, including exchange, the whole financial fabric of the alliance will collapse. This conclusion will be a matter not of months but of days." [18]

Thus all through the summer the British pressed for promises of regular credits, of a size calculated to disturb intensely the American Treasury. " The monthly money question seems easier," Northcliffe cabled on August 16, " but we shall have an anxious winter in regard to finance. McAdoo is being accused in some newspapers of spending

[17] Comment by Sir William Wiseman, May 23, 1933: " An excellent example of the diplomatic effectiveness of the intimate relations between Balfour and House. Warned by Balfour, House brought the key persons together. The matter was arranged by them and not by House, who did not touch technical details. But the interposition of House was an indispensable preliminary."

[18] Page to Lansing, July 20, 1917, *F.R., 1917, Suppl. 2,* I, 553. (Communicated by Lord Northcliffe to Colonel House, *I.P.,* III, 105.)

the nation's money like a drunken sailor." [19]   Mr. McAdoo, on his side, in answer to the Allied demands replied, naturally, that he was responsible to the American taxpayers and must be able to show that all funds advanced were for expenditures necessary to victory.

He asked accordingly for the creation of some sort of interallied finance council or purchasing board, which would certify to him the absolute necessity of what was asked and indicate the priority of needs. The situation was complicated by the fact that the confusion in Allied demands was such as to give the appearance of a pell mell scramble for priority of funds and supplies. Furthermore the withdrawal of Morgan and Company as purchasing agent for the British and French Governments, a step occasioned by the proper feeling that with America in the war a private American firm ought not to exercise what amounted to official functions, had left a gap in organization that was not filled until the end of August. Both the British and French representatives in the United States emphasized the need of better coördination.

" The demands for money, shipping and raw materials come from the Allies separately "—so ran a British memorandum—" and without reference to one another. Each urges that their own particular need is paramount, and no one in America can tell where the next demand will come from and for how much it will be. . . . At present, confusion reigns not only in the Administration Departments, but in the public mind. There is, on the one hand, a feeling that some of the money and material is not needed for strictly war purposes, and, on the other hand, some genuine alarm is felt that even the resources of the United

[19] Northcliffe to Wiseman, August 16, 1917, *I.P.*, III, 114.

States will not be able to bear the strain. German agents . . . are encouraging the idea that it would be better to conserve American resources for the protection of America, rather than dissipate them in a quarrel with Europe." [20]

The French High Commissioner, André Tardieu, believed that existing interallied bureaux could be utilized and developed into a general interallied conference for the coordination of demands. The United States Government on its side must assume complete control of all essential industries:

" The old organization has disappeared and the new one has not been set up as yet. Whence a general condition of uncertainty concerning prices as well as terms of delivery. . . . Supplying the Allies with considerable advances of money, the United States may properly ask to be assured that money so advanced is actually and fully devoted to war needs. The Allies, working in coöperation with the United States may also properly ask that, as regards the negotiating of their orders, they should be protected as to prices against any exaggerated claims from the producers. . . . Assurances should be given to the American Government that the orders of the Allies are not such as to hamper the industries which are necessary to the United States. Assurances should be given to the Allies that the carrying out of the orders in the United States shall not be hampered or delayed by orders from the American Government." [21]

The general principles of Tardieu's plan were later carried into effect. But there were long delays in its execution. In the United States the War Industries Board had broad planning functions, but previous to the reorganization of the following spring lacked the power to super-

[20] Wiseman Memorandum on Anglo-American Relations, August, 1917, Y.H.C., cited in *I.P.*, III, 107.
[21] Tardieu Memorandum, May 27, 1917, *I.P.*, III, 109-110.

vise and execute. The Allies, on their side, delayed the formation of the interallied council that McAdoo asked for. They may have feared that it would mean the sacrifice of the financial autonomy of London and Paris, the substitution of the dollar for the pound. A conference of Allied representatives in Paris, after discussing Mr. McAdoo's proposals, drafted a plan which in its main lines met the desires of the United States. But the Allied Governments refused ratification, apparently because of the extent of the powers that would be conferred upon the commissioners.

President Wilson realized acutely the unsatisfactory character of the situation and the difficulties under which both the Allied missions in America and the American officials themselves were working:

"Wilson urged strongly," Wiseman reported of a conference on July 13, "that more information, both as to actual financial needs and general policy of the Allies, must be given to the United States Government. He pointed out that there was much confusion and some competition in the demands of the various Allies. Specifically, so far as the British are concerned, he pointed out that there was no one who could speak with sufficient financial authority to discuss the whole situation, both financial and political, with the Secretary of the Treasury. All these things should be remedied as soon as possible. He was thoroughly in favor of the scheme proposed by McAdoo for a council in Paris. This council, composed of representatives of the Allies, should determine what was needed in the way of supplies and money from America. It should also determine the urgency of each requisition and give proper priority." [22]

The Allied missions faced the situation courageously and finally with success, but they lived through the nightmare

[22] Notes on interview with Wilson, July 13, 1917, *I.P.,* III, 108.

that the necessary credits might not be forthcoming. " Loan to us strongly opposed by powerful section of Congress," cabled Northcliffe. " If loan stops, war stops." [23] Tardieu's picture of the summer from the French point of view is illuminating:

" Without means of payment in dollars . . . the Allies would have been beaten before the end of 1917. America's entry into the war saved them. Before the American soldier, the American dollar turned the tide. . . . For Europe, what a stream of gold! But its approaches were crowded. Banker of her Allies since 1914, England came first. France, who had suffered more than England, wanted to be served equally well. The others pressed behind, a clamoring crowd whose enormous estimates frightened the Treasury officials. . . . Associated, but not Allied, the United States had authorized its Secretary of the Treasury to grant advances to Europe, but not to enter into definite undertakings. . . . This independent policy was justified and strengthened by the unbridled competition of the borrowers, by their ever-outstretched hands, by the astuteness of their ever-increasing demands. American mistrust increased when . . . both London and Paris, on the ground of their financial autonomy, stubbornly opposed the American proposal for an interallied finance board. . . . Every day my Government called upon me to obtain regular agreements, which it considered indispensable. Every day the Treasury told me, as it told my colleagues, that it did not intend to enter into any binding agreements. The American Congress had limited the object, the amount, the form of financial assistance. No one could complain that this assistance was not forthcoming. But no one had the right to count upon it." [24]

In late August the creation of a purchasing commission in Washington to take over the functions formerly exercised for the British Government by Morgan and Company,

[23] Northcliffe to Phillips, October 10, 1917, Steed, *Through Thirty Years*, II, 143.

[24] Tardieu, *France and America*, pp. 227-229.

alleviated certain difficulties. The Allies delayed the agreement for one reason or another and the American Treasury
had chafed for several weeks until it was accomplished.
Northcliffe cabled, "Government greatly pleased, and as a
result expressed intention of helping us in every way possible." [25] This commission did not in any way meet the plan
of McAdoo for an interallied council to correlate Allied
demands, but it went far to replace the very effective purchasing agency organized by Stettinius for Morgan and
Company which had lapsed in April. It obtained offers at
the best current prices, submitted them to the representatives
of the Allies and supervised the purchases made, the Allies
themselves determining technical details. The purchasing
agreement, signed by the United States, Great Britain, France
and Russia, greatly facilitated all buying operations and
resulted in important economies. It did not touch the major
problem of coördinating Allied demand with American
supply.

Early in September, at the suggestion of House, enthusiastically supported by Northcliffe and Wiseman, the British
Government sent Lord Reading to take up with the American Treasury the whole financial situation. Northcliffe himself was not a member of the Government and, fully occupied with a thousand and one details of industrial coordination, was not in a position to handle finance as well.
Both Wilson and McAdoo had insisted that the British send
someone of high official position and who could speak with
more authority than their experts in Washington. Lord
Reading, occupying high judicial and political position, the

25 Northcliffe to Wiseman, August 24, 1917, *I.P.,* III, 122-123.

close friend of the Prime Minister, an able financier, was admirably qualified. He created the happiest impression and established relations of such value that three months later he was to become Ambassador.

" He was able," cabled Northcliffe to the Prime Minister, " to obtain fifty million dollars for Canadian wheat, which really was an inroad on the basic principle that every cent of money advanced to the Allies should be spent in the United States. This achievement of Reading is in my opinion one that could not be brought about by anyone not possessed of Reading's ability, charm, and tact in handling these difficult people. . . . [He] will, I am convinced, be able to achieve all that is humanly possible." [26]

This success was inevitably limited. Reading obtained the necessary credits, but himself insisted that the situation would not be satisfactory until or unless a complete system of coördination were developed. As the American military organization progressed, with consequent demands for materials from every American department, the danger that Allied needs would be passed over became acute. The problem of supply was to equal or surpass that of finance. At the end of October Lord Reading drafted a comprehensive memorandum on the whole situation, admitting the gravity of the outlook, although " it is, of course, much too soon to say that the impossible will not be achieved." He emphasized three factors likely to govern the situation in the succeeding months:

" (A) The officials of the United States Treasury are nervous and oppressed. Pending the result of the forthcoming Liberty loan and even thereafter they will hesitate to

[26] Northcliffe to Lloyd George, September 30, 1917, *I.P.*, III, 178-179.

commit themselves. I believe that for the present we shall always get our money in the end, but it will probably be at the expense of constant importunity and some anxiety. Nothing will be clear-cut, and each Ally will be struggling for itself. A time will probably come when we shall have to ask the Treasury to take risks which will appear unjustifiable from the strictly financial standpoint. (B) Mr. Crosby stated plainly that the requirements of their own Departments must come first. Any shortage of funds, therefore, will fall mainly on the Allies. (C) I told Mr. Crosby that what will save the United States Treasury, as it has saved ours in the past, will be the material limitations on what it is possible to buy. Goods will not in fact be forthcoming on a sufficient scale to absorb the vast credits to which the Departments and the Allies are becoming entitled. This will save the financial position. But the same trouble will crop up in another form. The Ministry of Munitions is more likely to be embarrassed by shortage of supplies from America than is the Treasury by shortage of dollars. . . ."

Lord Reading concluded with emphasis upon the core of the difficulty: " The growing lack of coördination between the programme of the Administration here and the programme of the Allies is probably, on every ground, the biggest question in front of us." [27] His comment was enforced by a report from the British Ambassador: " What is most serious is that there . . . is no coördinating authority here nor has this country any certain means of becoming informed, not only of their own war needs but of the war needs of the Allies as a whole. The war is still conducted by pigeonholes in departments." [28]

[27] Reading Memorandum, *I.P.,* III, 180-182.
[28] Spring Rice to Balfour, October 23, 1917, *Spring Rice,* II, 414.

3

Just as the vital peril faced by the Allied armies in the spring of 1918 led to the development of the supreme command, so the financial and economic dangers that threatened America's relations with the Allies forced a system of coordination in those fields. Lord Reading's ominous phrase at the close of his report, " growing lack of coördination," made a deep impression upon the War Cabinet. The Allied programme must be made sufficiently definite to permit the Americans to work toward it intelligently. America must be made to realize that her contributions would be more efficient if applied to the existing Allied armies rather than to the American organization that was still in the making.

The problem essentially was one of a technical character and it was ultimately solved by technical experts. But diplomatic preparation was first necessary in order to remove the obstacles which kept the American and Allied experts apart. Reading and Wiseman agreed that the one person capable of smoothing the road was Colonel House; and they urged that House be sent to Europe at the head of a mission designed to bring the chiefs of the important American departments or war-making agencies into personal contact with their opposites in Europe.

" Would the President consider the advisability of sending plenipotentiary envoys to London and Paris, with the object of taking part in the next great Allied Council, bringing their fresh minds to bear on our problems, discussing and giving their judgment on some of the questions I have raised, and also to arrange—if that be possible—for some machinery to bridge over the distance between Washington and the theatre of war? " [29]

[29] Wiseman to House, September 26, 1917, *I.P.*, III, 184.

The British Prime Minister had already suggested that the United States take a more active part in the larger questions of war policy. He wanted American help in devising some plan of military coördination that would offer better hope of success than the existing *guerre d'usure* principles of the British staff.

" He was quite clear in his mind," wrote Sir Henry Wilson on August 23, " that we were not winning the war by our present plans, and that we never should on our present lines; but he did not know how, or what we should do, and he had no means of checking or altering Robertson's and Haig's plans though he knew they were too parochial. He said that he was not in the position, nor had he the knowledge, to bring out alternative plans and to insist upon their adoption, as it would always be said that he was overruling the soldiers." [30]

In any developments he might have in mind, American support would be of great political importance to Mr. Lloyd George. " I have talked things over with him [Sir William Wiseman]," he wrote Colonel House on September 4, " with the special purpose that he should explain to you what I think about the present situation. He will go straight to see you on arrival. Very briefly I think it is essential to the cause of the Allies that a representative of the United States of the first rank should come over here officially as soon as possible to take part in the deliberations of the Allies over their future plans of campaign. Needless to say it would be a source of the utmost satisfaction to us if you were to come yourself." [31]

[30] Sir Charles Edward Callwell, *Field Marshal Sir Henry Wilson,* II, 10.

[31] Lloyd George to House, September 4, 1917, *I.P.,* III, 187.

Following Reading's suggestion of an American mission, Mr. Lloyd George agreed that it would be preferable to a single representative. The French and Italians joined in urging the desirability of the mission. They intimated strongly that it should be headed by House. The British War Cabinet felt "that in view of the forthcoming international conference it was of great importance that a man in the complete confidence of the President should visit Western Europe in order to obtain first-hand information in regard to the position of the Allies, and Colonel House seemed to them the only suitable person." [32]

The suggestion of a war mission, designed to set up machinery of coördination, was approved by the President after very slight hesitation. He realized that it might lead to an increase of Allied influence over our war effort and, as House reported on October 13, "he has no intention of loosening his hold on the situation." [33] But he appreciated keenly the need of improved coöperative effort. Other questions than finance were acute. The whole problem of arranging the transportation of American troops and supplies must be faced.

"Tonnage conditions," cabled Balfour, "will be the deciding factor in the extent of spring operations in every theatre of war. . . . It is of paramount importance that adequate arrangements should be made for provisioning and transporting the powerful army America is preparing, without reducing the tonnage now devoted to supplying the Allied

---

[32] *I.P.*, III, 195. See also Frazier to House, October 12, 1917; Wiseman to Drummond, October 13, 1917; Balfour to House, October 14, 1917; Reading to Wilson, October 15, 1917, *ibid.*, III, 195-198.

[33] House Diary, October 13, 1917, *I.P.*, III, 203.

forces already engaged, lest such reduction should weaken them in the same proportion that the American army will strengthen them." [34]

Another problem which could be settled only through complete coöperation was that of embargo policy as it related to neutrals. It was, in view of the attitude of America as a neutral, one of considerable delicacy. The British desired to establish in London an Allied blockade council, and wished to include American representatives.[35] Machinery must be organized to coördinate the export licensing system of all the nations at war with Germany; decisions must be taken on matters of high policy regarding the rigorous restriction of exports to neutrals. Questions of such importance could not be settled by cable.[36]

On October 13 Wilson decided that the mission, led by House, was necessary. He appointed General Bliss and Admiral Benson to represent the Army and Navy; the Assistant Secretary of the Treasury, Oscar Crosby, to be in charge of financial problems; Vance McCormick, Chairman of the War Trade Board, to be in charge of embargo and blockade problems. The Shipping Board and Food Administration were represented by Bainbridge Colby and Alonzo Taylor respectively; Thomas Nelson Perkins, legal adviser to the War Industries Board, represented the Priority Board in discussions on priority of shipments. The mission sailed from Halifax on the cruiser *Huntington* and arrived in London November 7.

The coming of an American war mission to Europe coincided with a double blow to Allied fortunes. On October

[34] Balfour to House, October 11, 1917, *I.P.*, III, 190-193.
[35] Balfour to House, September 15, 1917, Y.H.C.
[36] *I.P.*, III, 194.

24, the Italian army cracked at Caporetto, and through the breach the enemy poured down on the plain of Friuli. Complete disaster was narrowly averted. In a month the Italians lost three-quarters of a million of effectives. On November 8, the Bolsheviks seized control of the Russian Government, and at once made it evident that the Allies could no longer count upon Russian assistance. The Russians proposed an immediate armistice on all fronts.

The initial effect of the Italian disaster was to hasten plans for improved military coördination that had already been under discussion. The British and French Prime Ministers met the Italian Premier, Orlando, and his Foreign Secretary, Sonnino, at Rapallo, where on November 7 an agreement was signed creating an interallied organization, the Supreme War Council (*Conseil Supérieure de Guerre*). It was conceived primarily in a military sense and owed its creation to a military crisis, but it was essentially a political body composed of the Prime Minister and a member of the Government of each of the great Powers whose armies were fighting on the Western Front. It was to act "as an agency for the adoption and maintenance of a general policy for the Allies in the prosecution of the war, consistent with the total resources available and the most effective distribution of those resources among the various theaters of operations." [37]

The Supreme War Council, as constituted, was by no means an adequate military substitute for a unified command in the field, and the French, although their Chamber rati-

[37] Tasker H. Bliss, "The Unified Command," *Foreign Affairs*, December 15, 1922, 6; Paul Painlevé, *Comment j'ai nommé Foch et Pétain*, pp. 233-269; Callwell, *op. cit.*, II, 13-34.

fied it, regarded it as an unsatisfactory half-step. In England, on the other hand, it was opposed on the ground that it would mean the surrender of national to interallied control. It was looked upon also as evidence of Lloyd George's hope to get military control out of the hands of the professional soldiers, especially Robertson, whom he was known to distrust and whom he held largely responsible for the carnage of the *guerre d'usure*.

This discontent in both France and England was not skilfully handled by the parliamentary leaders. The Painlevé Cabinet, accused of incompetency and deprived of popular confidence, was overthrown and for several days France was without a responsible government. Whether the new Clemenceau Ministry, regarded by many as the child of desperation, could conquer the increasing confusion was a matter of doubt.[38] The British Prime Minister likewise faced the probability of defeat in Parliament. " Lloyd George stopped in Paris," writes Wiseman, " on his way back from Rapallo and made an important speech at a breakfast in Paris, in which he severely criticized the Allied bungling and in particular the inefficiency of the high command of the British Army, thereby stirring up great resentment in Parliament circles friendly to the Army. This speech of Lloyd George caused a real ministerial crisis in England and to save himself Lloyd George had to get support from Wilson for his idea of the Supreme War Council." [39]

[38] Raymond Poincaré, *Au Service de la France, L'Année trouble*, pp. 352-376; Painlevé, *op. cit.*, pp. 270 ff.; Tardieu, *France and America*, pp. 234-235.

[39] Wiseman to C. S., August, 1932. Text of speech in *F.R., 1917, Suppl. 2*, I, 358-366.

Thus at the moment the Americans touched the shores of Europe they found the Allies under the shadow of military defeat and political indecision. The firmness of Clemenceau and the parliamentary skill of Lloyd George, who capitalized Wilson's insistence on interallied coöperation, triumphed over the immediate danger of collapse. But it was in the midst of confusion that the American war mission began the conferences designed to arrange a permanent system of coördination.[40]

Those conferences fell into two periods: preliminary meetings with the British in London, which lasted until November 21; and the general Interallied Conference at Paris, at which eighteen nations were represented, from Belgium to Siam. In London the work consisted largely of individual conversations between the American members and their British opposites. It was easy to exchange information, for the conferences were of the frankest sort, but more difficult to decide policy. Minor questions could be settled, but decisions upon major policies affecting several departments could not be taken. "Had the Supreme War Council," wrote Bliss, "been functioning at the time of its arrival, the American Mission would have found its work easier. As it was, the members had to obtain their information piecemeal from various representatives of the different governments, put it together and reconcile conflicting views as best they could."[41]

[40] Comment by Sir William Wiseman, August, 1932: "Emphasize the chaos existing at the time of the visit of the first American War Mission to Europe and the great need of fresh initiative in Allied Councils."

[41] Bliss, in *Foreign Affairs*, December 14, 1922, 7.

The Americans pressed strongly, first, for some definite indications of the priority of Allied needs, and, second, for permanent machinery that would permit the settlement of the larger questions and the execution of decisions after they were made. Northcliffe and Tardieu, from their experience in the United States, gave strong support to the demand. " Unless there is swift improvement in our methods here " wrote Northcliffe to Lloyd George, " the United States will rightly take into its own hands the entire management of a great part of the war. It will not sacrifice its blood and treasure to the incompetent handling of the affairs of Europe." [42] House reported to the President: " Northcliffe has been splendid. . . . With this combination of Wiseman, Reading, and Northcliffe, things are being accomplished with more rapidity than I have ever experienced here." [43] In a published statement Tardieu insisted that a permanent interallied organization was indispensable:

" When each of the Allied Governments sends its missions to ask the aid of Americans, the United States gains the impression that affairs in Europe are in chaos. There should be at once a Council of the Allies, which with full knowledge of the situation after a careful study of all the circumstances, military and political, should transmit to the American Government *en bloc* the requirements of the various nations filtered, correlated, and justified." [44]

From their individual conversations and from what Mr. Lloyd George told them at the conference of November 20, the American delegates gathered that man-power and ship-

[42] Northcliffe to Lloyd George, November 15, 1917, in N. Y. *Times*, November 16, 1917.

[43] House to Wilson, November 16, 1917, *I.P.*, III, 240.

[44] Quoted in *The Times*, London, November 19, 1917.

ping were the two most urgent problems. "The Prime Minister frankly stated that the sooner the Republic can send over the largest number of troops the better. He was anxious, he said, to know how soon the first million could be expected in France. America has promised to launch 6,000,000 tons of shipping during the coming year. Here again time is of the essence of their usefulness." After these items came food and American assistance in maintaining a strict blockade. Underneath all as an invariable assumption lay the contribution of American credits.[45]

The mission left London for Paris, better instructed as to Allied needs but disappointed at the absence of definite conclusions and the delay in creating permanent machinery. They were determined to see that if humanly possible, things were "buttoned-up" before they left. That determination was one of America's major contributions to victory. As Paul Cravath observed, although because of the defection of Russia and the Italian disaster "there is greater need than ever for a close and sympathetic coördination of the efforts of Great Britain, France, and Italy," progress in that direction, to say nothing of coöperating with America, was slow. "This is due," he added, "to the ineradicable mutual suspicion and differences in temperament and method between the British and the French. The relations with Italy are complicated by her own peculiar ambitions in the war which make full coöperation between her and France and England very difficult." Writing immediately after the Inter-

---

[45] London *Times,* November 21, 1917. The *procès-verbal* of the meeting is published in the *N. Y. Times Current History,* July, 1925; *F.R., 1917, Suppl. 2,* I, 366-384.

allied Conference, a prejudiced witness perhaps, but certainly representing the sentiment of the American mission, he commented:

" My observations led me to believe that the recent conferences in Paris would have accomplished very little in the direction of the arrangements for coördinated effort had it not been for the presence of the American delegates and their patient but firm insistence upon conclusions being reached while the conferences were together . . . although the work of forcing effective coördination has only begun." [46]

The Franco-American Commissioner also bears witness to the pressure exerted by the Americans. " When Americans fall in love with an idea, even if their enthusiasm does not last, it is always intense. In 1917 and 1918, they had a passion for the organization of interallied war machinery, the weight of which was not always borne gladly by Europe." [47]

However much or little credit the Americans should be given for the process of hastening coördination, it is certain that the Paris conference marked the decisive crossroads in the path to Allied victory.

" Nations remember only the high spots of wars," wrote Tardieu. " What did they grasp of the tragic period of 1917-18? The Rumanian disaster, Caporetto, the British Fourth Army, the Chemin des Dames. Were those the decisive events of the great struggle? No! The essential things were the problems of transportation, rotation of shipping and submarine sinkings, the financial problem, the problems of coöperation. Any shortcoming in the adjustment of effort, any breakdown in the machinery of supply, might have left our soldiers weaponless." [48]

[46] Cravath to House, December 6, 1917, *I.P.,* III, 294.
[47] Tardieu, *op. cit.,* p. 235.
[48] *Ibid.,* p. 224.

Colonel House judged the importance of the achievement in similar terms. " The good the Conference has done," he wrote as he sailed for America, " in the way of coördinating the Allied resources, particularly the economic resources, can hardly be estimated. Heretofore, everything has been going pretty much at sixes and sevens. From now there will be less duplication of effort. . . . No one excepting those on the inside can know of the wasted effort there has been. This Conference may therefore well be considered the turning point in the war even though the fortunes of the Allies have never seemed so low as now." [49]

The Interallied Conference was planned for accomplishment and not rhetoric. It was agreed by Clemenceau, Lloyd George, and House that the plenary conference should meet only to be welcomed by Clemenceau, who promised that his speech would be brief. As delivered it consisted of five sentences, concluding: " The order of the day is work. Let us get to work." The French Foreign Secretary then explained that the work of the conference would be carried on in the small committees of technical experts which had already been organized. Eight minutes after Clemenceau had called the meeting to order, it adjourned, the committees immediately going into executive session. Within five days the vital questions had been isolated and, at least so far as basic problems were concerned, decisions taken.

The understanding reached as to man-power was that the Americans would place in France by the end of the year 1918 at least thirty divisions, or approximately a million men, available for the early campaign of 1919, with another

[49] House Diary, December 1, 1917, *I.P.*, III, 293.

million ready to replace and reënforce them.[50] Of equal
importance perhaps, although not so widely recognized,
were the promises of American naval assistance. Allied naval
morale was certainly touched if it was not shaken by the
experience of the Battle of Jutland. The Americans insisted
upon active offensive operations against the submarine
menace and promised assistance in surface ships that would
offer reasonable assurance against a second offer of battle
by the German High Seas Fleet. They agreed to send over
at once a division of battleships to join the British Grand
Fleet.[51] With the exercise of some pressure they persuaded
the British to coöperate in closing the North Sea to submarines by carrying out the American plan of a mine

[50] Pétain Memorandum, *I.P.*, III, 259. Comment by Sir William
Wiseman, August, 1932: "If you examine the report of the
mission I think you will find that the Allies asked the United
States to have in Europe by June, 750,000 men of all classes and
by October 1,000,000 men of all classes. Pershing in December,
1917, had only about 100,000 men in Europe. The program seemed
in December, 1917, to be impossible of accomplishment. As a
matter of fact, however, I believe you will find that the United
States of America had over 1,000,000 men in Europe by June,
1918, and over 2,000,000 there by October, 1918. This most
striking effort was, of course, to a great extent made possible
by the ability of the British to furnish tonnage far in excess of
what was contemplated in December, 1917." See Report of
General Bliss, *F.R., 1917, Suppl. 2*, I, 386-391; also annex to his
report giving the conclusions of the conference of December 1,
ibid., 442-445.

[51] Comment by Commander Carter, chief aide to Admiral Benson,
May 12, 1933: "On our arrival we found the British naval
officers extremely disturbed by the efficiency of German gun fire
as demonstrated in the Battle of Jutland, and quite uncertain as
to the probable outcome of a second capital naval encounter. It
seemed vital to reëstablish confidence by the agreement to send
over enough American ships to assure surface superiority."

barrage. A definite plan of offensive operations was approved, in which American forces would participate, and it was tentatively agreed that the American Atlantic fleet be sent to European waters in the spring if conditions warranted.[52]

Agreement was further reached in blockade policy and methods of rationing neutrals. "The blockade authorities of the four countries," reported Mr. McCormick, "understand each other from the point of view of commodities, industry, trade, and exchange. Any question that may arise in those directions will from now on be trivial and easily settled by cable. There remain only questions of policy, which change with the progress of the war, and under these circumstances, future negotiations ought to be greatly simplified as compared to those of the past."[53]

But the real importance of the Conference lay in the fact that from its committees sprang permanent interallied machinery, capable of carrying out the decisions taken or modifying them as occasion arose. It arranged for the immediate organization of the Interallied Council on War Purchases and Finance. This represented the nearest approach possible to the plan of Mr. McAdoo for solving the problem of confusion in Allied demands for financial aid. It was designed to coördinate purchases by the Allies, to serve as a clearing house for information as to Allied needs for loans, and to develop a unified policy relating to

[52] Benson Report, *F.R., 1917, Suppl. 2,* I, 384-386.
[53] McCormick Report, *F.R., 1917, Suppl. 2,* I, 400-409. For the operation of the Allied Blockade Committee, see *F.R., 1918, Suppl. 1,* II, 936-1012. Crosby Report in *F.R., 1917, Suppl. 2,* I, 392-400.

credits granted to the Allies by the United States. It sat in
London and Paris under the presidency of the American
representative, Mr. Crosby, and worked in close coöperation
with the other interallied boards. The fact that this council
did not succeed in forcing absolute financial unity is believed by Tardieu to have resulted in more loss to the
debtors than to the creditors.[54]

In other fields, he adds, " the Americans finally had their
way." The Maritime Transport Council, seated in London,
supervised the general conduct of Allied transport and was
authorized to obtain the most effective use of tonnage by
planned distribution, while leaving each nation responsible
for the management of the tonnage under its control.[55]
The Interallied Naval Council was created in order " to
insure the closest touch and complete coöperation between
the Allied fleets." The Food Council, composed of the
representatives of the food controllers of the Allied countries, was authorized primarily to allocate stocks of food and
to prepare transport programmes. The Interallied Petroleum
Conference supervised the distribution of oils. In the following summer the Interallied Munitions Council was
set up.[56]

The actual process of coördination was carried through
not by the diplomatists but by the technical experts. Delay

[54] Tardieu, *op. cit.*, p. 235.
[55] Sir Arthur Salter, *Allied Shipping Control*, pp. 144-150.
[56] The diplomatic documents relating to the coöperation of the
United States with the Allied Powers are printed in *F.R., 1918,
Suppl. 1*, I, as follows: Maritime control, 498-534; supply and
distribution of food, 535-558; raw materials and munitions, 589-
616; oil, 617-623.

and disappointments were not absent. But the final outcome justified the earlier efforts of the diplomatists to remove the obstacles that impeded the creation of adequate machinery. "After four years of experiment and dispersion," says Tardieu, " control reached something in the nature of perfection towards the end of 1918. Had the war lasted another year, the machinery would have been running with incredible smoothness." [57]

4

The most obvious failure of the Interallied Conference lay in the larger field of policy, comprehending all the other fields, economic and political as well as purely military, in which the war had to be waged. The failure is not surprising, for the difficulties resulting from national unwillingness to submit to international control were tremendous. At least a beginning was made through the organization of the Supreme War Council.

The Americans were dissatisfied with the lack of executive powers given to that body. President Wilson vigorously urged unity of military control. At the moment when opposition to its creation appeared in England, he cabled to House: " Please take the position that we not only approve a continuance of the plan for a war council but insist on it. We can no more take part in the war successfully without such a council than we can lend money without the board Crosby went over to join." [58] The President's support, according to Bliss, House, and Wiseman, saved the Council

[57] Tardieu, *op. cit.,* p. 235.
[58] Wilson to House, November 16, 1917, *I.P.,* III, 220.

and the Lloyd George Government,[59] but the control established by the Council was not effective.

" If this war is to be won," wrote House in his report to the
President, " better team work between the Allies must be
effected. . . . The diplomatic end of such an undertaking
[the defeat of Germany] is nearly as great as the military
end, and General Pershing is beginning to realize this.
Unless a change comes for the better the Allies cannot win
and Germany may. . . . The Supreme War Council as at
present constituted is almost a farce. It could be the efficient
instrument to win the war. . . ." [60]

General Bliss was equally emphatic:

"A military crisis is to be apprehended culminating not
later than the end of next spring, in which, without great
assistance from the United States, the advantage will probably lie with the Central Powers. This crisis is largely due
to the collapse of Russia as a military factor and to the recent
disaster in Italy. But it is also largely due to the lack of
military coördination, lack of unity of control on the part
of the allied forces in the field. This lack of unity of control results from military jealousy and suspicion as to ultimate national aims. Our allies urge us to profit by their
experience in three and a half years of war; to adopt the
organization, the types of artillery, tanks, etc., that the
test of war has proved to be satisfactory. We should go
further. In making the great military effort now demanded
of us we should also demand as a prior condition that
our allies also profit by the experience of three and a half
years of war in the matter of absolute unity of military
control. National jealousies and suspicions and susceptibil-
ities of national temperament must be put aside in favor
of this unified control, even going, if necessary (as I be-

[59] Bliss to C. S., June 14, 1928, *I.P.,* III, 255; House to Wilson,
November 20, 1917; *ibid.,* III, 224. Wiseman to C. S., August,
1932, Y.H.C.

[60] House Report, December 14, 1917, *I.P.,* III, 300-302.

17

lieve it is), to the limit of unified *command*. Otherwise, our dead and theirs may have died in vain." [61]

The functions of the Council were confused and its power uncertain because of the confusion of motive and circumstance that attended its creation. The French had looked forward to the unified command and with the accession of Clemenceau to power hoped to attain it by conferring executive powers on the Council. Mr. Lloyd George welcomed the Council, partly, at least, as a means of withdrawing control over military policy from the British Chief of Staff, Robertson, whom he did not trust. He insisted that the Council proper should be composed of representatives of the civil governments, and he appointed as British military adviser not Robertson but Sir Henry Wilson. Thus it was not clear whether the Council was to be a political body directing the high policy of the war or primarily a military body, directing operations; and if the latter, how it was to work efficiently in view of the fact that the military advisers were not to be the Allied chiefs of staff and there was to be no executive head.

" No one fully understood it," wrote General Bliss, " not even its creators. Military men, and most others who thought at all about it, believed that it would be a sort of Aulic Council, making and directing military plans—in short, another step to disaster. Moreover, the French believed that it was a British scheme to get control of the French armies, and the British thought the same about the French." [62]

Clemenceau and Pétain made a determined effort to work toward real unity of military control, suggesting the elimina-

[61] Bliss Report, December 14, 1917, *I.P.*, III, 303-304; *F.R., 1917, Suppl. 2*, I, 387.
[62] Bliss to C. S., June 14, 1928, *I.P.*, III, 254.

tion of the Prime Ministers and other political representatives from the Council, which would thus consist of the Commanders-in-Chief and the Chiefs of Staff as the active and controlling members, and the appointment of one of them as executive officer.[63] This plan would approach the unified command, for the executive officer would have almost the powers of a generalissimo. It was supported by Bliss, who in a memorandum of November 25 insisted that " to ensure real efficiency, this unity of control must be effected through a purely military council, it being assumed that one or more of the principal Allied nations may be unwilling to place their military forces under a single Commander-in-Chief." [64] The plan was certain to arouse the opposition of the British. President Wilson refused to enter the quarrel. He cabled: " I favor the most effective methods obtainable whether directed by one man or not." [65]

The French plan was certainly the most effective proposed from the military point of view, but it was not obtainable in the political sense. Mr. Lloyd George dared not accept a plan which the British would regard as a renewal of the disastrous experiment of the previous spring, when Nivelle was given control of British troops. Moreover he was determined that the Council should be under political control, since it was impossible to separate problems of general policy from those of military strategy. It was just this separation, he contended, that accounted for the waste and failures of

[63] House to Wilson, November 23, 26; Memorandum of November 25, 1917, *I.P.*, III, 251-3, 257-60.

[64] Bliss Memorandum, *I.P.*, III, 253.

[65] Wilson to House, December 1, 1917, *F.R., 1917, Suppl. 2,* I, 331.

the preceding years. Nor would he put his Chief of Staff
on the Council as military adviser. He insisted upon Wilson,
" an intimate friend of Foch and much trusted by the
French Staff—a happy augury for the new coöperation . . .
a man whom Mr. Lloyd George understood and valued, for
he had many qualities akin to his own—unflagging optimism, for one thing, and a talent for explicit statement
rare among tongue-tied soldiers." [66] But at the moment he
did not dare attempt to supersede Robertson with Wilson
as Chief of Staff.

Thus Lloyd George came to Paris determined to oppose
the French plans for changing the Rapallo Agreement.

" Lloyd George is angry," wrote Sir Henry Wilson in his
diary on November 27, " and says that he will have a row
with Clemenceau tomorrow, and if Clemenceau does not
give in he [Lloyd George] will go straight back to London.
Lloyd George certainly must show his teeth. . . . Clemenceau will give in tomorrow. He is in no position to quarrel
with Lloyd George." [67]

The prophecy was accurate, although the " row " did not
develop. Early in the morning of November 28 the British
Prime Minister explained to House the reasons that compelled him to insist upon the Rapallo Agreement, to exclude
the Chiefs of Staff, and to emphasize the political com-
plexion of the Council. He asked House to tell Clemenceau
that unless the French accepted the Rapallo Agreement as
binding he would have to return to London.

" Clemenceau agreed to yield to Lloyd George," wrote
House, " as to the Chiefs of Staff, but said with a sardonic

[66] John Buchan, *A History of the Great War*, IV, 173-174.
[67] Callwell, *op. cit.*, II, 32.

smile, ' It vitiates the entire plan. What I shall do is to put on a second or third rate man instead of Foch, and let the thing drift where it will.' . . . I remarked that it was hard enough to fight the Germans and we had best not begin fighting among ourselves, and if Lloyd George insisted upon such a Supreme War Council as had been suggested but which was not supreme, we would have to yield because of his difficulties at home. The differences between George, Robertson, and Haig make it impossible to carry out the general desire for complete unity of military action." [68]

Although Clemenceau did not carry out his threat of replacing Foch with a " second or third rate man," for he appointed Foch's Chief of Staff, General Weygand, it is true that the British attitude " vitiated " the plan for effective unity of military control. The committee of military advisers proved to be strong—Weygand, Wilson, Bliss, Cadorna. It collected at Versailles a mass of important information, and developed plans which were ultimately of value to Foch after he became Commander-in-Chief. But, lacking executive functions and separated from, if not at odds with, the Commanders-in-Chiefs, it was not the body that finally coördinated strategic operations on the western front. The most important of its recommendations, the creation of a general reserve, although approved by the Allied Governments as well as by Pershing and Bliss,[69] was disregarded by Pétain and Haig and never put into operation. Unity of military control was forced only by the German victories of the following spring, and it came in the simple form of conferring upon an individual, General

[68] House Diary, November 28, 1917, Y.H.C., printed in part in *I.P.,* III, 262.

[69] Pershing to House, February 27, 1918, Y.H.C.

Foch, first powers of " coördinating the action of the Allied Armies on the Western Front," and shortly afterwards a real supreme command, although power of appeal to their governments was left to the national Commanders-in-Chief.[70]

The coördination of military action was thus developed outside of the Supreme War Council and would probably have resulted from the threatening German offensive had there been no Council; in the end nevertheless, the conception of Lloyd George was largely justified by the political rôle which it developed. During the spring of 1918 it gradually assumed the position of a general interallied committee of direction, drawing its authority from the fact that its members were the Prime Ministers and the Foreign Ministers of the controlling Allied Powers. Where it did not decide, it offered opportunity for discussion that led to compromise, as in the dispute between Pershing and the French over the creation of an independent American army. In coöperation with the various interallied boards it built up a comprehensive economic control. It made announcements of a political nature, attempting to coördinate the Allied political attitude toward the enemy. Finally, at the time of the armistice it took complete charge of the Allied case. After the German surrender, the Supreme War Council, soon merging into the Supreme Council of the Peace Conference, became in effect the executive commission for the administration of European affairs.

The relation of the United States to the Supreme War Council was never clearly defined. General Bliss sat as one

[70] Bliss, in *Foreign Affairs,* December 15, 1922, pp. 16-28; Ferdinand Foch, *Memoirs,* pp. 247-279; Georges Clemenceau, *Grandeur and Misery of Victory,* pp. 27-46.

of the military advisers from the first meeting of the Council. Colonel House represented the United States at the meeting in December, 1917, and as Wilson's personal representative sat with the Prime Ministers. But after his return to the United States the President appointed no one in his place. Mr. Arthur Frazier, Counsellor to the Paris Embassy, attended meetings of the Council, an example of a Democratic Administration adopting the practise of using a " listener " which in different circumstances was to be followed by the Republicans. The President emphasized the fact that the United States was not represented on the political side, and objected warmly to the issuance of political manifestoes by the Council except when accompanied by the statement that they represented Allied and not American policy. The Allies made efforts to persuade the United States to send a political representative, especially in the spring when it was hoped that Pershing might be overruled. Wilson did not yield.[71]

Political relations between the Supreme War Council and the United States were none the less almost as close as though an American member were sitting upon it. The President received the reports of Mr. Frazier and by reason of the personal intimacy existing between himself and House was able to bring his own opinions, informally but effectively, to the notice of Balfour. When the all-important question of the armistice arose it was taken for granted that House, as Wilson's representative, would sit in the Council meetings with the Prime Ministers and the Foreign Secretaries.

[71] House to Wilson, May 20, 1918, *I.P.*, III, 447. Also Lloyd George to Reading, May 18, 1918, *I.P.*, III, 446.

5

The coördination of Allied and American effort formed the most important diplomatic problem of the later phases of the war. It was met and solved by men who for the most part were not professional diplomats. Upon its solution depended Allied victory. Only gradually was its significance really appreciated and only gradually effective steps taken. From the time of the Balfour and Viviani missions it was seen that permanent Allied missions must be established in the United States. Almost immediately the Americans insisted that if they were to supply the demand for credits and supplies, the requisitions must come in some orderly and systematic manner, and that if the American contribution were to equal what the Allies believed essential to victory there must be a correlation between demand and supply.

The Reading mission confirmed this insistence and led to the despatch of the American war mission to the Interallied Conference, where the problem of interallied coordination was finally attacked with vigor. The European Allies, who for three years had muddled along with unsystematic machinery of coöperation, under American pressure overhauled it, tightened the gears, and added the necessary new parts. The United States, under European pressure, undertook a system of state control of industry hitherto undreamed of. American representation on the interallied boards carried the essential conduits from America to Europe. Finally, under the Supreme War Council an interallied government was set up, ruling over the fortunes of the greater part of the world. Thus the war was won. It needed only an equal unity of peace policy to make of the final settlement as great a triumph.

Chapter VII

CONFLICT OF WAR AIMS

1

Every nation, once at war, pursues a double purpose so obvious that generally we do not stop to formulate it. It seeks first of all to defeat the enemy; next to capitalize the victory in political terms at the peace conference. Although the first of these purposes is primarily developed by the military arm, it lies also in the diplomatic field. President Wilson was no exception to the general rule, and at the moment when the United States entered the war, expressed this double purpose, which he never failed to keep before himself: first, the defeat of German military imperialism; second (and in time merely, not in importance), the establishment of a peace worthy of the preceding effort and sacrifice. In order to defeat Germany in the circumstances that prevailed when America entered the war, successful coördination of American contributions with those of the Allies was essential. The President appreciated the necessity clearly, and gave to those responsible for meeting it all the power and support he could. The development of a peace policy was his own particular, almost his personal, task. It was his ultimate fate to lead the nation triumphantly to complete victory in the war, and to see his plans for the peace disfigured and repudiated. Yet his contribution to the peace settlement was without question the greatest achievement of his career.

In a political sense war, at least in the past, has been simply a violent method of attaining national aims which have presumably existed in time of peace—an instrument of national policy. This was true of the World War, even though no one Government in Europe desired the general war and all of them slithered into it, propelled by circumstances greater than themselves. Once in and compelled to pay the price of war, they looked around to see what advantage they might draw in the future from the tremendous disadvantage of the present. They formulated war aims. In the case of the European nations the war aims naturally were largely in terms of territorial acquisitions or *irredenta*. What had been merely a dream of peace-time policy now became an object of immediate aspiration, attendant only upon victory. Nor was the United States exempt from the inevitable workings of this process. Brought into the war very much against the desires and hopes of the President, our Government developed a policy which, while it aimed at permanent peace, would not have been developed except for the stimulus of war.

The United States had no territorial ambitions like those of the European states. She had a very direct interest in virtual control of the Caribbean and the approaches to the Panama Canal and would doubtless insist upon whatever means might be necessary to maintain it. But in general, American policy was dominated by the desire above everything for peace, whether in Mexico, in the entire western hemisphere, or in the world. This was not so much because of the peace-loving nature of the American people, for our history has been characterized by lawlessness and violence.

Rather it resulted from the security of the United States provided by geography and the resources of its territory. Neither by fear nor by greed were the Americans impelled toward war. On the other hand the rapidly developing relations with other countries and the growth of foreign trade made a régime of international tranquillity quite as much a purpose of enlightened *Realpolitik* as an object of abstract idealism.

President Wilson's interests in foreign policy at the time of his inauguration were not lively, and his inaugural address contained no reference to anything except domestic problems. Insofar as he was compelled to face foreign questions inherited from the previous administration his attitude was primarily negative. He was anxious to avoid stressing the material strength of the United States or its commercial interests abroad. He abhorred the term " dollar diplomacy." " We can afford to exercise the self-restraint," he said, " of a really great nation which realizes its own strength and scorns to misuse it." [1] He reversed the Republican policy of coöperation with European nations in the Far Eastern consortium. He was determined to repeal the Panama Tolls exemption. At Mobile on October 27, 1913, he set forth plainly a self-denying declaration: the United States would never acquire another square inch of territory at the expense of a neighbor. There was implicit in his tone the promise that the smaller nations of the Americas might rest secure in the conviction that not merely their

[1] Address to Congress, August 27, 1913, *Congressional Record,* 63rd Congress, 1st Session, Vol. 50, 3803-3804.

territory but their " policy " should be free from the domination of the United States.[2]

There was in this attitude the germ of a positive policy. It was inspired not by weakness but by the desire to live and let live. Mutual understanding and confidence would be the foundation of mutual and active coöperation. To the conception of such a development Wilson soon advanced. During the early months of his administration he developed confidential negotiations with the British regarding the Tolls controversy and the Mexican imbroglio. The satisfactory issue of those negotiations undoubtedly impressed the President with the possibilities that might result from the frank and friendly coöperation of the more powerful nations. He was influenced to some extent by Ambassador Page, who constantly stressed the service to the world that could be rendered by an intimate understanding between Great Britain and the United States:

" It is a time," wrote the Ambassador, " for some great constructive, forward idea—an idea for action. If the great world forces could, by fortunate events and fortunate combinations, be united and led to clean up the tropics, the great armies might gradually become sanitary police, as in Panama, and finally gradually forget the fighting idea and at last dissolve." [3]

Wilson was much more deeply influenced by House, who not merely supported with vigor the ideas of Page but insisted that Germany must be brought into the Anglo-American understanding. German coöperation was essential not only because of her material strength and influence,

[2] Baker and Dodd, *The Public Papers of Woodrow Wilson*, I, 64-69.

[3] Page to House, August 28, 1913, *I.P.*, I, 240-241.

but because the plan offered a means of liquidating the increasing mutual distrust of Triple Alliance and Triple Entente. When Sir William Tyrrell, Grey's secretary, came to Washington in December, 1913, to discuss Panama Tolls, the possibility of an understanding among Great Britain, Germany, France, and the United States that might clear away misunderstanding and lead to a limitation of armament was frankly discussed. Tyrrell encouraged the attempt and gave assurance "that England would coöperate [in limitation of armament] with Germany cordially, and had been ready to do so for a long time." Wilson was so far impressed with the possibilities inherent in the situation that he sent House abroad in the spring of 1914, to lay the suggestion before the Kaiser and the British Government.[4]

The outbreak of the World War put an end, for the moment, to any such plan. Perhaps it would have been destined to failure in any case. But it indicates how far and rapidly President Wilson's mind had travelled. His representative had offered not, indeed, an alliance, but at any rate the cordial coöperation of the United States with European Powers in an effort to stabilize and organize international relations. He suggested a complete rupture with tradition; not the entrance of the United States into the European political system, but the creation of a new world system in which the United States would take active part.

Not less significant in the evolution of Wilson's attitude toward a positive American policy was the drafting of the so-called Pan-American Pact in the autumn of 1914. The effect of the Mobile speech of 1913 had been apparent in

[4] House Diary, December 2, 1913, *I.P.,* I, 243.

the growth of cordial feeling toward the American government in South American countries. The willingness of the President to accept the A. B. C. mediation in the dispute with Mexico seemed an earnest of his sincerity. Circumstances were favorable for developing a permanent understanding among the states of North and South America. Colonel House was convinced that the situation was ripe for an enlargement of the Monroe Doctrine, which the South American States regarded as a humiliating, unilateral anachronism, into a veritable league for security and peace of all American states. Wilson accepted House's plan for a Pan-American Pact enthusiastically and on December 16, 1914, went so far as to sketch the essential articles of an agreement or covenant. The first article carried the essence of the plan and when Wilson wrote it he wrote the birth-certificate of Article X of the League of Nations: " Mutual guarantees of political independence under Republican form of government and mutual guarantees of territorial integrity." [5] During the following months the plan was actively discussed with the Ambassadors of the A. B. C. Powers, who received it at first with enthusiasm. Difficulties and delays followed until the United States was caught in the World War and entered into plans for a larger combination.[6]

[5] House Diary, December 16, 1914, *I.P.,* I, 209-210. Cf. Art. X of the League Covenant: " The members of the League undertake to respect and preserve as against external aggression the territorial integrity and existing political independence of all members of the League. . . ."

[6] *I.P.,* II, 210-234.

But the historical importance of the draft Pan-American Pact must be emphasized. It familiarized the mind of President Wilson with the idea of active American coöperation in a scheme of international organization. What he considered in the spring of 1914, when he sent House to Europe, was a limited coöperation with the European States, aimed primarily at a limited objective, naval and military disarmament. The Pan-American Pact, limited geographically to American States, was far broader in its political scope and aimed at a permanent and organized system of coöperation for the preservation of peace and security. When these two ideas were fused in Wilson's mind, the result was a policy aiming at the organization of all the states of the world in a system of security and peace such as at first he planned simply for the Americas.

The factor which forced this conclusion upon Wilson was his growing fear that the United States would be compelled to enter the war. He was determined that if we became involved America's effort should be based upon a broader principle than the defense of purely national rights. Equally important was his hope that by putting forward a programme of international security he might find means to facilitate effective mediation between the belligerents. As early as the autumn of 1915 Wilson was beginning to work on the idea of a real league of nations. He was stimulated, evidently, far more by the letters of Sir Edward Grey than by the movement in the United States sponsored by the League to Enforce Peace. On November 12, 1915, he referred to a paragraph of a letter from Grey, suggesting that the President might propose a league the members of

which would bind themselves to side against any Power
which broke a treaty or refused in case of dispute to adopt
some other method of settlement than that of war. "I think
the principle quoted from his letter of September 22," wrote
Wilson, "contains the *necessary* programme."[7] A month
later, in sending House abroad to discuss the possibility of
American intervention he insisted that America was not
interested in the territorial questions of Europe but in the
guarantees of permanent peace. "The only guarantees that
any rational man could accept, are (a) military and naval
disarmament and (b) a league of nations to secure each
nation against aggression and maintain the absolute freedom
of the seas."[8]

Thus before the end of the year 1915 Wilson contemplated American participation in a league of nations.
Of this he gave formal indication to the Allies on January 9,
1916, cabling to House: "Would be glad if you would
convey my assurance that I shall be willing and glad when
the opportunity comes to coöperate in a policy seeking to
bring about and maintain peace among civilized nations."[9]
During the spring there were indications in his public
speeches of his increasing sense of America's interest in international affairs. "America can not be an ostrich with its head
in the sand. America can not shut itself out from the rest of
the world."[10] Finally on May 27, 1916, came his public an-

[7] Wilson to House, November 12, 1915, Y.H.C.; Grey to House,
September 15, 1915, *I.P.*, II, 89.

[8] Wilson to House, December 24, 1915, Y.H.C.

[9] Wilson to House, January 9, 1916, Y.H.C.

[10] Address at Des Moines, February 1, 1916, Baker and Dodd,
op. cit., II, 73. Cf. "America is now going to be called out into

nouncement of an international policy: "We are participants whether we would or not, in the life of the world. . . . We are partners with the rest." The speech culminated in the demand for a league to preserve peace, the very words suggesting a direct descent from the Pan-American Pact: "a virtual guarantee of territorial integrity and political independence."[11]

This speech was conceived as part of the plan of American armed mediation, an invitation to the Allies to accept Wilson's intervention. At the time that he made it the possibility of our entering the war was in the back of his mind. Thus almost a year previous to the entrance of the United States into the war, the President had publicly outlined certain principles which he believed would serve to justify American participation in world affairs. These he elaborated in his speech of January 22, 1917, when he set forth the broad terms of a desirable peace, insisted upon the principle of the Monroe Doctrine for the entire world, and demanded a concert of Powers capable of maintaining international tranquillity and the rights of small nations.[12]

These principles Wilson took for his text on April 2, 1917, in asking Congress to declare that a state of war existed with Germany. It is true that he now declared that the German imperial government must be defeated. It was no longer to be a "peace without victory." But the elevated purpose of the war and final utilization of the victory must

---

an international position such as she has never occupied before," Address at St. Louis, February 3, 1916, *ibid.*, II, 117.

[11] Speech of May 27, 1916, Baker and Dodd, *op. cit.*, II, 184-188.

[12] *Senate Document,* 685, Sixty-fourth Congress, 2nd Session.

18

not be forgotten in the heat of the struggle and the ideals of peace time must be kept alive:

" Our object now, as then, is to vindicate the principles of peace and justice in the life of the world as against selfish and autocratic power and to set up amongst the really free and self-governed nations of the world such a concert of purpose and of action as will henceforth ensure the observance of those principles." [13]

2

The literary quality of Wilson's speeches on war aims was much finer than anything delivered in any of the European belligerent countries. This may have proceeded in part from his native gifts and acquired powers, for he was one of the really great orators of the half-century following the death of John Bright. It also resulted from the fact that he believed intensely in what he said. His phrases rang with passionate conviction. He was certain not merely of the possibility but of the necessity of what he advocated. " How else [than by a League] " he wrote privately in May, 1916, " can we secure the deliberate consideration of all situations that may threaten war and lay a foundation for the concerted action of nations against unjustifiable breaches of the peace of the world? " [14]

In Allied countries a great many speeches on war aims were delivered and in almost all of them, as in all the belligerent nations, the war was set forth as a crusade for justice. The attack upon Serbia by Austria-Hungary and the violation of the neutrality of Belgium by Germany, per-

[13] *F.R., 1917, Suppl. 1,* 195-205.
[14] Wilson to House, May 18, 1916, Y.H.C.

mitted the Allies to insist that they were fighting for the rights of small nations and for the sanctity of treaties. It need not be assumed that then or ever was there in the consciousness of the Allied statesmen any sense of insincerity. They also were passionately convinced that theirs was the cause of justice and of permanent peace.

But their practical interpretation of an abstract programme of peace and justice was bound to be different from that of Wilson. They formed a coalition, each state certain to frame its own interpretation of such a programme. For a variety of reasons they had not settled upon a definite final scheme, expressing the common desire. Their expressions must perforce be couched in vague terms, except for such points as the restoration of Belgium. Unlike the United States, each nation, with the exception of Great Britain, had clear territorial aspirations. The extent of these aspirations varied with the chances of complete victory. They might or might not conflict with the aspirations of another ally or with the abstract principles of " justice " that formed the grist of public speeches. In any event, lest they be accused of waging a war of annexations, they did not dare publish them. From such territorial aspirations America was freed by the fact of geographical position.

The diplomats of the Entente were impelled toward a crystallization of war aims, partly because it was their natural function to be ready when peace should come (and who could tell when it might come?), to produce a programme capitalizing in the national interest the prospective victory. These war aims were determined by policy resting upon historical tradition, conditions of security, economic advantage. They were also compelled to accept as part of their programme the war aims of allies or prospective allies. It was the diplomats' business to aid the military by securing new friends or solidifying the enthusiasm of old. Their only effective means of pressure when they negotiated with a neutral Power that was considering the possibility of entering the Alliance, was a promise that the aspirations of that Power should be satisfied. Thus it happened that as neutrals entered the Alliance a whole string of promises had to be made and a new quota of war aims added. Each Power of the Alliance had its major war aims, the points of peculiar interest to itself, and its minor war aims, the points upon which it had promised help to an Ally. The major war aims of one Power became the minor aims of its Ally. Contradictions and inconsistencies could not be avoided.

This process was illustrated by the negotiations between the original Allies and Italy which culminated with the entrance of the latter into the war in May, 1915. Italy had been offered partial satisfaction of her territorial ambitions by Austria-Hungary if she would remain neutral. She was offered far wider territories (at the expense of Austria), and control of the northern Adriatic, by the Allies if she would join them. The arrangement with the Allies was consummated by the Treaty of London, April 26, 1915. Incidentally the interests of the Serbs, for and with whom the Allies were fighting, were seriously jeopardized by the treaty and they were told nothing of it. Similarly in August, 1916, after long hesitations, Rumania entered the war on the side of the Allies. But she did so only after receiving in the Treaty of Bucharest, which also was kept secret, promises of extensive territories to fulfil her national ambitions, again at the expense of Austria-Hungary, an enemy, as well as at that of Serbia, a friend.

The original Allies did not fail to consider their own interests. Russia, which would not have embarked upon war to acquire control of the Straits, once the war started was loath to lose the opportunity of securing them. By the end of 1914 she intimated to France and Great Britain that their formal approval of this aspiration was desired. It was at the moment of the Dardanelles expedition; Russia's enthusiastic coöperation and the solidity of the alliance was of the first importance. In March, 1915, the claim was approved. A year later an exchange of letters, generally called the Sykes-Picot Treaty, sanctioned the further Russian claim to extension of territory into northern Asia Minor, the French claim to control of Syria, and the British claim to control of Mesopotamia. In the spring and summer of 1917, just as the United States was entering the war, Italian claims to a portion of the old Turkish Empire, which had been reserved in the Treaty of London, were roughly defined in the Treaty of Saint Jean de Maurienne. In the meantime, by an exchange of letters, Japan was given a free hand in the ultimate fate of Shantung and a promise of the German colonies of the eastern seas north of the equator. Less formal, but actually as binding, was the understanding that France should recover Alsace-Lorraine. Finally France and Russia informally agreed that each should have a free hand in disposing of German territories bordering the frontier of each.

Such were the so-called "secret treaties," which the objective observer is apt to regard as representing much more accurately the war aims of the Allies than the rather indefinite phrases of their public speeches. There was nothing so innately evil in them as some American critics have believed. They were the result of a natural, perhaps an inevitable, process and one followed by Germany in acquiring the military assistance of Turkey and Bulgaria. They were in several cases negotiated by so high-minded a statesman as Sir Edward Grey. It is true that he confessed his dislike for such diplomatic processes, but he asserted with reasonably complete justification that in the circumstances of war they were necessary.[15] To secure the defeat of the enemy in this desperate struggle any and every available tool must be used.

Whatever the justification of the secret treaties, it may be seriously questioned whether the sum total of their terms, after inconsistencies had been ironed out, did not contradict the public declarations of the Allies. It is certain that their general trend was contrary in spirit to, and many of their details subversive of the principles laid down by President Wilson. Sooner or later the conflict between the war aims of the United States and those of the Allies must be recognized and fought out or compromised.

3

President Wilson knew the general sense of Allied war aims, even if he did not keep in his mind the details of the different treaties. In his testimony before the Senate Foreign Relations Committee, August 19, 1919, after he returned from Paris, the President stated that he was first informed of the secret treaties as a whole at the Peace Con-

[15] *Grey,* II, 166.

ference: " The whole series of understandings was disclosed to me for the first time then." Questioned as to the promises made to Italy and Rumania and the agreements regarding the partition of Asiatic Turkey, he was definite in his disclaimer of any knowledge previous to his trip to Paris.[16]

Colonel House believes that in his testimony the President was confused and quite evidently forgot the facts. " There was nothing to be gained by a misstatement, and it is clear to me that he spoke from conviction." [17] Wilson was certainly informed of the secret treaties. The fact is vouched for by Balfour, and in a letter of January 30, 1918, addressed by Balfour directly to Wilson, the then British Foreign Secretary explained to the President the circumstances in which the Treaty of London had been drafted and attempted some justification of it. The letter was written in response to a hint from the President to Wiseman that he would like Balfour's views on the treaty.[18] An equally clear indication of Wilson's knowledge of another aspect of the secret treaties is found in his own cable of December 1, 1917, in which he makes reference to plans " for divisions of territory such as have been contemplated in Asia Minor." [19]

[16] *Senate Document* 106, Sixty-sixth Congress, 1st Session.
[17] Colonel House to C. S., April 9, 1928, *I.P.,* III, 62.
[18] Balfour to Wilson, January 30, 1918. Cf. Balfour to House, July 17, 1922, Y.H.C.: " He [Mr. R. S. Baker] is certainly wrong in his statement that Mr. Wilson was kept in ignorance by me of the secret treaties, an error which I feel the more acutely, because it is a calumny which, if I remember rightly, I have already publicly contradicted."
[19] Wilson to House, December 1, 1917, *F.R., 1917, Suppl. 2,* I, 331.

Other evidence is to be found in House's diary, where he sets forth a long discussion of the treaties with Balfour, on April 28, 1917, during the latter's visit to Washington, and records a conversation *à trois* the following evening, when Balfour and House joined Wilson for dinner. " The ground we covered was exactly the same as Balfour and I had covered." Four days before Wilson had himself remarked, " it would be a pity to have Balfour go home without a discussion of the subject." [20] The only issues of territorial importance that were not touched in the conference were the disposition of the German colonies and the settlement in the Far East. The discussion with the President on April 29 lasted from eight until half-past ten. It is thus clear that even though nothing was said about promises to Japan, Wilson was fully informed of the character of the Allied war aims and its contradiction of his own programme. References to the subject in his own letters bear witness to his keen realization of that contradiction. On July 21, 1917, he wrote very plainly: " Our real peace terms—those upon which we shall undoubtedly insist, are not now acceptable to either France or Italy (leaving Great Britain for the moment out of consideration)." [21]

On the other hand, at the moment of American entrance into the war, Wilson was not in a position to attempt any protest against the secret treaties nor any compromise with the Allies in the matter of war aims. He has been strongly criticized as a catspaw of Allied policy; some critics have argued that he should have come to an understanding with

[20] House Diary, April 26, 28, 30, 1917, *I.P.*, III, 43-49.
[21] Wilson to House, July 21, 1917, Y.H.C.

the Allies before he committed the nation to war. But this was quite obviously impracticable. The United States had its own quarrel with Germany, wished to make war as efficiently as possible, and found the most efficient method in close military coöperation with the Allies.

" Could any satisfactory agreement have been reached? " writes Colonel House. " I doubt it. Meanwhile, Germany would have sunk our ships and we should have been standing idly by, waiting for a termination of negotiations regarding the secret treaties. As it was, the United States entered the war promptly and efficiently, but as an associate Power, uncommitted to any agreements made between the Allies. Our hands were untied and we were free to do as we would at the peace table. If any criticism is to be made, should it not be of what we failed to do there, and not what we failed to do before we entered the war? " [22]

Wilson himself was convinced of the inadvisability of raising with the Allies any such contentious topic as war aims, at a moment when complete unity of military purpose was vital. He recognized the pitfalls attending public discussion of war aims and referred to " grave possibilities of danger " in the plans suggested for a debate between the New York *World* and the *Berliner Tageblatt* on war aims. He puzzled over the difficulties of saying what he wanted to say without raising an issue. " How shall I say it," he wrote previous to his Flag Day speech of June 14, 1917, " without seeming directly to contradict Cecil and Ribot if I am to add, as I feel that I must, the terms (in general phrase, as in the address to the Senate) upon which we in this

[22] House to C. S., April 9, 1928, *I.P.,* III, 62-63.

country think that a settlement should be made when we win?" [23] Six weeks later he wrote:

"*England and France have not the same views with regard to peace that we have by any means.* When the war is over we can force them to our way of thinking, because by that time they will among other things be financially in our hands; but we cannot force them now, and any attempt to speak for them or to our common mind would bring on disagreements which would inevitably come to the surface in public and rob the whole thing of its effect. I saw all this too plainly in a conversation with Viviani." [24]

Hence the President was careful to avoid speaking for the Allies and careful always to refer to the United States not as an "allied" but as an "associated" power. The expression occurs, apparently for the first time, in a letter of June 15, referring to the Flag Day speech: "I do not think that it contains anything to which our Associates in the war (so I will call them) could object." [25]

Another reason for avoiding, at the moment, any conflict with the Allies over war aims lay in the propagandist value of Wilson's speeches. A united front was essential in order to carry through the policy of weakening German will to continue the war by driving a wedge between German Government and people. This policy had been attempted by the Allies and was taken up by Wilson, with ultimate effects of the first importance. Very quickly the speeches of the President became the text of Allied propaganda in the Central Powers. Coördination of war aims thus seemed as important as coördination of material effort;

[23] Wilson to House, June 1, July 21, 1917, Y.H.C.
[24] Wilson to House, July 21, 1917, Y.H.C. Italics are Wilson's.
[25] Wilson to House, June 15, 1917, Y.H.C.

so far as possible, differences between the United States and the Allies must be avoided.

In his first war speech, April 2, Wilson indicated his intention of appealing over the head of the German Government to the people. " We have no quarrel," he declared, " with the German people. We have no feeling towards them but one of sympathy and friendship." He insistently sounded the note that the war was one of liberations of peoples, " the German people included," from the military masters whom they might and must renounce if they wished peace. House constantly encouraged Wilson to develop this appeal. " Imperial Germany should be broken down within as well as from without," he wrote to Wilson on May 30.[26] " Give the German liberals every possible encouragement so they can tell the German people that ' here is your immediate chance for peace because the offer comes from your enemies, who will treat with you at any time you are in condition to express your thoughts through a representative government. On the other hand, the present government is offering you peace through conquest, which of necessity has all the elements of chance and cannot be relied upon.' "[27]

There were thus two aspects of Wilson's speeches on war aims. The one was ultimate and constructive, designed to provide a charter for a new and better world order; in the end it would be subject to Allied criticism, perhaps hostility. The other was immediate and destructive, designed to stimulate German discontent with the German Government, a moral weapon of war against the enemy.

[26] House to Wilson, May 30, 1917, *I.P.,* III, 133.
[27] House Diary, May 19, 1917, *I.P.,* III, 132.

Two clear opportunities were given the President during the summer of 1917 to develop the destructive factors in his policy. The first was on Flag Day, June 14. He summarized the main points of his speech in a letter written just as he began the draft:

" I should like to say in substance just what you say in your letter," he wrote House, " ' that the military masters of Germany have no intention of making peace upon any other basis than that of conquest,' that they already hold Middle Europe from Bruges to Constantinople,[28] that Belgium, Poland, Austria-Hungary, European Turkey, and a portion of the Balkan States are completely in their power, and that they intend that they shall remain so, meaning to take a gambler's chance, stand pat if they win, yield a parliamentary government if they lose." [29]

Such was the central theme of the speech of June 14, delivered, as Wilson wrote, " in a downpour of rain to a patient audience standing in the wet under dripping umbrellas." [30] With the same emphasis that he used to attack the German Government, the President appealed to the people: " We are not the enemies of the German people. . . . They did not originate or desire this hideous war . . . we are vaguely conscious that we are fighting their cause, as they will some day see it, as well as our own. They are themselves in the grip of the same sinister power that has now at last stretched its ugly talons out and drawn blood from us." The speech won tremendous applause, not merely because of the vitriolic attack upon the Imperial Government

[28] In the speech this became " From Hamburg to the Persian Gulf the net is spread."

[29] Wilson to House, June 1, 1917, Y.H.C.

[30] Wilson to House, June 15, 1917, Y.H.C.

but because of the implication that Wilson would not make peace with that Government. It has little significance in the development of his ultimate peace programme, but it is important as foreshadowing exactly the line he was to take in the armistice negotiations. "If they fail," Wilson concluded, referred to the existing German Government, "the world may unite for peace and Germany may be of the union." [31]

No direct result of this speech was apparent in Germany, but very shortly a second opportunity was given Wilson to emphasize his theme of "war on the German Government, peace with the German people." During the spring suggestions of a peace of compromise had come from Austria. They were stimulated by the Russian demand for a peace without annexations or indemnities and enforced by the conviction that the Hapsburg Monarchy could be saved by an early peace. "Another winter campaign," wrote the Foreign Minister, Count Czernin, "would be absolutely out of the question . . . in the late summer or in the autumn an end must be put to the war at all costs." [32] In Germany itself, a demand for a compromise peace was formulated and put forward in the Reichstag, under the leadership of the Centrist Erzberger who was in touch with Czernin and hoped to prepare the way for mediation by the Pope. The Erzberger *bloc* was able to muster enough votes to carry, on July 19, a resolution that might have formed the basis of a peace of reconciliation: "With such a peace," the resolution declared, "forced acquisitions of territories, forced requisi-

[31] Text of speech of June 14, *F.R., 1917, Suppl. 2,* I, 96-100.
[32] Ottokar Czernin, *In the World War,* p. 164.

tions and political, economic, or financial oppressions are inconsistent." [33]

The terms of the Reichstag resolution were not far in principle from Wilson's policy. But they would by no means have satisfied France, and the German military leaders would not hear of them.

" The future will show," writes Czernin, " what superhuman efforts we have made to induce Germany to give way. That all proved fruitless was not the fault of the German people, nor was it, in my opinion, the fault of the German Emperor, but that of the leaders of the German military party, which had attained such enormous power in the country. Everyone in the Wilhelmstrasse, from Bethmann to Kühlmann, wanted peace; but they could not get it simply because the military party got rid of everyone who ventured to act otherwise than as they wished." [34]

Czernin's assertion seems justified by the event. No attention was paid by the German military leaders to the Reichstag vote. Bethmann was forced out of the Chancellorship, and his successor, Michaelis, accepting the domination of the army group refused to permit any interference with high policy by the Reichstag. Ludendorff's power was greatly enhanced. [35]

The attitude of the German military party appeared to justify Wilson's refusal to discuss peace with them or with any but a representative German Government. He was able to reiterate this determination when, early in August, the Pope, who was in touch with the Austrian and the German

[33] Erzberger, *Erlebnisse,* pp. 251 ff.; Stovall to Lansing, July 20, 1917, *F.R., 1917, Suppl. 2,* I, 139; Payer, *Von Bethmann bis Ebert,* pp. 23-38.

[34] Czernin, *op. cit.,* p. 362.

[35] Ludendorff, *The General Staff,* II, 446-476.

Centrist movement for peace, issued an appeal to all the belligerents, calling for a settlement based upon the principles of complete restoration of occupied territory, disarmament, and international arbitration.[36]

Given the firmness of the Allies on the one hand and of the German Government on the other, against any peace of compromise, the chance of capitalizing the Pope's appeal so as actually to end the war was practically non-existent. But it provided an opportunity for a restatement of Wilson's position, and also some danger of diplomatic misunderstanding between Wilson and the Allies. The latter were troubled. They may have feared that a conciliatory reply from Wilson would weaken the war spirit in Allied countries. They made a discreet suggestion that he let them know what he was going to say before he said it.[37]

Wilson was rather bellicose, not that his feelings were hurt by the suggestion that the Pope might assume the rôle of mediator but because of his growing conviction, partly intellectual in origin, partly emotional, that no lasting peace could be made with the existing Government of Germany. "I do not know," he wrote, "that I shall make any reply at all to the Pope's proposals, but I am glad to let Mr. Balfour know what it would be were I to make one." He then outlined his objections to the conditions suggested. Although recognizing the lofty purpose of the Pope and expressing general sympathy with his desire to end the war, he insisted that there was no indication that the terms he

[36] F.R., 1917, Suppl. 2, I, 161 ff.; Czernin, op. cit., pp. 146-162; Valentin, Deutschlands Aussenpolitik, pp. 334, 336; Erzberger, op. cit., pp. 269 ff.

[37] Wiseman to House, August 11, 1917; House to Wilson, August 13, 15, 1917, Y.H.C.

put forward would meet the views of any of the belligerents; discussion would be " a blind adventure." The terms,
in fact, constituted no settlement but merely a return to
the *status quo ante* and would leave affairs in the same condition that had originally led to war.

The great objection which the President stressed, was that
" the absolute disregard alike of all formal obligations of
treaty and all accepted principles of international law which
the autocratic régime still dominant in Germany has shown
in the whole action of this war," forbade the possibility of
accepting any assurances from that Government:

" The present German Imperial Government is morally
bankrupt; no one will accept or credit its pledges; and the
world will be upon quicksand in regard to all international
covenants which include Germany until it can believe that
it is dealing with a responsible government. I see no other
possible answer."

The sincerity of Wilson's feeling is indicated by the spon-
taneity of the language: " I am rushing this through my
typewriter," he added " (and through my mind too, for
that matter), on a desperately busy day, and may not have
expressed my conclusions very happily, but I am in no uncertainty as to their substance." [38]

Within the week Wilson had decided to make a public
reply to the Pope in the sense he had sketched and completed a first draft. " It should be as brief as possible. I
center it, therefore, on one point: That we cannot take the
word of the present rulers of Germany for anything." He
continued, however, to reiterate his appeal to the German
people and emphasized the assurance that the political or

[38] Wilson to House, August 16, 1917, Y.H.C.

economic annihilation of a liberalized Germany was not desired. He even disavowed explicitly threats made in certain Allied quarters of waging an economic war against Germany after the peace. " Punitive damages," he wrote, " the dismemberment of empires, the establishment of selfish and exclusive economic leagues, we deem childish." [39] Again he was restrained by the Allies' attitude from going far into the positive aspects of his peace programme. " I have not thought it wise to say more or to be more specific because it might provoke dissenting voices from France or Italy." [40] As it was, he did not discuss the content of the speech with any of them and postponed sending them copies until it was too late to make changes.

" I did not dare submit it to our associates across the sea more than twenty-four hours before I made it public. I felt morally certain that they would wish changes which I could not make. I was confirmed in that view when Jusserand the next day went up in the air because it seemed to exclude economic punishment of Germany after the war. It will work out this way as well as any. The differences of opinion will be less embarrassing now than they would have been if I had invited them beforehand." [41]

4

Avoidance of serious misunderstanding with the Allies was thus, until the autumn of 1917, secured by an emphasis upon the destructive aspect of Wilson's policy, the diplo-

[39] The word " childish " on House's suggestion, he changed to " inexpedient " in the speech as delivered, House to Wilson, August 25, 1917, *I.P.,* III, 164. Text of speech in *F.R., 1917, Suppl. 2,* I, 178-179.

[40] Wilson to House, August 22, 1917, Y.H.C.

[41] Wilson to House, September 2, 1917, Y.H.C.

19

matic attack upon Germany: a weapon of war and not a programme for peace except in the negative and most general
sense. He was estopped from active prosecution of a positive war aims policy lest trouble with the Allies should result. But it was certain that the formulation of a reasonably
definite positive policy could not long be postponed. President Wilson seems to have reached this conclusion at the
moment when he faced the difficult problem of answering
the Pope's peace note without offense to the Allies. At all
events, in the same letter in which he reported that the
French Ambassador "went up in the air," because of
differences of opinion, he suggested to Colonel House that
the time had come to formulate carefully and in detail
America's war aims.

The President realized that such formulation would throw
into high light the aspects of the settlement which divided
America from the Allies. He thought of the conflict with
their war aims as a judicial conflict, referred to the " litigants," but it was to be none the less a conflict:

" I am beginning to think," he wrote, " that we ought to go
systematically to work to ascertain as fully and precisely as
possible just what the several parties to this war on our
side of it will be inclined to insist upon, as part of the final
peace arrangement, in order that we may formulate our own
position either for or against them and begin to gather the
influences we wish to employ—or at least, ascertain what
influence we can use; in brief, prepare our case with a full
knowledge of all the litigants." [42]

Thus originated the Inquiry, the special American organization formed to define American war aims. It was designed
not merely to formulate the American case and crystallize

[42] Wilson to House, September 2, 1917, Y.H.C.

American policies, but also to study the probable policies of
the Allies and prepare to meet them where they conflicted
with American policy. Wilson's purpose was stimulated by
the news that had come to him that the other Governments
were taking steps to " get their cases ready and their pipes
laid." It was natural that the President should ask Colonel
House to take charge of organizing a staff for this purpose, partly because in matters of foreign policy he and
House worked as partners, partly because House more than
anyone else was in close touch with Allied leaders and was
obviously qualified to be the one to work out the detailed
aspects of the final settlement with them.

The general political situation forbade the maintenance
by the Allies of a purely negative attitude on war aims.
The call to the Socialists' Congress at Stockholm in July
had disturbed labour circles in England and France. The
Russian Revolution, with the resulting demand for a peace
of compromise, tended to force the Allies to come out into
the open in order to justify the continuation of a bloody
and indecisive war by a more specific statement of war aims.
As yet no adequate comment, or at least no comment satisfactory to Russia, had been made to the Russian note of
May 1, suggesting a repudiation of aggressive war aims;
far less to the suggestion of the Petrograd Soviet: " Peace
without annexations or indemnities, on the basis of the self-
determination of peoples." [43] In November the Kerensky

[43] *Izvestia*, May 15, 1917, cited in *Russian-American Relations,*
17; *F.R., 1917, Suppl. 2*, I, 53, 71; see also *F.R., 1918, Russia,*
I, 86 ff. President Wilson replied sympathetically to the Russians
on May 22 but had insisted that " wrongs must first be righted
and then adequate safeguards must be created to prevent their
being committed again."

Government was overthrown and power seized by Lenin and Trotsky. The Bolsheviks proposed an immediate armistice and on November 20 addressed a formal request to the Allied Ambassadors in Petrograd to consider immediate peace negotiations.[44]

The Bolshevist demand for peace came precisely at the moment of the convening of the Interallied Conference in Paris. Gathered together to discuss the coördination of military and economic efforts, the Allied statesmen were forced to consider this diplomatic problem. The defection of Russia would have tremendous military effects. Could diplomacy prevent it? If not, could diplomacy take any steps or make any statements that might offset the moral effects of the Bolshevist appeal upon labor in England and France?

Wilson and House, both of whom felt in the spring that any attempt to coördinate war aims would be unwise, were now convinced that circumstances compelled it. Some answer must be given to Russia and it must be other than purely negative. The Russian Ambassador in Paris, not representing the new Government but cognizant of the situation, urged a joint Allied statement. In England Lord Lansdowne had pleaded for a statement that the Allies would negotiate with Germany on the basis of certain guarantees.[45] In France Briand, not then in office, argued that Germany had shown greater intelligence than the Allies by constantly keeping before her people the one idea that she was fighting to prevent her economic extinction and to preserve her territory

[44] Francis to Lansing, November 22, 1918, *F.R., 1918, Russia,* I, 244.

[45] In the London *Daily Telegraph,* November 29, 1917. See Page to Lansing, November 30, 1917, *F.R., 1917, Suppl. 2,* I, 327.

from dismemberment. She had neglected no opportunity to impress upon her people that they must continue to fight, because if the Allies were successful the condition of the German people would become one of abject servitude. The Allies ought to formulate their war aims in concrete form, said Briand, so that they could say to Germany: " Here are our war aims, this is what we are fighting for; if you are willing to accept them we will have peace to-morrow." [46]

But the heads of the Allied Governments found it impossible to frame a statement of any diplomatic value upon which they could agree. Mr. Lloyd George was committed too far to the British Conservatives to support any plan for a liberal restatement of war aims in the unsympathetic atmosphere of Paris. Clemenceau, primarily interested in reviving the drooping spirit of the French army, feared lest any manifesto might be regarded as a suggestion of defeatism. The Italians refused to abate a jot of their territorial claims.

House's efforts to secure agreement upon even the mildest manifesto were fruitless. On November 30 he submitted for Wilson's approval the following: " The Allies and the United States declare that they are not waging war for the purpose of aggression or indemnity. The sacrifices they are making are in order that militarism shall not continue to cast its shadow over the world, and that nations shall have the right to lead their lives in the way that seems to them best for the development of their general welfare." [47]

[46] House-Briand conference, House Diary, December 3, 1917, I.P., III, 279-280.

[47] House to Wilson, November 30, 1917, I.P., III, 282.

Wilson cabled immediate approval:

" The resolution you suggest is entirely in line with my thought and has my approval. You will realize how unfortunate it would be for the conference to discuss peace terms in a spirit antagonistic to my January address to the Senate.[48] Our people and Congress will not fight for any selfish aim on the part of any belligerent, with the possible exception of Alsace-Lorraine, least of all for divisions of territory such as have been contemplated in Asia Minor. I think it will be obvious to all that it would be a fatal mistake to cool the ardor of America." [49]

No action was taken on the American resolution. " England passively was willing," reported House to the President, " France indifferently against it, Italy actively so. They were all willing to embody what I suggested if certain additions were made to which I could not agree. It was decided finally that each Power should send its own answer to its Ambassador at Petrograd." [50]

5

From the failure of the Interallied Conference to agree upon a restatement of war aims resulted the Fourteen Points. At the very moment of the decision not to issue a joint declaration, House cabled Wilson urging him to postpone any statement he planned to make on foreign affairs, until he had a direct personal report of conditions in Europe. " I

[48] January 22, 1917, the " peace without victory " speech. It is important to note that even after entering the war Wilson on various occasions harks back to this speech as expressive of the essence of his policy. Cf. his letter to House of June 1, 1917, *supra*, p. 269.

[49] Wilson to House, December 1, 1917, *F.R., 1917, Suppl. 2*, I, 331.

[50] House to Wilson, December 2, 1917, *I.P.*, III, 285.

sent this cable to the President," House endorsed on the copy, " because I had in mind his making a statement giving our war aims. I tried to get this done at Paris, but failed. The next best thing was for the President to do it." [51] Like Wilson, House was bitterly disappointed by the unwillingness of Allied leaders at this time to adopt and express publicly a liberal policy that would guarantee a peace of reconstruction rather than one of conquest. Referring to Clemenceau's request that he close the Interallied Conference with a short speech, House confided to his diary:

" I wish I could say what I would really like to say, but with the reactionary crowd I find here I do not dare to do so. More would be lost than could be gained. . . . I have determined to wait until my return and ask the President to say with all the authority back of him what ought to be said at this time." [52]

President Wilson, the moment he read the written and listened to the oral reports of the American war mission, decided that something must be done to correct the failure of the Interallied Conference to meet the diplomatic issue. The Bolsheviks were actively negotiating for a separate peace. Germany must not be permitted to pose as the victim of Allied imperialist aspirations. On December 13, the *Manchester Guardian* published the essential texts of the secret treaties which the Bolsheviks had found in the Russian Foreign Office and released. Some corrective was necessary to justify Allied sacrifices in the war and to maintain the enthusiasm of liberal and labor circles. If in the process

[51] House to Wilson, December 1, 1917, *I.P.,* III, 286.

[52] House Diary, December 2, 3, 1917, Y.H.C.; printed in part in *I.P.,* III, 291.

and because of their increasing dependence upon the United States the Allies could be pledged to support Wilson's principles, a double advantage would be gained.

It has been suggested that the Fourteen Points resulted from Wilson's refusal to let anyone but himself state the purposes of the war.[53] The suggestion gives a false impression of the situation. It is true that Wilson did not trust the French and the British to formulate an adequate counter to the Russian proposals in a liberal sense. " I should be afraid of the formulating," he wrote on January 2, 1918.[54] But he would have preferred a joint Allied-American statement. It was only after the failure of the Interallied Conference to produce one that he tried his own hand.

The Fourteen Points speech was designed primarily as a weapon of war diplomacy, a manifesto framed with the Russian and the labor situations primarily in mind, a " counter," as Wilson expressed it, to proposals for what he regarded as an unsatisfactory peace, as illustrated by the Russian-German negotiations. It was also a positive platform for a satisfactory peace, a charter of the new international organization to be set up by the Peace Conference. But it was only later that its ultimate importance as such became obvious, when the Germans by appealing for peace on the basis of the Fourteen Points made of them the legal and moral foundation of the settlement.

Wilson utilized largely for his speech a report prepared by the Inquiry, the members of which were instructed to reduce general propositions to brief formulas, to isolate the

[53] Jules Jusserand, Le sentiment Américain pendant la guerre, p. 147.
[54] Wilson to House, January 2, 1918, Y.H.C.

critical territorial issues, and to draft specific recommendations in accord with the principles of Wilson's policy. The
first part of the Inquiry's report outlined the diplomatic
situation and the points that needed emphasis in the proposed diplomatic offensive against Germany. It urged the
President to " show the way to Liberals in Great Britain
and in France, and therefore restore their natural unity of
purpose. These Liberals will readily accept the leadership
of the President, if he undertakes a liberal diplomatic offensive, because they will find in that offensive an invaluable
support for their internal domestic troubles." The second
part of the report consisted of a statement of terms on eight
territorial issues: Belgium, Northern France, Alsace-Lorraine, Italian frontiers, the Balkans, Poland, Austria-Hungary, Turkey. It concluded with a paragraph suggesting that
out of the existing anti-German alliance a League of Nations
was already developing: " Whether this League is to be
armed and exclusive, or whether there is to be a reduction
of armaments and a cordial inclusion of Germany will
depend upon whether the German Government is in fact
representative of the German democracy." [55]

The speech of the Fourteen Points was drafted on January
5, 1918, in a little more than two hours steady work. The
President had called Colonel House down to Washington
a day or so before and together the two men went over
House's impressions of the current situation in Europe,
especially the Russian problem and the attitude of the Allies
towards it. They studied also a mass of memoranda sup-

[55] Inquiry Report, Y.H.C. Cf. the final sentence with Wilson's
armistice notes, *infra,* p. 356.

plied from European sources by House, as well as the comprehensive although hastily constructed Inquiry report. It is apparent that the choice of the material and the points to be covered was largely made by House; the arrangement was chiefly Wilson's and the phraseology characteristically and almost entirely Wilsonian. The President placed the general terms before the territorial, except that he reserved for his final peroration the League of Nations, the cornerstone of the whole new international organization.

Certain points in the speech raised especial difficulties in the President's mind. He feared the opposition of the Senate to Point III, which called for " the removal, so far as possible, of all economic barriers and the establishment of an equality of trade conditions." He was determined to insert Point II, the Freedom of the Seas, although he knew that it would arouse British opposition. As first drafted, the speech did not carry a specific reference to Alsace-Lorraine; a second draft was not positive: " if Alsace and Lorraine were restored to France, Germany should be given an equal opportunity." It was only the day before the speech that he revised this clause to its final form. Even so it was indefinite, although it was interpreted at the time and later by Wilson himself as meaning the return of the provinces.[56] The Russian paragraph was written with especial care, for in a sense that problem formed the main *raison d'être* of the speech; it was based upon discussions which House had carried on

[56] " All French territory should be freed and the invaded portions restored, and the wrong done to France by Prussia in 1871 in the matter of Alsace-Lorraine, which has unsettled the peace of the world for nearly fifty years, should be righted, in order that peace may once more be made secure in the interest of all."

with the Russian Ambassador. The paragraph on Poland was framed to come as near as possible to one drafted by the Polish National Council, which had been presented to the Interallied Conference in Paris and which the diplomats there had refused to publish. The only paragraph shown to any representative of the Allied Governments was that concerning the Balkans. This was taken to Vesnitch, head of the Serbian Mission. He criticized it strongly because the break-up of Austria-Hungary was not demanded; the President decided nevertheless to make no change and delivered the paragraph as first written.[57]

At the last moment Wilson was almost deterred from giving his speech by the news of Lloyd George's war aims speech before the Trade Union Congress on January 5. The British Prime Minister realized, on returning from the Interallied Conference, the compelling necessity of some pronouncement, in view of the Russian situation and the publication of a memorandum upon war aims by the British labour conference. On January 5 Balfour cabled that the British Government desired to be released from certain pledges which were made to the labor leaders earlier in the war, a relief that was indispensable for the development of man power on the western front. " Finally the negotiations arrived at a point at which their successful issue depended mainly on the immediate publication by the British Government of a statement setting forth their war aims." [58]

[57] See House Diary, January 5, 1918, which describes in detail the drafting of the speech, *I.P.*, III, 325-335. Text of the speech, *F.R., 1918, Suppl. 1*, I, 12-17.

[58] Balfour to House, January 5, 1918, *I.P.*, III, 340.

The Lloyd George statement was made on January 5 and published in the American papers that afternoon. For a few moments Wilson " thought the terms which Lloyd George had given were so nearly akin to those he had worked out that it would be impossible for him to make the contemplated address before Congress." [59] He soon decided however that the situation had been rather improved than otherwise. The similarity of tone was enough to suggest to some critics that Wilson based his Points upon Mr. Lloyd George's speech.[60] But the documentary evidence of complete independence is final. The President's address was already drafted before he knew that the Lloyd George statement was to be made.

The address as delivered on January 8 evoked a storm of enthusiasm in the United States, which in view of later developments and the attitude taken in certain quarters toward Wilsonian policy is surprising. It was praised by Theodore Roosevelt and Morris Hillquit, by Mr. Frank Simonds and Mr. Myer London. The New York *Tribune* declared editorially that " the President's words are the words of a hundred million. . . . Today, as never before, the whole nation marches with the President." The co-operation of America with Europe, which in two brief years was to be anathematized, drew fulsome praise:

"As Lincoln freed the slaves of the South half a century ago, Mr. Wilson now pledges his country to fight for the liberation of the Belgian and the Pole, the Serb and the Rumanian. For the long suffering populations of Alsace-

[59] House Diary, January 9, 1918, *I.P.*, III, 341.
[60] See " The Genesis of the Fourteen Commandments," *North American Review*, February, 1919, presumably by George Harvey.

Lorraine and the Italian Irredenta the words of the President of the United States are a promise of freedom after a slavery worse a thousand times than that of the negro. . . . President Wilson has done nothing finer; there is nothing more admirable in American history than his address of yesterday. In a single speech he has transformed the whole character and broken with all the tradition of American policy. He has carried the United States back to Europe; he has established an American world policy and ideal of international policy throughout the civilized world. . . ." [61]

Apart from the extraordinary and beautiful irony of the New York *Tribune* heaping such praise upon a Democratic President for a policy which in the presidential campaign of 1920 the *Tribune,* together with all other Republican organs, regarded as a betrayal of American independence, the editorial touches the very spot that makes the speech significant in the history of American and Wilsonian policy. For the first time Wilson regards the territorial terms as America's business, lays down territorial conditions as a prerequisite of American coöperation. In his speech of May 16, 1916, he had called for a League of Nations, in that of January 22, 1917, for the protection of free peoples, great and small. But except for the mention of Poland in the latter he did not refer to territorial problems. Even after America entered the war he was not inclined to be caught in what he regarded as local details. On August 22 he wrote that he would like to say but dared not for fear of offending France or Italy, " that their territorial claims did not interest us." [62] But with the study of Allied territorial claims by the Inquiry and his increasing appreciation of the conflict

[61] N. Y. *Tribune,* January 9, 1918.
[62] Wilson to House, August 22, 1917, Y.H.C.

between those claims and the principles of his policy, his interest in territorial problems was necessarily aroused. The United States, by the speech of January 8, was obligated to full participation not merely in the general world problem of preserving the peace but in the local problems peculiar to Europe which might disturb the peace. Wilson himself was now consciously committed to this policy and wrote three weeks later, in response to criticism that America was meddling, that he was inclined to "attempt to show that each item of a general peace is everybody's business." [63]

The Allies were pleased by the speech as a weapon in the diplomatic war against German propaganda; they hailed it as "another notable contribution in the drumfire on the enemy's moral position." But the invasion by Wilson of detailed points of European interest disturbed them. Some resentment against Wilson's attempt to define and limit Italian aspirations was reported by the American Ambassador in Rome, who also noted critical voices in France. The President was irritated but not disturbed by the ultimate prospect of a diplomatic contest with his present partners. He was certainly not deluded by the hope that it would be easy to persuade them to accept his terms. "If we have to fight an all-Latin combination," he wrote on January 31, "we must fight it. I trust they will have no stomach for such a combination as we could form against them." [64]

Even in England, where the Wilsonian programme stood far better chances of acceptance, sceptical voices were raised. They admitted his prophetic qualities, praised the "spiritual

[63] Wilson to House, January 31, 1918, Y.H.C.
[64] Wilson to House, January 31, 1918, Y.H.C.

insight and divination of the greatest American President since Abraham Lincoln," but they were not ready to adopt the Fourteen Points as a political programme. Even such liberal organs as the *Manchester Guardian* and the *Westminster Gazette* were suspicious of the Freedom of the Seas. Others entered definite reservations regarding the League of Nations. " The chief criticism which cautious thinkers may be disposed to make upon it [the President's speech]," said *The Times,* " is that, in its lofty flight to the ideal, it seems not to take sufficient account of certain hard realities of the situation. . . . Some of the proposals which Mr. Wilson puts forward almost appear to assume that the reign of righteousness upon the earth is already within our reach." [65]

The Allied Governments were polite in their attitude toward the President's programme but they made no move to adopt it as their own. In each state appeared reservations regarding the particular points that touched the national interest. Nor during the succeeding months was there a tendency to develop as between the Allies and the United States any common programme for ultimate peace. The immediate effect of the speech in Russia and in Germany was equally disappointing. The Bolsheviks sneered at Wilson's generalizations and rejected his specific conditions. They distrusted Entente annexationist plans and were just as suspicious of American capitalism. " We are equally hostile," said Trotsky on February 10, " to the Imperialism on both sides, and we do not agree to shed any longer the blood

[65] Cf. Mr. Lloyd George on the Freedom of the Seas, Address to Trades-Union delegates, January 18, 1918, *The Times,* London, January 19, 1918, p. 7.

of our soldiers in the defense of the one side against the other." [66] The German Chancellor, Count Hertling, gave no indication of a willingness to make concessions and scolded both Wilson and Lloyd George. " Only a victor speaks to the vanquished in such language," he said of their speeches. " Our military situation was never so favorable as at present. Let the Entente bring new proposals." [67]

But the solvent effects of the Fourteen Points upon German determination shortly became apparent, combining with the difficulty of negotiations with Russia and increasing food troubles to precipitate serious industrial and pacifist manifestations in the Central Powers. Although the German and Austrian Governments refused Wilson's specific terms they were obliged to accept tentatively the general propositions which were received with some enthusiasm by liberal opinion in Germany.[68] Mr. Carl Ackerman reported from Berne that the speech of the Fourteen Points had had the most important effect of any public address since the United States entered the war. He cited the following reasons:

" It separated absolutely, and I think permanently, the people and the Liberals from the Annexationists, the Military Leaders and the War Industrial magnates; it forced the Austro-Hungarian Government to recognize the peace movement in that country and cemented the Dual Monarchy to the German Liberal party; it gave more momentum to the revolutionary movement, which is under way in Germany,

[66] *Proceedings of the Brest-Litovsk Conference* (Washington, 1918), 172.

[67] Hertling before the Reichstag committee, January 24, 1918, *F.R., 1918, Suppl. 1,* I, 42.

[68] Valentin, *op. cit.,* pp. 368-369.

than the Russian revolution; it increased the possibilities of success for the present confidential negotiations which are taking place with Bulgaria; and it made a tremendous impression upon the small European neutrals. . . . The war has reached the decisive period. To my mind the problem facing the United States is this: How far can the United States go in encouraging the peace movement and the reform forces within Central Europe without weakening the determination of the Allies to fight until a just peace can be concluded. The solution is: War, relentless war with armies and speeches against the German War government but peace with the democratic, or reform, peace forces." [69]

6

All during the spring, President Wilson carried on what the British termed his " drum-fire " on the German Government. At the same time that he insisted upon the impossibility of dealing with the " military masters " of Germany he built a fire back of Ludendorff by appealing to the peoples:

" The tragical circumstance is that this one party in Germany is apparently willing and able to send millions of men to their death to prevent what all the world now sees to be just." [70]

He ordered the study of German Socialist press and speeches by the State Department, and in his speeches used the arguments and even the phrases of the dissidents in enemy countries against their own Governments.

In his speech of February 11 he promised that " every territorial settlement involved in this war must be made

[69] Ackerman to House, February 4, 1918, *I.P.,* III, 355-357.
[70] Address delivered before Congress, February 11, 1918, *F.R., 1918, Suppl. 1,* I, 112.

20

in the interest and for the benefit of the populations concerned." In that of April 6 he declared: " I am ready,
ready still, ready even now, to discuss a fair and just and
honest peace at any time that it is sincerely purposed—a
peace in which the strong and the weak shall fare alike.
But the answer, when I proposed such a peace, came from
the German commanders in Russia, and I cannot mistake
the meaning of the answer." [71] Finally on September 27,
when Germany was beginning to crack, came the reiterated
declaration that there could be no bargain or compromise
with the existing Governments of the Central Empires:
" We cannot ' come to terms ' with them." But in the same
breath he promised an impartial justice that " must involve
no discrimination between those to whom we wish to be
just and those to whom we do not wish to be just . . .
no leagues or alliances or special covenants and understandings within the general and common family of the league of
nations . . . no special economic combinations within the
league and no employment of any form of economic boycott
or exclusion." [72] So long as the German armies were victorious the effect of these words could not be measured,
but once Germany faced defeat it turned to Wilson as to a
saviour.

The Allied Governments may have appreciated the cor-
rosive value of the President's diplomacy. But they were
certainly disturbed by the fear lest he commit them to a
policy of renunciation they were not prepared to adopt.

[71] *F.R., 1918, Suppl. 1*, I, 108 ff.; 200 ff.

[72] Address in opening the Fourth Loan Campaign, *F.R., 1918,
Suppl. 1*, I, 316 ff. For Wilson's preparation for this speech,
see House Diary, September 24, 1918, *I.P.*, IV, 66-67.

There were clear indications of their intention to employ a punitive and discriminatory trade policy against Germany after the war.[73] As the chances of success increased, their territorial aspirations hardened. In the spring, the gulf between Wilson and the Allies became apparent when the Supreme War Council issued a statement upon general policy which by no means satisfied the President. He dissociated himself promptly, although privately, and made it clear that any political statement from the Allies carried the approval of the United States only if specifically expressed. " He would have had no objection to joining with the Allies," cabled Wiseman, " in a general declaration of war policy but only after such declaration had been carefully considered by him in view of the special position of America." [74]

That Wilson would eventually bring the Allied Governments to the acceptance of his programme he never doubted. He received increasing assurances of the support of liberal and working-class opinion in France and Great Britain. A message from the American Embassy in London carried word that British Labour leaders were prepared to follow any course " suggested " by Wilson; that he had " only to signify " his wishes.[75] He was encouraged by the increasing sentiment favoring a League of Nations in Great Britain and France. The British Government itself was now seriously considering the Phillimore Report on a League of Nations and sent a copy to the President. There would

[73] Wiseman to Reading, August 16, 1918, *I.P.*, IV, 62.

[74] Polk to Frazier, February 5, 1918; statement to Allied Ambassadors in Washington; Wiseman to Foreign Office, February 19, 1918, *I.P.*, III, 363-365; *F.R., 1918, Suppl. 1*, I, 81-82.

[75] Frazier to Lansing, March 18, 1918, Y.H.C.

evidently be difficulties with the British over the form of the League, but if the principle were accepted as the corner-stone of the peace the success of the Wilsonian programme was assured. Liberals abroad were coming to see this and insist upon it.

The situation was summarized brilliantly by a British historian:

"A League of Nations was the fundamental war aim; the rest were only machinery to provide a clean foundation for it. Unfortunately this was not fully recognized at the time by any Allied Government save America, and M. Clemen-ceau went out of his way to declare the conception un-balanced and unpractical. Yet it was the only practical ideal before the world, in the sense that it was the only one which met the whole needs of the case. If a statement of war aims was meant to solidify the Alliance and drive a wedge be-tween Prussianism and the German people, then a sound internationalism must be the first item in the programme. It offered the Allies an enduring union, based on coöperation instead of rivalry; it offered the German people security for their rights of possession and development so soon as they discarded their false gods; it offered a world weary of strife some hope of a lasting peace." [76]

To bring the Allied Governments to an acceptance of this programme now became the dominating purpose of Wil-son's policy. With the turn of the military tide, in the summer of 1918, it was apparent that the destructive ele-ments in his speeches had accomplished their purpose. The German people had lost faith in their own leaders and turned to Wilson and the Fourteen Points as a harbor of refuge. Such willingness to follow the new prophet from over the seas could hardly be explained except as a death-

[76] Buchan, *A History of the Great War,* IV, 156-157.

bed conversion. Germany accepted Wilson because she was *in extremis*. Whether France and Great Britain, in the full flush of victory, would permit America to define the political consequences of victory was more than doubtful. " Unity of purpose and of counsel," said Wilson on September 27, " are as imperatively necessary in this war as was unity of command in the battlefield." [77] But it was even more difficult to attain. For in the military field the Allies were forced into unity by the threat of a general disaster; whereas in the political field they were separated by their individual interests.

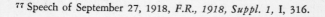

[77] Speech of September 27, 1918, *F.R., 1918, Suppl. 1*, I, 316.

Chapter VIII

THE APPEAL TO WILSON

1

The imposition of final defeat upon a tired enemy is not entirely a military task. The development of negotiations which without yielding any essential fruits of victory will shorten the period of fighting, is a vital function of diplomacy. The Central Powers were worn out by the effects of the Allied blockade; after July, 1918, they faced certain defeat because Foch disposed of an overwhelming superiority in fighting effectives. Except for President Wilson's manipulation of political factors, however, the German debâcle would have been postponed and the war would have continued for weeks, perhaps for months, beyond November 11.

Wilson appeared before the German people in 1918 with a sword in his right hand and the olive branch in his left. If they insisted upon making force alone the deciding element he would accept the challenge and abide the issue. When the German Government answered his Fourteen Points with the Treaty of Brest-Litovsk imposed on Russia, he declared: "There is, therefore, but one response possible from us: Force, Force to the utmost, Force without stint or limit, the righteous and triumphant Force which shall make Right the law of the world, and cast every selfish dominion down in the dust." [1] But if the German people would accept the principles of his Fourteen Points, especially if they would throw off the dominion of their "military masters," he promised them protection against political annihilation and the just treatment to which every nation has a claim. [2]

Because of Wilson the Germans accepted an armistice in November, whereas if they had had to deal with France and Great Britain only they would have fought on in desperation. They saw in him a saviour from the destructiveness of Allied wrath. Through him as an intercessor they hoped to avoid the penalties ordinarily paid by the defeated after a prolonged and exhausting war. Later they made the charge that Wilson betrayed them. "We now realize that we were misled by President Wilson's Fourteen Points, held out to Germany as a bait for accepting the terms of this devastating truce." [3] The charge, although not unnatural, is equally untrue. A survey of the facts shows that the Fourteen Points were accepted by German leaders after careful consideration, as a desirable alternative to the continuation of the fighting in which German armies were doomed to unabated slaughter, with an unconditional surrender as the only possible outcome. Wilson's terms were not dangled as a lure. They were brought forward frankly as a means by which useless carnage might be stopped.

[1] Address at opening of third Liberty Loan campaign, Baltimore, April 6, 1918, *F.R., 1918, Suppl. 1*, I, 203.

[2] Address of September 27, 1918, *F.R., 1918, Suppl. 1*, I, 316 ff.

[3] Chancellor Hitler's *Völkischer Beobachter*, quoted in N. Y. *Herald Tribune*, June 29, 1933.

2

The shadow of defeat hung low over German military leaders in the early summer of 1918, even before the definite turn of fortune became apparent to the general observer.[4] By the collapse of Russia and Rumania in 1917 Germany had been able to add forty divisions to her armies on the west front, and for the first time since 1914 disposed of a superiority in man-power over the Allies. This superiority approached 200,000 and offered Ludendorff good hope of crushing the Allied lines before the Americans arrived in numbers.[5] But although victorious in the spring offensives, he could not break the front. The opportunity was lost never to return. In July, the final offensive on the Marne was stopped, the Germans were compelled to operate again upon the defensive. From then on the sheer weight of Allied armies, reinforced by America, was bound to be overpowering. On August 8, the Allies delivered a counter-offensive of tremendous force which began the general advance that ended only with the armistice.

Germany's last chance even of a stalemate thus disappeared. The difficulty of securing replacements became increasingly apparent.[6] The effect of the Allied blockade was manifest in the shortage of raw materials and food.[7] After

---

[4] According to the Crown Prince Rupprecht, Ludendorff after the failure of the April drive had no longer material grounds for victory, Hans Delbrück in *Ursachen des Deutsches Zusammenbruchs,* III, 353 (hereafter cited as *Ursachen*).

[5] Ludendorff, *Ludendorff's Own Story,* II, 165; *Ursachen,* III, 6.

[6] *P.H.A.,* No. 57, p. 83.

[7] *Ursachen,* III, 88.

four years of heroic effort Germany was war-weary, had reached a stage of national anæmia which could not endure the news of retreat on the fighting front. Bolshevist and defeatist propaganda doubtless weakened the will to victory, already blunted by the prospect of an unending war.[8] Austria was breaking industrially, lacking food and facing a collapse of her transport system. The Austrian Chief of Staff insisted that to continue the war was sheer nonsense. Bulgaria and Turkey were barely hanging on.[9]

As early as April, Ludendorff confessed disappointment to himself, recognized that " the enemy's resistance was beyond our strength." [10] He continued however to conceal the true situation from the civil Government. At the Spa Conference of July 3, the Kaiser and Chancellor drafted a plan for the future disposition of Belgium which assumed the attainment of German military ends.[11] When Kühlmann, Foreign Secretary, admitted on June 25 in the Reichstag that " an absolute end of the war can hardly be expected through purely military decisions alone, without any diplomatic negotiations," Ludendorff joined in the Conservative hue and cry that led to his dismissal.[12] In the middle of July when his successor, Hintze, put to Ludendorff at General Headquarters the formal and definite question as to whether he was certain of finally and decisively beating the enemy in the offensive, Ludendorff repeated his

---

[8] Ludendorff, *op. cit.,* II, 422; Karl Friedrich Nowak, *Collapse of Central Europe,* p. 45; Valentin, *Deutschlands Aussenpolitik,* pp. 381-383.

[9] Nowak, *op. cit.,* pp. 39-43; 180-188.

[10] Ludendorff, *op. cit.,* II, 232.

[11] *Ursachen,* III, 318.

[12] Nowak, *op. cit.,* pp. 153 ff., also Appendix III.

question and answered, " I can reply to that with a decided Yes." [13]

Not until the German Council of August 14 was any hint of the true situation brought before the civil Government. For the first time Ludendorff then confessed that he was no longer certain of winning peace through a vigorous offensive; he none the less expected to bring the enemy to terms by a strategic defensive on French soil. The Crown Prince Rupprecht and the Crown Prince Wilhelm were less optimistic, and gave the representative of the Foreign Office, Baron von Lersner, the impression that every additional day of warfare was a step towards ruin. At the full Council, which included besides the Kaiser and Army chiefs the Chancellor and Foreign Secretary, the Chancellor reviewed the general situation in rather gloomy colors, which so far as Austria was concerned were confirmed by the attitude of the Emperor Karl and his Foreign Secretary, who had joined the conference. In the long run the Allies were obviously bound to win because of their practically inexhaustible supplies of men and raw materials. Hintze asked for the inauguration of a peace move and the limitation of war aims. The Supreme Command agreed to an approach to a neutral Power, preferably Holland, but asked postponement until some success had been achieved on the western front; it insisted that whatever powers of negotiation were given to Hintze should be limited by the maintenance of war aims established in view of victory.[14]

[13] *P.H.A.*, No. 2, p. 20.

[14] Nowak, *op. cit.*, pp. 162-168; *Ursachen*, p. 351; *P.H.A.*, No. 2, p. 19. Ludendorff maintains that he was entirely willing at Spa to give Hintze a free hand in the question of war aims

It can hardly be doubted that Ludendorff was not entirely frank with the civil officials. The representative of the Supreme Command attached to the civil Government, Colonel von Haeften, later reported that if Ludendorff had spoken in the same way to the statesmen as he had to him, the Foreign Secretary must have realized that it was high time to start peace negotiations. A fortnight later Mertz asked Ludendorff directly whether the Foreign Office was fully apprised of the real situation. Ludendorff replied: " I couldn't bring myself to it, for if I told them the truth, they would completely lose their heads." [15] This lack of complete confidence between the military and civil leaders was destined to have important consequences. The eyes of the latter were opened so suddenly later on that they had no fair opportunity to prepare the way diplomatically for an armistice appeal. The precipitate action into which they were forced by the military had the most disastrous consequences at home and abroad.

The Austrian leaders were not encouraged by any misapprehension of their own situation. The Emperor Karl and Count Burian came to Spa desirous of a direct appeal for peace to all the belligerents at the earliest possible moment. The Germans begged them to wait, promising neutral mediation at the next favorable opportunity. But desperation was driving Austria out of German control. Count Burian, contrary to the agreement with Germany, took up separate negotiations with Turkey and Bulgaria in the hope of winning their support for a direct appeal for peace. On

---

(*The General Staff and its Problems,* II, 585) but the contention is contradicted by the official documents.

[15] *Ursachen,* III, 348-349.

August 21, a draft of a peace note was submitted by Austria. The Emperor Karl apparently preferred the direct method of general appeal to neutral mediation, since he hoped that through it he might appear to the peoples of the Hapsburg Monarchy as the peacemaker.[16]

3

The Austro-Hungarian note, issued on September 14, was published in the European newspapers the following day. It called upon all the belligerents to put an end to the horrible indecisive struggle by immediately opening a "confidential non-binding conversation" at a conference in a neutral country. Coming at the moment of the Bulgarian debâcle and just before the launching of the Allied offensive in the Argonne, the Austrian note created hardly a ripple abroad. President Wilson answered briefly that the American terms had been repeatedly stated and he could not entertain a proposal for a conference upon a matter concerning which he had made his position plain.[17]

The failure of the Austrian appeal rendered more difficult the German attempts to secure neutral mediation. In this direction the Foreign Office made little progress, whether because of the diplomatic incapacity alleged by Ludendorff or because the German armies had been unable to provide

[16] *P.H.A.*, No. 4, pp. 24-30. The contents of various documents in the archives have been summarized and are presented under the title "Chronological Review of the Development of the Austro-Hungarian Peace Proposal."

[17] Text of Note in Minister of Sweden to Lansing, September 16, 1918, *F.R., 1918, Suppl. 1,* I, 306-309. For the reply, *ibid.,* 309-310.

the favorable opportunity desired.[18] At the end of the month both Hindenburg and Ludendorff, apparently independently, reached the conclusion that they could wait no longer. An armistice must be had, even if it meant appeal to one of the belligerents.[19]

The Foreign Office had already drafted a plan of direct appeal to President Wilson for a peace based upon the Fourteen Points. They reckoned, however, upon adequate time for its development, so as to avoid the appearance of precipitate action. But on September 29 Ludendorff described the military situation in terms that made an immediate step seem vital. The Foreign Secretary gathered that a catastrophe impended. Apparently the entire civil Government was taken by surprise.[20] Ludendorff continued his pressure for immediate action. On October 1 he insisted, " Today the troops are holding their own; what may happen tomorrow cannot be foreseen." On the same day at half-past one Hindenburg agreed to postponing the armistice appeal for a day to permit the formation of a new Government. Half an hour later Ludendorff asked that the note be sent at once; no delay should be made for the new Government. Grünau wired to Berlin, " He [Ludendorff] said he felt like a gambler, and that a division might fail him anywhere at any time. I get the impression that they have all lost

[18] *P.H.A.*, No. 5, p. 30, Ludendorff, *Das Scheitern der neutralen Friedensvermittlung* (Berlin, Mittler, 1919), *passim*.

[19] Ludendorff, *Das Friedens- und Waffenstillstandsangebot*, p. 44; *P.H.A.*, No. 14, p. 36.

[20] *P.H.A.*, No. 12, p. 34; *Ursachen*, I, 23, 261, 266-267; VIII, 285-289. Erzberger, *Erlebnisse*, p. 321; Valentin, *op. cit.*, p. 379.

their nerve, here." On October 2 Ludendorff wired that the army could not wait forty-eight hours longer.[21]

Whether, as Payer suggests, Ludendorff suffered a nervous collapse or whether, as he himself maintains in his later defense, he had reasoned grounds for demanding an immediate armistice to "show us where we stood," [22] his insistence hampered if it did not upset effective diplomatic procedure. He hoisted the white flag at a moment most unpropitious from the political and diplomatic point of view.[23] Whether more deliberate action could have secured better results for Germany may be questioned; but if a last-ditch defense by the German people was to be successfully undertaken, as both Ludendorff and the new Chancellor, Prince Max, planned, Ludendorff's impetuosity made it impossible.

Prince Max of Baden, a liberal and long an advocate of a peace of reconciliation, proceeded to form a Government based upon parliamentary principles. He protested strongly against sending the note. He needed time to organize his Government; he wished to prepare the country for a "back-to-the-wall defense"; he was uncertain about accepting the Fourteen Points as a basis of peace, for he was under no illusion as to the significance of that program in relation to the integrity of the Empire. "An armistice offer," writes Prince Max, "made any such peace step as I had contemplated impossible. I begged him [Haeften] to get General Ludendorff to change his mind. I must at least demand

[21] *P.H.A.,* Nos. 21, 22, 23, 27, pp. 40-42.

[22] Payer, *Von Bethmann bis Ebert,* 88; Ludendorff, *General Staff,* II, 613.

[23] *Ursachen,* III, 353.

a fortnight to prepare the political ground at home and abroad." [24] On October 3 the new Chancellor sent a definite warning to the Supreme Army Command. Was the military situation so critical that action for the purpose of bringing about an armistice and peace must be inaugurated at once? Did the Supreme Army Command realize that the inauguration of a peace move under pressure of a critical military situation might result in the loss of the German colonies and German territory, such as Alsace-Lorraine and the Polish districts of the eastern provinces? Did General Headquarters agree to the text of the enclosed note? In conference with Hindenburg Prince Max insisted that he would consent to the despatch of the note " only on the condition, that the Supreme Command states in writing . . . that the military situation on the Western Front no longer admits of a postponement of the dispatch of the note." [25]

Hindenburg's reply sent the same day was emphatic. " The Supreme Command persists in its request . . . urging the immediate despatch to our enemies of the peace proposal. . . . The situation is daily growing more acute, and may force the Supreme Army Command to very serious decisions. . . . Every day's delay costs the lives of thousands of brave soldiers." [26]

On the night of October 3, much against his will, Prince Max sent the appeal for an armistice to President Wilson. " I fought against the note," he insisted before the council of Ministers on October 6, " First, because I thought the time premature; secondly, because I wished to turn to the

[24] Prince Max of Baden, *Memoirs,* II, 5, 24 ff.

[25] *P.H.A.,* No. 32, p. 4; Prince Max, *op. cit.,* pp. 18-19.

[26] *P.H.A.,* No. 33, p. 48.

enemy in general. Now we must quietly consider the consequences." Later he explained to Scheidemann: " I sent it because I was forced by the Supreme Command. I was opposed to this over-hasty cry for rescue, but have taken all the responsibility." [27]

Responsibility for the appeal for an armistice at this time must rest with Ludendorff. With him also must rest the responsibility for selecting Wilson as the one to appeal to and for accepting the Fourteen Points as the basis of the peace.[28] The point is of capital importance, for if the appeal had been to the Allies in general terms, it is probable that a brusque refusal would have been the answer, as in the case of the Austrian appeal of September 14. Prince Max would then have been given a chance to attempt his plan of calling upon the fatherland to fight in the last ditch. Ludendorff, a great tactician but a poor strategist whether on the field of arms or politics, chose to appeal to Wilson, perhaps believing him easy to handle diplomatically and hoping to gain from him a respite for his hard pressed troops.

Thereby he made it impossible to stop the German stampede towards peace. For Wilson would be careful, in the circumstances, not to close the negotiations with a summary negative. With the Fourteen Points as a haven of refuge, German opinion, whether that of the man in the street or of the parliamentarian, would not let go this chance of peace. When Ludendorff who had forced the appeal

[27] *P.H.A.,* No. 35, p. 49; Philipp Scheidemann, *Der Zusammenbruch,* p. 184. See also Prince Max, *op. cit.,* p. 22.

[28] The note as sent to Wilson was almost identical with that drafted by Ludendorff.

realized what its consequences would be and tried to stop
negotiations, he found that it was too late. A more astute
politician, if his object were to rouse the country to national
defense, would have been very slow to engage in diplomatic battle with Wilson, at the moment when the latter
had captured the leadership of liberal and peace-loving
forces, alike in the Central Powers and among the Allies.

4

The German note sent through the Swiss Government by
Prince Max on the evening of October 3, requested

" the President of the United States to take steps for the
restoration of peace, to notify all belligerents of this request,
and to invite them to delegate plenipotentiaries for the purpose of taking up negotiations. The German Government
accepts, as a basis for peace negotiations, the program laid
down by the President of the United States in his message
to Congress of January 8, 1918, and in his subsequent pronouncements, particularly in his address of September 27,
1918. In order to avoid further bloodshed the German Government requests to bring about the immediate conclusion
of a general armistice on land, on water, and in the air." [29]

President Wilson, apparently, regarded it as a matter of
course that the request should come to him personally rather
than to the Allied leaders. He did not take them into his
confidence. They waited in Paris for his reply to the German
offer, not without nervousness lest he should be caught in
what at first they regarded as the " German peace trap." [30]

[29] Text of note, Swiss Chargé to Wilson, October 6, 1918, *F.R.,
1918, Suppl. 1,* I, 338.

[30] Frazier cabled on October 7 that Lloyd George " was exceedingly anxious to find out whether President Wilson had

The President was not completely taken by surprise, although neither he nor the Allied leaders had any idea of the plight of the German armies and nation as pictured by Ludendorff. After all, they were only three months from the threat of German victory on the Marne. All during the summer preparations had been made for another year of war. As late as September 12 Lord Reading cabled to Wiseman, as though it were good news: " The general view among military chiefs in France is that with great effort the war might be ended in 1919 and that all energy should be concentrated in this direction." [31] But only a week later the Bulgarian front in Macedonia cracked, and on September 28 the Bulgars, requesting an armistice, accepted terms which amounted to unconditional surrender. The Austrian cry for peace was accompanied by the news of Allenby's victorious advance against the Turks. Germany's allies were giving up the struggle. At the moment of Germany's appeal, Marshal Foch indicated that events might

replied to the German proposal and earnestly hoped that the President would send Colonel House over at the earliest moment. . . . The foreign representatives are remaining in Paris over to-morrow in the hope that something may be heard from President Wilson." On the following day he reported that Lloyd George had told him that they " would remain another night in Paris in the hope of receiving word from Mr. Wilson," Frazier to Lansing, October 7, 8, *F.R., 1918, Suppl. 1,* I, 344, 346. The President, however, gave them no advance information as to the character of his reply. Cf. Callwell, *Field-Marshal Sir Henry Wilson,* II, 133 ff. On the 5th, Sir Henry noted that the Germans had agreed to treat on the basis of the Fourteen Points and adds, " pretty piece of impertinence." And later, " Lloyd George took the line that we pandered and bowed much too much to President Wilson."

[31] Reading to Wiseman, September 12, 1918, *I.P.,* IV, 57.

move more rapidly than had been expected. "We are on the slope of victory," he said to Frazier in Paris, "and victory has sometimes a way of galloping."[32]

Opinion in the United States and Allied countries was generally in favor of a direct negative to the German appeal. The note was almost universally spoken of as a "manœuver" to catch Wilson in a "negotiated peace." Despatches from abroad indicated that Allied opinion expected and hoped that the President would send back an immediate denial to the appeal for negotiations. "According to the *Evening News,*" ran a London despatch, "both Lloyd George and Clemenceau are of the opinion that the proposal to suspend military operations, which is regarded everywhere as impelled by military necessity, and a scheme by which Germany hoped to be able to extricate and regroup her armies, ought to have been addressed to Marshal Foch."[33] Sir Henry Wilson, Chief of the British Staff, wrote in his diary, "A few good home truths would do the President good."[34] In the United States Senate, the peace offer was "peremptorily spurned. . . . In spirited discussion of the latest enemy proposals, Senators participating in a two hours debate declared it an insidious attack and voiced a demand for its immediate rejection." Senator Lodge, supported by Senator Poindexter, declared that "the plain English of it is, that an armistice now would mean the loss of the war."[35] It is almost certain that had Germany appealed

[32] Frazier to House, October 5, 1918, Y.H.C.
[33] *N. Y. Times,* October 8, 1918.
[34] Callwell, *op. cit.,* II, 134.
[35] N. Y. *Tribune,* October 8, 1919; *I.P.,* IV, 76.

to anyone else but Wilson and on any other basis than the
Fourteen Points the appeal would have been refused.[36]

The President felt that in the name of humanity this
chance of negotiations must not be lost. He immediately
called Colonel House on the telephone and received from
him the warning that if the Allies permitted this opportunity to go by and the German resistance stiffened, the
popular demand for peace during the winter might result
in giving to Germany easier terms than could be arranged
at the moment.[37] On October 7 Wilson summoned House
to Washington and read to him and Lansing a draft of his
reply to Germany. House disapproved it, as not emphasizing
sufficiently the need of adequate guarantees for thorough-
going acceptance of the Fourteen Points. The President
failed to appreciate, according to House, the " nearly unanimous sentiment in this country against anything but unconditional surrender. He did not realize how war-mad our
people have become." Wilson was discouraged. " After
arguing the matter some half hour or more," wrote House,
" he said that I might be able to write something and embody what I had in mind, but he had to confess his inability
to do so." But the following day, after reading the reports
of the Senate debate and of the French Socialist Convention
in Paris, as well as the *Manchester Guardian* and London
Daily News, he produced a revised draft. " There was not
much left of the original," recorded Colonel House.[38]

[36] " I am informed on good authority," cabled Frazier, " that
word was passed down by the French Government to the press
in Paris to adopt an uncompromising attitude toward the peace
proposals of the Central Empires," Frazier to Lansing, October 8,
1918, *F.R., 1918, Suppl. 1,* I, 345.

[37] House to Wilson, October 6, 1918, *I.P.,* II, 75.

[38] House Diary, October 9, 1918, *I.P.,* IV, 77-79.

The note was published on October 9. Contrary to the advice of his secretary, Tumulty, who had urged a decided refusal, and to the prophecies of the *Times,* which reported Washington as convinced that the President would reject the German appeal, Wilson intimated that the United States was ready to consider it seriously.[39] But the Central Powers must furnish adequate guarantees. He asked whether they accepted the Fourteen Points and subsequent addresses as a definite basis for the peace, any discussion being merely for the purpose of working out the practical details of their application. This was not so much a question as a notification that the United States would not consider any discussion of the Fourteen Points themselves. He called for the evacuation of France and Belgium as a preliminary to any armistice. Finally he referred back to the point he had raised in various speeches, that although German political institutions were not the business of the United States, it was impossible to negotiate with the " military masters " of Germany: " The President also feels that he is justified in asking whether the Imperial Chancellor is speaking merely for the constituted authorities of the Empire who have so far conducted the war." [40]

Hindsight has found in this and the later armistice notes of Wilson a diplomatic skill which brought Germany to early surrender. Contrary to almost universal judgment he was able to maintain and develop negotiations which undoubtedly shortened the war without any sacrifice of Allied

[39] Joseph P. Tumulty, *Woodrow Wilson as I Knew Him,* p. 315; New York *Times,* October 8, 1918.

[40] Text of note, Lansing to Swiss Chargé, October 8, 1918, *F.R., 1918, Suppl. 1,* I, 343.

military advantage. André Tardieu has praised the astuteness which turned the offer designed by Ludendorff as a means of saving his army, into the prelude of German surrender.[41] It was not so much shrewdness on Wilson's part as a simple adherence to straightforward ideas. He would not, just because the military map was changing, refuse any sincere offer of peace based upon a programme he had himself proposed. The only point to determine was whether Germany recognized her defeat and was sincere in her appeal.[42]

5

The best indication of the diplomatic effectiveness of the Wilson note is to be found in the confusion it created in German Headquarters. Prince Max and Solf, the new Foreign Minister, realized that acceptance outright of Wilson's conditions meant the defeat of Germany and would lead to peace terms that up to now no one in Germany had dreamed of considering. But in the public state of mind they dared not break off negotiations. The Army command was still more embarrassed. They had hoped that the appeal would bring an immediate armistice; a breathing space would save the retreating armies and enable Germany to negotiate with an effective armed force in reserve. But Wilson's note seemed to point not toward a breathing space but toward surrender.

On October 9 a conference was held between the military and civil chiefs. The former were not coherent. The mili-

---

[41] Tardieu, *Truth about the Treaty,* pp. 52-54.
[42] House Diary, October 15, 1918, *I.P.,* IV, 83.

tary situation was described as unfavorable, because of the lack of replacements; but Ludendorff disapproved of a *levée en masse* since the labor service could not be diminished. He no longer talked of an immediate collapse, spoke of holding the front for three months, of having six hundred tanks by spring. Colonel Heye pressed for the continuance of negotiations: " I do not fear a catastrophe, but I want to save the Army, so that we can use it as a means of pressure during the peace negotiations." [43]

It was on the basis of this principle that it was decided to draft a reply to Wilson which would accept his conditions, with an implied reservation that might make it possible to save the German armies. The note was sent on October 12. It accepted flatly the Fourteen Points as the basis of the peace, asking assurance that the Allied Governments also agreed.[44] It expressed readiness to evacuate occupied territory and left it to the President to " occasion the meeting of a mixed commission for making the necessary arrangements concerning the evacuation." It informed the President that the negotiations were being carried on by a Government which had the support of the majority of the Reichstag. " The Chancellor, supported in all of his actions by the will of this majority, speaks in the name of the German Government and of the German people." [45]

Germany's note of October 12 gave the appearance of a wholehearted acquiescence in Wilson's conditions. It made

[43] *P.H.A.*, No. 38, pp. 53-57.

[44] This counter-demand, quite as important to Wilson as to the Germans, was proposed by Hindenburg, *P.H.A.*, No. 41, p. 59; Prince Max, *op. cit.*, p. 75.

[45] Text of note, Swiss Chargé to Lansing, October 14, 1918, *F.R., 1918, Suppl. 1*, I, 357-358.

a real concession in its definite acceptance of the Fourteen Points, for the original note might have been interpreted as merely a readiness to talk them over. But it concealed a very serious counter-proposition which could have vital military results. The proposal of " a mixed commission " to debate the conditions of evacuation, if accepted with the suspension of hostilities, would have robbed the Allied armies of their existing advantage in position. Ludendorff suggested that it would be possible to put forward counter-proposals at the meetings of this commission and evidently believed that if the Allies did not agree to them he could resume the war on the line of the Franco-German frontier.[46] Thus Germany was yet far from surrender.

News of the German note reached Wilson on October 13, while on a visit to Colonel House. They were dining together, when House was called to take a telephone message from the Military Intelligence in Washington, reporting that the Germans had accepted the President's terms. " It seemed to me," wrote House, " that the war was finished, certainly finished if we have the judgment to garner victory." [47] Wilson agreed, but after returning to Washington and studying the German note he realized that the problem was not simple. The President faced the discontent of the Allies, who had drafted a joint note to him urging that simple evacuation of invaded territory would not be a sufficient basis for an armistice.[48] Even without this warning he

[46] P.H.A., No. 43, p. 62; Prince Max, op. cit., II, 73-74.
[47] House Diary, October 13, I.P., IV, 81-82.
[48] Text of note in F.R., 1918, Suppl. 1, I, 353. Frazier reported on October 9 that " in a conversation with Lloyd George and Bonar Law this morning, I noted a tone of disappointment that the

would probably have appreciated the joker contained in the proposal for a mixed commission. The United States could not engage separately in any discussion of the question of evacuation, which must be left to Allied military leaders. Germany must not be allowed to manœuver into a position where she could resume fighting. But Wilson must make his reply sufficiently encouraging to bring the Germans to a definite agreement and the negotiations to an immediate culmination. He was not affected by the demand for " unconditional surrender " that appeared in the metropolitan and eastern newspapers and on the floor of the Senate, but he was determined not to permit the Germans any loophole for escaping the Allied military attack.

Wilson again called Colonel House to Washington in order to discuss the form of his note, which was drafted during a long conference on the morning of October 14. The President did not find the process easy and it was not facilitated by his realization that it would probably determine the success or failure of the effort to shorten the war. " I never saw him more disturbed," wrote Colonel House.

" He said he did not know where to make the entrance in order to reach the heart of the thing. He wanted to make his reply final so there would be no exchange of notes. It reminded him, he said, of a maze. If one went in at the right entrance, he reached the center, but if one took the wrong turning, it was necessary to go out again and do it over. . . . [He was] anxious not to close the door, and yet desired to make the note as strong as the occasion required. He fell back time and again on the theory offered when the last note was written: that was, if Germany was

---

President had not left the terms of armistice to the military men," *ibid.*, p. 351.

beaten, she would accept any terms. If she was not beaten, he did not wish to make terms with her. . . . Neither did he desire to have the Allied armies ravage Germany as Germany has ravaged the countries she has invaded. The President was especially insistent that no stain of this sort should rest upon the Allied arms. He is very fine in this feeling and I am sorry he is hampered in any way by the Allies and the vociferous outcry in this country. It is difficult to do the right thing in the right way with people clamoring for the undesirable and impossible." [49]

At the end of the morning the President called a conference of House, Lansing, Baker, and Daniels to discuss the final form of the note. They approved it and it was sent off in the afternoon.

Wilson's second note bluntly rejected the suggestion of a mixed commission to negotiate the terms of evacuation. They " must be left to the judgment and advice of the military advisers of the Government of the United States and the Allied Governments." No armistice would be granted which did not provide " absolutely satisfactory safeguards and guarantees of the maintenance of the present military supremacy of the armies of the United States and of the Allies in the field." Nor could there be any agreement so long as German submarines continued to sink passenger ships at sea and the retreating armies committed wanton destruction. The note finally referred to the Mount Vernon speech of July 4, which demanded the " ' destruction of every arbitrary power anywhere that can separately, secretly, and of its single choice disturb the peace of the world. . . .' The power which has hitherto controlled the German nation is of the sort here described. . . . It is indispensable that

[49] House Diary, October 15, 1918, *I.P.*, IV, 82-83.

the governments associated against Germany should know
beyond a peradventure with whom they are dealing." [50]

The second Wilson note threw consternation into the
German camp. It made plain that Wilson, like the Allies,
demanded the complete defeat of Germany.

" In a single page," writes André Tardieu, " the whole poor
scaffolding of the German Great General Staff is overthrown.
The Armistice and peace are not to be means of delaying
a disaster and of preparing revenge. On the main question
itself the reply must be Yes or No! If it is no, war will
continue, as it has gone on for the last three months, by
Allied victories. If it is yes, the military capitulation must
be immediate and complete by the acceptance pure and
simple of terms which will be fixed by the military advisers
of the Allies alone." [51]

Prince Max is equally emphatic in describing the effects
of Wilson's terms:

" Not a word in this terrible document recalled the high
office of Arbitrator to which the President had aspired even
after the entry of America into the war. First the bow to
the Allied generals; then the abuse of our army and our
navy; the demand for the termination of the intensified
submarine war; and finally in dark and equivocal words the
appeal to the German people to take its fate into its own
hands, and thus to fulfill the preliminary condition required
for the conclusion of peace.

" Wilson's note altered the situation in Germany funda-
mentally. The internal peace which had been newly cemented went to pieces. With our offer longing for peace
became the ruling passion of the masses. Many had only
dammed up their impatience into a momentary self-control.
Only the supposed nearness of peace had kept them back

[50] Text of note, Lansing to Swiss Chargé, October 14, 1918,
F.R., 1918, Suppl. 1, I, 358-359.
[51] Tardieu, op. cit., p. 54.

from unpatriotic words and deeds. And now disappointment worked like the bursting of a dam." [52]

For a week the German leaders debated. Ludendorff, who had started the armistice ball rolling but who had regained some confidence by October 9, now became bellicose. The exchange of notes had not developed the situation as he expected. Acceptance of Wilson's demands meant not a breathing space in which he could save his armies, but their practical surrender:

" Before accepting the conditions of this note, which are too severe, we should say to the enemy: Win such terms by fighting for them. . . . I believe now as before, that if it is in any way possible, we must bring about negotiations for an armistice. But we should only enter upon such armistice negotiations as will permit an orderly evacuation of the country—consequently a respite of at least two or three months. Further we should not accept any conditions that would appear to make the resumption of hostilities impossible. That this is the intention, we cannot fail to see from the note. The terms are meant to put us out of the fight." [53]

Hindenburg warned the Chancellor by telephone, on October 20, that Wilson's terms meant complete defeat: " Even if we should be beaten, we should not really be worse off than if we were to accept everything at present." In the army the sentiment of the officers generally seemed to favor answering the note by force of arms.[54]

But the Ministers had lost confidence in the judgment of the military leaders, especially Ludendorff. His statements were vague and contradictory. He had bewailed the lack

[52] Prince Max, op. cit., p. 89.
[53] P.H.A., No. 57, pp. 98-99.
[54] P.H.A., No. 63, p. 105; Valentin, op. cit., p. 392.

of replacements. Now he had learned that he could have reinforcements of 600,000 within a short time; he seemed hopeful and happy, remarked Scheidemann, because he was promised 600,000 men to present to the death-dealing machines of the enemy. Delbrück maintained that " Ludendorff was such a muddlehead that he never knew what he really wanted." [55] The Foreign Minister, Solf, pointed out that at the beginning of the month the Supreme Army Command urged the Government to beg for an armistice. Against his will and conviction the Chancellor assumed responsibility for this step. After the Wilson reply General Headquarters had still adhered to their demand. " Now an answer from Wilson has arrived which puts us face to face with the most serious of decisions, and at once the picture undergoes a change—showing that we can now hold our own, that if we can survive the next four weeks, we shall even be in a much better position than before. . . . What is the real reason, a thing can be done now which a short time ago was declared impossible? " [56]

Despite the protests of the military leaders the Government decided to yield to Wilson. Ludendorff's explanation that the scarcity of men was not so great as they had supposed did not impress them. They received " intimations from a most impartial source, according to which the hopes expressed yesterday by General Ludendorff are not shared even by his *entourage*." [57] But most vital of all, the morale of the nation was broken. Wilson's notes had aroused irri-

[55] Scheidemann, *op. cit.,* pp. 180-187; *Ursachen,* III, 320.
[56] *P.H.A.,* No. 57, p. 99.
[57] Solf to Minister of War, October 18, 1918, *P.H.A.,* No. 62, p. 104.

tation because of apparent interference with Germany's constitutional development, and in army circles renewed determination, which might or might not have been justified. But they had also pointed the path to an early peace and German opinion could think of nothing else. " Ludendorff . . . wanted to go back; so did I " wrote Prince Max, " but here there was no room to turn." [58]

On October 20, the German Government sent their third note, embodying the acceptance of Wilson's conditions. To give point to the process of democratization, upon which the President had insisted, the Chancellor introduced into the Reichstag an amendment to Article 11 of the Constitution, which provided that the right of decision in questions of war and peace was to be vested solely in the people. Thus he could contend that he had met Wilson's demand for the elimination of " the arbitrary power that can separately and secretly disturb the peace of the world." He furthermore made a special point of presenting the new Ministers to the Kaiser. " The new government has been formed in complete accord with the representation of the people based on equal, universal, direct and secret franchise. . . . In future no government can take or continue in office without possessing the confidence of the majority of the Reichstag. The responsibility of the Chancellor . . . is being legally developed and safeguarded." [59] Orders had been sent to

[58] Prince Max, op. cit., II, 152.

[59] The historian may note what Prince Max could not publicly refer to, that the note itself was disapproved by Hindenburg, who refused to give up the submarine warfare without counter-concessions. The German people, he insisted, were " forced to capitulate and thus delivered to destruction before making their last

cruising submarines to cease the sinking of passenger ships, and to the retreating forces to respect private property. There was tacit acceptance of Wilson's insistence that the terms of the evacuation must be left to the military advisers of the Allies.[60]

The decision of the Government to send the note of October 20 sealed the fate of Germany. The Supreme Army Command continued to insist upon rejection of what it described as humiliating demands. But each day it became more difficult to break off negotiations. "This time," writes Tardieu, "Germany bound hand and foot is rivetted to Wilsonian dialectics. Since she does not break, she gives herself up."[61] When the German Government sent the note of October 20 it realized clearly that Wilson's conditions meant that Germany would not be able to resume the war. On October 23, Wilson agreed to communicate his correspondence with Germany to the Allies. On the 27th a fourth German note concluded: "The German Government now awaits the proposals for an armistice, which is the first step toward a peace of justice, as described by the President in his pronouncements."[62]

In Germany there has long persisted the contention that German armies were not defeated but betrayed; that Ger-

---

and final exertion," *P.H.A.*, No. 63, p. 105. This over-riding of Hindenburg indicates better than anything else the transfer of power to the civilians.

[60] Nowak, *Collapse,* p. 286 ff. Text of note, Swiss Chargé to Lansing, October 22, 1918, *F.R., 1918, Suppl. 1,* I, 380-381.

[61] *P.H.A.*, No. 82, pp. 118-119; Tardieu, *op. cit.,* p. 58.

[62] Wilson note of October 23, Lansing to Swiss Chargé, October 23, 1918; German note of October 27, Swiss Chargé to Lansing, October 28, 1918, *F.R., 1918, Suppl. 1,* I, 381-395.

many was lured into the armistice by promises that were not kept. Something is to be said, certainly, for the argument that it would have taken Allied armies costly weeks, perhaps months, of the severest fighting to have imposed upon Germany the terms that were incorporated in the armistice of November 11. When Marshal Foch was asked on November 3 what would happen if the Germans refused to sign, and how long it would take to drive them back across the Rhine, " he answered, opening both arms, a familiar gesture with him: ' Maybe three, maybe four or five months. Who knows? ' He never alluded to a final blow in the next few days." [63]

But the German armies were so close to absolute defeat that continued fighting could merely have postponed the ultimate result at tremendous cost of life, perhaps the miseries of armed invasion for the German people. The German armies were not betrayed. Their own military leaders started the process which ended in the armistice of November 11. Ludendorff hoped, it is true, merely to win a breathing space for recuperation. He hoped by matching his diplomatic wits against the simple-minded Wilson to save his armies, through political action, from a fate which the military force and genius of Germany could not avert. His plan failed. Wilson was not caught in the lure. Once Ludendorff had started the peace-making process he could not stop it, for the material and moral condition of Germany and German public opinion demanded that it continue. But there was in this process nothing of bad faith.

[63] Mantoux to House, July 6, 1920, *I.P.*, IV, 91. Paul Mantoux acted as interpreter for the Supreme War Council.

Nor was Germany lured into the acceptance of the Fourteen Points. The Government had ample opportunity to discuss the possible significance of Wilson's principles, realized that they were nebulous, and might have insisted upon an immediate elucidation or a future discussion. Prince Max knew and stated that the Fourteen Points meant that Germany would lose important territory, Alsace-Lorraine, the Polish corridor, her colonies. So clearly did the Government appreciate these facts that it prepared a memorandum dealing with them and asking from Wilson guarantees regarding the Fourteen Points. But the memorandum was never sent, lest it interrupt the negotiations for an armistice. The military leaders were so intent upon an armistice that the Chancellor was not permitted to make the speech he had drafted, reserving German rights under the Fourteen Points. The representative of the Supreme Command, Haeften, declared that "the definition of the Fourteen Points would endanger the whole armistice action." The Germans were not deceived by the Fourteen Points; they refused to ask themselves or Wilson what their bearing might be. "My speech," writes Prince Max, "would have aroused Germany to the startling consciousness that it had never considered what Wilson's programme really meant." [64] Therefore the military leaders would not let him deliver it.

Wilson had achieved a brilliant diplomatic success, one not generally recognized at the moment and of which he himself seems to have been scarcely conscious. He had turned Ludendorff's plan to save German armies into a process which led rapidly and successfully to German sur-

[64] Prince Max, op. cit., II, 32-42.

22

render. It was not an unconditional surrender; by agreement the Germans were to acquire legally and morally the right to appeal to the Fourteen Points. But it guaranteed that Germany could bring no pressure through military force, for her army was to be helpless.

6

President Wilson's interchange of notes with Germany was purely personal to himself and the United States. He committed himself to nothing more than a willingness to transmit his correspondence to the Allies, in order that they might act upon Germany's conditional acceptance of his terms. His note of October 23 reads:

" The President has, therefore, transmitted his correspondence with the present German authorities to the Governments with which the Government of the United States is associated as a belligerent, with the suggestion that, if those Governments are disposed to effect peace upon the terms and principles indicated, their military advisers and the military advisers of the United States be asked to submit to the Governments associated against Germany the necessary terms of such an armistice as will fully protect the interests of the peoples involved and ensure to the associated governments the unrestricted power to safeguard and enforce the details of peace to which the German Government has agreed, provided they deem such an armistice possible from the military point of view." [65]

Both the German and Wilson's approval of the terms agreed upon in this correspondence was conditional; in the case of the Germans upon the Allied approval of the Fourteen Points, in the case of Wilson upon Allied willingness

[65] Wilson note of October 23, Lansing to Swiss Chargé, October 23, 1918, *F.R., 1918, Suppl. 1,* I, 382.

" to effect peace upon the terms and principles indicated."
Furthermore the development of the negotiations was dependent upon the provision that the Allies deemed " such
an armistice possible from the military point of view."

The fact is important and should be underlined, since
many have laid upon Wilson the responsibility for a premature peace.[66] Except for his influence, they insist, Foch
would have triumphantly invaded Germany and dictated
peace in Berlin. For some unexplained purpose the United
States was believed to have robbed the Allies of victory.
The criticism rests upon misconception and ignorance. What
Wilson offered the Allies was not peace but merely the opportunity to make peace through an armistice, if they wished.
He merely passed on to them Germany's appeal for an
armistice. He left them free to decide not to grant an
armistice if they disapproved it.

" Then was the time," wrote General Bliss, " for the Allied
Governments, or any one of them, to say, ' No, we are not
disposed to effect peace upon the terms and principles indicated ' and ' we shall not ask our advisers to submit for our
approval the necessary terms of such an armistice nor of
any armistice.' As a matter of fact, the Allies and Associated
Powers immediately consulted their military advisers." [67]

Allied leaders had watched with interest and some nervousness the exchange of notes between Germany and the

[66] Cf. Henri Mordacq, *Le Ministère Clemenceau*, II, 340. Mordacq's opinion, which is of importance as he was military representative on the staff of Clemenceau, is that the armistice terms
gave the Allies all that could have been expected from a continuation
of the fighting.

[67] Bliss, " The Armistices," in *The American Journal of International Law*, 16, p. 512.

United States. At the beginning they certainly feared lest Wilson commit himself to a course of compromise. The President was careful, however, to leave them with completely free hands. During the first days of October they were inclined to believe that victory was still distant and that an armistice would imperil their military advantage. But the situation changed rapidly and favorably, in both the military and diplomatic sense. On October 12 Clemenceau, Pichon, and Foch met to discuss terms that might be inserted in an armistice convention. President Poincaré protested in opposition to the armistice, writing to Clemenceau on the 14th that the Germans were simply seeking to gain time and an opportunity to " hamstring " the French army. But Clemenceau in a brief note replied that the decision must be made by the responsible leaders and intimated that any interference by Poincaré would lead to his own resignation.[68]

At a meeting of the military commanders held at Senlis on October 25, the proviso raised by Wilson, " provided they [the Allies] deem such an armistice possible from the military point of view," was settled apparently without any discussion. " We should have to go back to the days of Rome or earlier," said General Bliss, " to find a civilized nation refusing even to discuss terms upon which fighting

[68] Gabriel Terrail, *Les negociations secrètes et les quatre armistices,* pp. 221-222. As early as October 8, Foch had sent to Clemenceau a " résumé of the obligations which, in my opinion, should be imposed upon our foe ' in case the question arose of stopping hostilities, even momentarily,' " Foch, *Memoirs,* p. 451. The recommendations were discussed by Foch and the Prime Ministers of France, Great Britain, and Italy, Frazier to Lansing, October 9, 1918, *F.R., 1918, Suppl. 1,* I, 351.

might cease. It would be unheard of to say: 'No, we haven't killed enough of you, there are some towns we want to burn.' " [69] They proceeded to draft terms designed to give the complete protection to the military superiority of the Allies that Wilson stipulated.

Of all the military leaders, the only one opposed to the granting of an armistice, no matter what its terms, was General Pershing. He raised no question at the meeting of the generals on October 26, but four days later wrote to Colonel House protesting against an armistice and presenting a memorandum that set forth his argument for continuing the fighting. He emphasized the favorable military prospects of the Allies and the danger of permitting the Germans to withdraw from a critical situation. His memorandum was cabled to Washington but produced no support from the President nor the War Department. It was also laid before Clemenceau and Lloyd George, who treated it with scant attention. The former glanced at the memorandum and, remarking " Theatricals! ", handed it to Lloyd George, who, rather in character, ejaculated, " Politics." [70] Neither remark was fair to Pershing. More cogent was the criticism of Foch, who pointed out the contradiction between the memorandum and the letter, both written on the same day: the first insisting that an armistice would jeopardize victory, the second approving the Foch recommendations as a complete guarantee of ability to impose a satisfactory peace on Germany. With military loyalty Pershing accepted the decision against his opinion.

[69] Bliss to C. S., June 22, 1928, *I.P.,* IV, 95.

[70] Pershing letter and memorandum with endorsement by House, Y.H.C.

Thus by October 26, without any formal conference it was agreed by the Allies that terms should be offered to Germany.

" There seemed to be perfect agreement both between the Allied Governments and between the soldiers and states-men," wrote Paul Mantoux, " as to the desirability of con-cluding the armistice, provided, of course, that Germany accepted the conditions laid down, which amounted to little less than capitulation." [71]

Full responsibility for deciding upon the armistice thus rests with the Allied Governments and the Generalissimo. This was formally determined in the famous interchange of ques-tion and answer between Foch and House, after the terms were drafted:

" Will you tell us, M. le Maréchal," asked House, " solely from the military point of view, apart from any other con-sideration, whether you would prefer the Germans to reject or sign the armistice as outlined here? "

" ' War is waged,' replied Foch, ' merely to secure certain results.[72] If the Germans now sign an armistice under the general conditions we have just determined, those results are in our possession. This being achieved, no man has the right to cause another drop of blood to be shed.' " [73]

[71] Mantoux to House, July 6, 1920, *I.P.,* IV, 91-92.

[72] " On ne fait la guerre que pour ses résultats."

[73] Mantoux to House, July 6, 1920, *I.P.,* IV, 91; Foch, *op. cit.,* p. 463.

CHAPTER IX

THE DRAFTING OF THE ARMISTICE

1

The diplomatic aspects of the ending of the war fall naturally into three divisions. The first, covered in the preceding chapter, was marked by Germany's appeal for an armistice and her acceptance of the general terms laid down by President Wilson. The second includes the determination by the Supreme War Council of the Allies of the specific conditions of the armistice proper, which was signed by Marshal Foch and the German delegates on November 11. The third, and from a certain point of view the most important, was the successful effort of Colonel House to win from the Allies approval of the Fourteen Points which had already been accepted by the Germans; it culminated in the so-called Pre-Armistice Agreement, approved by both sides as the basis of the peace.

During the first phase of the diplomacy of the armistice, negotiations were carried on between Washington and Berlin. With the beginning of the second, when President Wilson transmitted his provisional understanding with the Germans to the Supreme War Council, the diplomatic centre was shifted to Paris and the responsibility for drafting conditions of an armistice was laid upon the Allies. As representative of the United States, Colonel House arrived in Paris on October 26. He was advised in military matters by General Bliss, in naval by Admiral Benson.

House and Wilson were in such close understanding that
the former was left with a completely free hand and without any instructions. When Wilson, who has been accused
of an inability to delegate powers to assistants, selected a
representative he left the matter in hand to him and gave
him full authority.[1] The only indication of Wilson's wishes
appeared in a cable of October 29, which simply endorsed
his public statements:

" My deliberate judgment is that our whole weight should
be thrown for an armistice which will not permit a renewal
of hostilities by Germany, but which will be as moderate and
reasonable as possible within that condition, because lately
I am certain that too much severity on the part of the Allies
will make a genuine peace settlement exceedingly difficult
if not impossible. . . . Foresight is better than immediate
advantage." [2]

With this attitude the Allied leaders did not disagree, partly
at least since they were anxious to produce armistice terms
that Germany could accept. House's initial impression was
that the French would be too severe, for Clemenceau on
October 26 expressed the " belief, which was also that of
Marshal Foch, that Germany was so thoroughly beaten she
would accept any terms offered. Haig does not agree." [3]
But on November 1 he cabled the President that both
Clemenceau and Lloyd George were as " moderate as Foch
will permit. They realize that the terms should not be
harsher than is necessary to fulfill your conditions regard-

[1] The student will also note the undeviating support given to
Pershing in his differences with the Allies and the complete elimination of political interference with military control.

[2] Wilson to House, October 29, 1918, Y.H.C.

[3] House Diary, October 26, 1918, *I.P.,* IV, 93.

ing the making of it impossible for Germany to renew hostilities." [4]

Wilson's correspondence with the Germans had stipulated that the terms of the armistice must be such as to preserve, in the opinion of Allied military advisers, the existing military advantage of the Allies. To the Commanders-in-Chief, therefore, was first referred the question of essential military conditions. On October 25 Foch called the commanders of the French, British, Italian and American armies to Senlis and asked for their opinion. There appeared at once a marked difference between the French and British, resulting from their differing experience and estimate of German powers of resistance. General Pétain demanded the disarmament of the German troops, with the exception of carrying arms, and the occupation by Allied armies of a broad strip of German territory as a pledge. He wished to specify a time for withdrawal so short that it would be materially impossible for the Germans to carry away their war supplies. The Germans should evacuate all invaded territory and Alsace-Lorraine, and permit the occupation of the left bank of the Rhine and a zone fifty kilometres back on the right bank. In his opinion such conditions represented the minimum that should be demanded. He did not think the Germans would accept them.

Field Marshal Haig insisted that if it were really desired to conclude the armistice, and in his opinion this was most desirable, much more moderate terms must be offered. The

[4] House to Wilson, November 1, 1918, *I.P.*, IV, III. The text of the cable as published in *F.R., 1918, Suppl. 1*, I, 438, is obviously garbled, and alters House's meaning. The above is taken from the carbon copy of the original.

Allied armies, although victorious, were worn out; Germany
was not broken in a military sense. He suggested merely
the evacuation of the invaded portions of France and Belgium and Alsace-Lorraine, together with the restitution of
rolling stock. The evacuation of Alsace-Lorraine, he felt,
was enough to seal the victory.[5]

Marshal Foch did not express his opinion at the conference of October 25, but at the close of the meeting drew
up his own terms which he sent to Clemenceau on the following day, terms which were not far from those ultimately
offered. He took as his mandate the phrase from Wilson's
note of October 23 which designated terms that would
" fully protect the interests of the peoples involved and
ensure to the Associated Governments the unrestricted power
to safeguard and enforce the details of the peace to which
the German Government has agreed." Foch looked upon
Haig's suggestions as quite inadequate, for the German
armies after evacuation would still be able to resume defensive warfare on their own borders and with much better
chance of success than in existing conditions. But he did
not agree that it was necessary to follow Pétain's suggestion
of depriving the Germans of everything but carrying arms.
He demanded an evacuation so rapid as to prevent them
from taking a large part of the material of war stored in
invaded territory, and a surrender of approximately one-
third of the German artillery and half of their machine-
guns; in addition the restitution of rolling stock and enough
more for train service on the left bank of the Rhine. The
left bank must be occupied by Allied troops although it

[5] Foch, *Memoirs*, pp. 459-460.

would be administered by local authorities; in addition the Allies must occupy bridgeheads on the Rhine and a neutral zone must be established to the east of it.[6]

General Pershing, although opposed to any armistice at all at this time, agreed that if terms were to be granted he would approve those of Foch.[7] But General Bliss disagreed strongly. He had already cabled his own views to Washington and now drafted a memorandum for the chiefs of government. He also discussed it at length with Foch. His formula was more stringent but much simpler, the only sure guarantee, he felt, of protection from a renewal of the war with Germany. This formula was contained in three words: disarmament and demobilization. He said to Foch: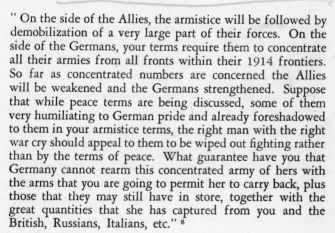

" On the side of the Allies, the armistice will be followed by demobilization of a very large part of their forces. On the side of the Germans, your terms require them to concentrate all their armies from all fronts within their 1914 frontiers. So far as concentrated numbers are concerned the Allies will be weakened and the Germans strengthened. Suppose that while peace terms are being discussed, some of them very humiliating to German pride and already foreshadowed to them in your armistice terms, the right man with the right war cry should appeal to them to be wiped out fighting rather than by the terms of peace. What guarantee have you that Germany cannot rearm this concentrated army of hers with the arms that you are going to permit her to carry back, plus those that they may still have in store, together with the great quantities that she has captured from you and the British, Russians, Italians, etc." [8]

---

[6] Foch to Clemenceau, October 25, 1918, *I.P.*, II, 143-144; Foch, *op. cit.*, p. 461.

[7] Pershing to House, October 30, 1918, Y.H.C.

[8] Bliss to C. S., June 14, 1928, Y.H.C.

Thus Bliss insisted that only the complete disarmament and demobilization of Germany would give complete security, and that if so much were accomplished no other armistice terms would be necessary. If Germany believed her case in the field were hopeless she would as soon accept such terms as those of Foch. " If she rejected this but would accept a much less complete disarmament, it was a fair presumption that she had in the back of her head the idea that some time she might want to resume the war." [9] Looking back at the armistice ten years later Bliss still insisted that the partial disarmament of Germany was a mistake, since she continued to be a peril in the eyes of the Allied leaders.

" No sooner was the armistice signed than the Allies became obsessed with a fear that Germany could rearm herself to such an extent, at least, as would make her very formidable, and for months this fear haunted the Peace Conference. It wasn't the partial disarmament of Germany that protected the Allies from this danger so much as it was the complete internal disruption of Germany following the signing of the armistice." [10]

But Bliss' contention received little support. Foch insisted that he knew every piece of equipment that Germany could lay her hands on and that it would be impossible for her to reëquip herself. The British were still less willing to accept the Bliss memorandum. Lord Milner, British War Secretary, admitted that the Germans would accept any terms, but wished to leave them some arms since he believed

[9] Bliss memorandum, October 28, 1918; Comment of General Bliss on armistice terms, June 14, 1928, *I.P.*, IV, 145-147.
[10] Bliss to C. S., June 14, 1928, *I.P.*, IV, 115.

Germany would have to serve as the bulwark against Bolshevism. Sir Henry Wilson, British Chief of Staff, was intent on making acceptance of the armistice easy for the Germans; he would take away their field artillery and machine guns, but would let them retreat with the honors of war, drums beating, colors flying, and infantry armament. " To get them out of France," he told Bliss, " I would build a golden bridge for them across the Rhine." [11] Opposed by the French and the British, unsupported by Pershing and the American War Department, the Bliss formula fell by the wayside.

While the military terms were thus being drafted by Foch, who consulted the generals but set down the conditions he liked, the naval terms were drawn up by the Interallied Naval Council and in this case largely under the influence of the British. Foch in his letter to Clemenceau had suggested very mild terms; the surrender of the seaworthy submarines, the withdrawal of the German surface fleet to Baltic ports, the occupation of Cuxhaven and Heligoland by the Allies.

The naval leaders were not satisfied with these terms. Admiral Benson, who represented the United States on the Naval Council, was convinced that the best guarantee of future world peace was to be found in a sharing of the command of the seas between Great Britain and the United States. " He was very anxious to have the United States maintain a fleet equal to that of Great Britain," writes Mrs. Benson. " He felt that by doing so the peace of the world could be maintained." [12] On the other hand, he was

[11] Bliss to House, October 28, 1918; Bliss to C. S., June 14, 1928, *I.P.*, IV, 116-117.

[12] Mrs. W. S. Benson to Colonel House, August 1, 1933, Y.H.C.

a determined although prudent advocate of limitation of
naval armament and believed that the opportunity should
be utilized to demand the surrender and the destruction
of the German battle cruisers, the most powerful naval arm
thus far developed. " I was in favor of sinking all German
naval warcraft," he wrote later. " The majority of the committee on naval terms wanted the vessels divided up. I did
not feel that after peace any naval armaments should be
increased." [13]

There was no disagreement between Benson and the
Allied naval leaders as to the need of stiffer naval terms
than those proposed by Foch. The Interallied Naval Council
insisted that in addition to their submarines the Germans
must surrender their battle cruisers, ten battleships, and
numerous light craft, cruisers and destroyers.

" If President Wilson's conditions are to be fulfilled,"
Sir Eric Geddes reported for the Naval Council, " and the
Germans are not to be in a position to renew the war under
better conditions than those at present existing, their fleet
must be cut down as proposed . . . the German fleet is
superior in battle cruisers to the Allies, and if those were
not handed over, the Allies would have to start to build
battle cruisers." [14]

Colonel House had the highest regard for Benson's judgment. He had worked with him during the Interallied Conference at the end of 1917, when he pressed for the creation
of the Naval Council; remembered the promptness with
which he guaranteed assistance to the Allied fleets at a
moment when British naval morale was low, and the energy

[13] Benson to C. S., June 16, 1928, *I.P.,* IV, 131.
[14] Minutes of Conversation, November 1, 1918, Y.H.C.

with which he insisted upon the North Sea mine barrage which the Allies regarded as impossible to lay, and which was nevertheless successfully accomplished.

" On my successive trips to Europe during the war," comments House, " the man most helpful to me was Admiral William S. Benson, Chief of Naval Operations. He was of the greatest possible service in the armistice negotiations, and I leaned on him heavily at that time. The outstanding characteristics of Admiral Benson were his good sense, his courage, and his extreme modesty." [15]

Although, like the other civil representatives on the Supreme War Council, House favored terms as lenient as consistent with Allied naval security, he was thus ready to accept the recommendations of the Naval Council. He believed, however, that it was for the British and not the Americans to assume the responsibility for them as against the protests of the French military leaders.

2

Clemenceau was willing to listen to the opinions of the generals and admirals, and even to follow them. But he was most insistent that the political chiefs must take definite responsibility for all final decisions. He spoke of the proposal that the whole matter be referred to Foch and discarded it. " If Foch decides, then the Governments are suppressed. I propose that we consult Marshal Foch and all others whose advice may be essential. Then we will transmit our conclusions to President Wilson." [16]

[15] House to C. S., May 3, 1933, Y.H.C.
[16] Minutes of Conversation, October 29, 1918, Y.H.C.

Actual decisions on all points of importance were taken by a small steering committee consisting of the heads of government, with Colonel House representing the United States. The latter suggested that much time could be saved if Clemenceau, Lloyd George, Orlando and himself could meet informally in the mornings, previous to the formal meeting of the Supreme War Council at Versailles. Lloyd George and Clemenceau accepted the suggestion and further agreed that no matter should be raised for debate at Versailles until decision upon vital issues, at least, had been reached in the small steering committee. Frequently the Foreign Secretaries, Balfour, Pichon, and Sonnino, were included, and, according to the character of the discussion, military, naval, and economic advisers. The meetings were held generally in the salon of Colonel House's headquarters, 78 rue de l'Université.[17]

Thus when the Supreme War Council met at Versailles drafts were ready for its approval and except upon a few

[17] Comment by Colonel House, May 3, 1933: "You should bring out clearly the reason why Clemenceau, Lloyd George, Orlando and I met in the mornings at my house, No. 78 rue de l'Université, during the Armistice proceedings and in the afternoons with the Supreme War Council at Versailles. This was done at my suggestion in order to avoid the endless debates of the other delegates that were going on day by day. Clemenceau approved the idea but said that since he was Prime Minister of France and, in a sense, the host of the visiting delegates, he could not invite Lloyd George, Orlando and me to meet in his office without inviting the others as well. He preferred that I invite the three of them to meet with me at my residence. This was done, and all questions were threshed out by the four of us in the mornings. In the afternoons our decisions were accepted by the Supreme War Council sitting at Versailles."

contentious points time was not lost in debate. " Its sole
function," writes Bliss, " was to trim the edges and round off
the corners, in doing which there was an opportunity to consider points raised by the smaller Powers that had not been
represented in the preparation of the drafts." [18] Clemenceau,
indeed, was rather inclined to regard the decisions of the
committee as authoritative. Once when Lord Milner complained that some resolutions drafted by the committee had
not been approved by the Supreme War Council at the afternoon meeting, the old Premier replied: " That is not necessary. The Supreme War Council met this morning and
passed upon those questions. Whenever the Prime Ministers
and Colonel House meet, the Supreme War Council meets,
and what we do is final." [19]

The steering committee had small leisure and it must be
accounted to the credit of the organization as well as to the
capacity of the men who composed it, that in a period of
no more than ten days it settled problems of the most varied
character and vital import: approval of the Turkish armistice,
drafting of the Austrian armistice, disposal of the Austrian
fleet, drafting of a fresh plan of campaign against Germany
from the south; all this was entirely beside the main business of the armistice with Germany and the consideration of
the Fourteen Points. The statesmen were human and they
also represented nations which, although allied, had each its
own point of view. Differences of opinion were often sharp
and sometimes expressive of extreme national sensitiveness.
The afternoon of October 30 was almost entirely taken up

[18] Bliss, " The Armistices," in *The American Journal of International Law,* 16, p. 509.
[19] House Diary, November 4, 1918, *I.P.,* IV, 99.

23

by a discussion as to whether the Turkish armistice should be signed by a British or a French admiral. The French maintained that the naval high command in the Mediterranean had always been theirs, and the prestige of signature should also be theirs, although the Turks had applied to the British for armistice terms. To this Lloyd George replied that when it had been a question of losing battleships in the Dardanelles the French had been quite willing to let the British take command; that the French had merely sent down a few colored policemen "to see that the British didn't steal the Holy Sepulchre!" The incident was quickly composed but it throws an interesting light on the differences of feeling that cropped up between the Allies as soon as the cement of German resistance disappeared.[20]

The Austrian armistice was drafted with speed and severity. "We have left the breeches of the Emperor," said Clemenceau on reading the terms recommended by the experts, "and nothing else." The original plan had been to transmit the terms to Austria through President Wilson, to whom Austria had appealed. But the Austrians were in such need of an armistice that they could not wait. Already on October 30 an Austrian officer had crossed the lines with a letter asking for immediate terms and a similar request by wireless had been received by the Italian command. Lloyd George pointed out that there would be great advantage in having disposed completely of Austria before dealing with Germany. He urged that the terms be sent without delay. "As soon as Austria is out, Germany will capitulate at once. Therefore we ought to act before President Wilson has time to answer."

[20] Minutes of Conversation, October 30, 1918, Y.H.C.

Thus it came about that the armistice with Austria was presented and accepted without any political implications. In the case of Germany, the notification that an armistice was ready was sent by Wilson, accompanied by a definite statement regarding the Fourteen Points. In the case of Austria, the process was carried through entirely by military officials and no mention was made of the Fourteen Points. Did the Fourteen Points, upon which as a basis Austria had sued for peace, apply to Austria or not? The question was never clearly settled and it was later to make trouble at the Peace Conference.

3

On October 29 the Prime Ministers, except Orlando who arrived a day later, and the Foreign Secretaries of the three principal Powers met with Colonel House for a preliminary discussion of the draft terms presented by Foch and by the Naval Council. They regarded them as too severe, especially the naval terms. Balfour at once expressed a doubt as to whether there was " the smallest prospect of Germany accepting those terms." " They won't the first day," responded Clemenceau, " but they will contrive somehow or other not to let the conversations drop." But even he thought the naval terms " rather stiff." [21]

Lloyd George then read out the terms drafted by the Naval Council, calling for the surrender of one hundred and fifty submarines, ten battleships, six battle cruisers, and lighter craft. " What are the Allies going to do," said House, " with the ships they take from Germany? " " They

[21] Minutes of Conversation, October 29, 1918, Y.H.C.

will divide them," said Lloyd George: " You can sink them if you like; you must take them away from Germany." " Well," continued Balfour, returning to his original criticism, " I do. not think Germany will agree to these conditions. They are stiffer than those imposed by Germany in 1871; you will have to beat them in the field worse than they are beaten now."

Lloyd George also raised the question of occupying the west bank of the Rhine, which seemed to him unnecessary and severe. He may have harbored the suspicion that the French were planning to turn a temporary occupation into permanent separation from Germany. But Clemenceau insisted that he could not maintain himself in the French Chamber of Deputies unless such occupation were stipulated in the armistice terms; the French army would also regard it as their due after so long an occupation of French territory by the Germans. He pledged his word of honor that France would withdraw after the peace conditions were fulfilled.[22] When House raised the argument that Germany might be driven to a state of Bolshevism by over-severe terms, and emphasized the consequent danger to the rest of Europe, Clemenceau refused to admit any danger of communism in France although " anything might happen in Italy." The military question was passed over for the moment, but it was definitely agreed that the naval terms should be " softened." [23]

[22] The promise was kept but it led to a bitter passage between Clemenceau and Foch at the Peace Conference.

[23] Minutes of Conversation of October 29, 1918, Y.H.C.; House Diary, October 29, 1918; House to Wilson, October 30, 1918, *I.P.*, IV, 118.

Marshal Foch's military terms were finally approved and incorporated with minor changes in the armistice, but not without long discussion. They were by no means rubber-stamped by the political leaders. On November 1 Foch and Weygand were called in to defend their recommendations. They met at House's apartment that morning in preparation for the formal meeting of the Supreme War Council in the afternoon.[24]

Foch had made one concession to British opinion in eliminating the bridgehead at Strassburg which he had planned. But Lloyd George was not satisfied; the terms were " rather stiff."

"All the great cities of western Germany will be in Allied hands. The conference must realize that we are making a very stiff demand. I ask Marshal Foch if it would not be possible to secure the bridgeheads required for military purposes without occupying the great cities."

The Generalissimo was adamant.

" Mainz is absolutely indispensable. Frankfort will not be occupied, although I admit that it will be within two miles of the occupied territory and under the guns of the Allies, I must insist also that Cologne is of tremendous importance, as it is the junction of many railways and the focus of the land communications of the Palatinate; therefore I regard Cologne as an indispensable bridgehead."

The discussion shifted to Haig's proposals, which provided merely for German evacuation of invaded territories and Alsace-Lorraine, leaving the west bank of the Rhine in German hands. Lloyd George summarized Haig's argument:

---

[24] The following paragraphs are based upon Minutes of Conversation held at 78 rue de l'Université, November 1, 1918, Y.H.C.

"Why do you wish to take more than the territories he had proposed? If you had those you would have in hand everything you desired in the West at the Peace Conference, and if the armistice broke down it would not be necessary for you to attack, but for the enemy to do so . . . the German army was by no means broken. Whenever you hit them they hit back and inflicted heavy casualties. They showed none of the ordinary symptoms of a disorganized army. Their retirement was effected in perfect order and was conducted with the greatest skill. . . . Field Marshal Haig did not assert that we should not be much better off if we could get the bridgeheads. The question he did raise, however, was as to whether the German army was in such a condition that the German Government would consider these drastic terms. . . . If we were not in a position to secure them, we ought to demand less drastic terms."

Marshal Foch returned to the basic condition laid down by President Wilson:

"The principle on which he had based his terms for an armistice was that you must not place the enemy in a better position than he now occupied, to resume the contest in the event of a breakdown of the armistice. Field Marshal Haig's conditions violated this principle since they put the enemy in a better position. If Germany should break off the peace negotiations, the Allies ought to be in a position to destroy her. The whole of the German system of defense, however, is based on the Rhine, and we cannot settle down during an armistice unless our perspective embraces the bridgeheads on the Rhine."

Colonel House, although not disposed to take from Germany more than was absolutely necessary, supported Foch. It was a military matter, he insisted, and must be determined by military judgment. But would not the Germans be able to carry on a defensive war even with the Rhine in the hands of the Allies? Foch replied that the bridgeheads and neutral zone on the east bank made all the difference. Orlando's suggestion of a neutral belt on the west bank instead of the east he opposed violently; this would enable the "enemy to entrench himself strongly on the right bank of the Rhine, and in order to attack him, we should have to cross the Rhine." But with the Rhine in Allied control Germany would be helpless.

The debate shifted to the probability of German refusal of terms and the consequences of refusal. Foch admitted that if he "was asked whether the German army was now ready (*en train*) to accept, his answer would be 'No.'" In reply to a question by Lloyd George as to whether Foch could continue to drive the Germans back all through the winter, he answered that undoubtedly the German army could take up a new position and "we could not prevent it. But he did not want to facilitate them in this task, as would be done by Field Marshal Haig's terms." He could certainly continue to drive them back and was determined to do so until the Allied armies were in a better position than that promised by Haig's conditions.

Clemenceau reiterated his conviction of Germany's inability to refuse whatever terms were offered. He was more confident than Foch:

"The situation of the Allies *vis à vis* the enemy had never been so crushing before. The American effectives were enormous. To-morrow the Allies would be able to march across Austria against Germany. He had little doubt that the first reply of the German Government would be to refuse our terms, but as we increased our advantages they would concede them."

Lloyd George finally yielded and agreed to the Foch proposals. It may have been that he merely desired their thorough clarification. At all events he stated that,

" after hearing the whole discussion, he was prepared to stand by Marshal Foch's document. He felt, however, that if, as the result of our demands, Germany should make up her mind to continue fighting, it was most important to let it be known to our soldiers that we had fully examined the contrary point of view put forward by Field Marshal Haig. . . . He would like it to be known that this view had been most carefully considered, and that a contrary decision had only been taken after all the generals had been consulted and on the unanimous decision of the Supreme War Council."

The naval terms as drafted by the experts gave to the heads of government quite as much difficulty as the military. The course of the debate illustrates beautifully the proverb that deals with feet and shoes. The French, a military nation, had demanded drastic military terms as against the protests of the British. The latter, dominating the Naval Council, proposed naval terms that seemed to Foch excessive. He was willing to see the submarines surrendered. But why ask the surrender of the surface fleet, battle cruisers and battleships, which had never played any part in the war? "Why make the armistice harder, for I repeat its sole object is to place Germany *hors de combat?*" Suppose that Germany proved willing to accept the necessary military terms, but refused the additional humiliation of the unnecessary surrender of her surface fleet. "It would not be right to ask the armies to fight again in order to secure these conditions." [25]

Sir Eric Geddes, who represented the views of the Naval Council, retorted that the terms as drafted were by no means excessive. It was a vital error to suppose that the surface

[25] Minutes of Conversation, November 1, 1918, Y.H.C.; Tardieu, *The Truth about the Treaty,* p. 67.

fleet had not been and might not be a factor of very great importance.

" Marshal Foch is wrong in saying that the submarines alone have hurt us. But for the [British] Grand Fleet the ships it is now proposed to take would have been out on the trade routes and inflicting great destruction on the Allies. They would even interrupt the arrival of American troops. Marshal Foch has no idea how much trouble the [German] High Sea Fleet has given us, because the [British] Grand Fleet has always held it in check. If these ships are not surrendered, the Grand Fleet during the armistice will be in the same state of tension as that of two armies opposed to each other in battle array in trenches."

But the British naval advisers did not receive the same support from Lloyd George that the French military advisers received from Clemenceau. The British Prime Minister was anxious to eliminate everything not absolutely necessary, lest it lead to a German refusal. He suggested that the naval advisers reconsider their recommendations on the basis of a compromise: the submarines and the battle cruisers to be surrendered, the battleships to be interned in neutral ports. " These conditions will appear much less hard to the Germans who, while they will know that they will never get the battle cruisers back, will assume that the battleships will be returned to them."

The naval advisers stood firm. At the full meeting of the Supreme War Council on the afternoon of November 2, Admiral Hope explained in much the same terms as those used by Geddes, the conviction of the Naval Council. Unless Germany were deprived of the warships designated, she would come out of the war stronger, in a naval sense, than she went in. Either the ships must be surrendered or interned under Allied surveillance. Surrender was much the preferable and safer course. Again the decision was postponed, at the request of Lloyd George, who contended that it was important to await the decision of Austria. If she accepted the armistice terms, stiffer terms could be put to Germany.[26]

The British Prime Minister cast about for another compromise, and insisted that the political leaders would have to take the initiative. " Our Admirals," he said at the meeting of November 2, " have got their tails up and will not move. We might suggest that instead of confiscating cruisers and battleships we intern the whole lot." The compromise was not suggested by the Americans, as was later asserted, although finally accepted by them. Internment would leave the ultimate disposition of the German navy to the Peace Conference, as suggested by House. Clemenceau preferred internment to surrender, which was evidently taken to mean the addition of the German ships to existing navies. " There will be no place in the Society of Nations," said he, " for a country with thirty-two dreadnaughts." Admiral Benson, the American representative on the Naval Council, advocated immediate destruction of the German navy; unable to secure it, he was willing to approve internment in place of surrender, provided it were understood that the ships were not returned to Germany:

" To intern the ten battleships," he told the statesmen, " will increase the probability of acceptance of the terms of the Armistice. In order to save life every possible effort should be made to submit such terms as will satisfy our requirements and at the same time bring an end to hostilities." [27]

[26] Terrail, *Les negociations secrètes,* pp. 244-246; House Diary, November 1, 1918, *I.P.,* IV, 130.

[27] Benson to House, November 2, 1918, *I.P.,* IV, 132; Minutes of Conversation, November 3, 1918, Y.H.C. Sir Eric Geddes, accord-

The compromise satisfied neither Foch nor Geddes. The former complained that the naval terms were still needlessly stiff. " Shall the war be continued for the sole advantage of interning these ships in a neutral port? . . . The German battleships never left their ports and naval warfare now is conducted by submarines. German battleships have no doubt kept the British fleet in home waters, but their action was virtual, not actual. Are we to continue the war simply to suppress this virtual influence? " Geddes, on the other hand, continued to insist that surrender of the dreadnaughts was essential. The Naval Council, he stated, would perforce accept any decision of the heads of Government, but could not approve the suggested compromise. Lloyd George finally proposed that Germany should surrender the submarines, but that all the other craft, battle cruisers as well as battleships, should be merely interned. Clemenceau, Orlando, and House agreed, provided the naval advisers could be persuaded to yield. Leaving the matter in this uncertain form, for the final ratification of the Supreme War Council, the conversation broke up, Lloyd George leaving at once for England.[28]

The military terms proposed by Foch and approved by the Prime Ministers were adopted by the Supreme War Council at the afternoon session of November 1. They provoked little discussion. The naval terms were brought up on the afternoon of November 4. The question was one of the

ing to Benson, favored the destruction of the fleet ultimately and stated that he did not believe any European Power wished to add it to existing navies.

[28] Minutes of Conversation of November 3, 1918; House Diary, November 3, 4, 1918, Y.H.C.

few which the steering committee had not put into definite shape for ratification. Lloyd George had left for London with the understanding that the revised terms, providing for internment instead of surrender, would be presented. But it had been also understood that the approval of the naval experts would be given, and this was not forthcoming. Clemenceau read the revised proposal to the full Supreme War Council, stating that the Council was free to change it. The compromise draft was approved without change. Both Geddes and Admiral de Bon, the French representative, made it clear that they did not like the alteration in their recommendations. "I want to state," said Geddes, "that the Naval Council withholding its approval, is merely submitting to the decision of the Ministers." [29]

The difference between surrender of the German ships and their internment with German caretakers on board, became obvious the next spring, when the caretakers opened the cocks and sank the fleet in Scapa Flow. The Americans bore the blame for the sinking of the fleet, since Wilson was believed to have protested against its surrender. The record is plain in its proof that it was the British Prime Minister himself who insisted upon internment. In truth, the suicide of the fleet saved the Allied Powers from the difficult decision of what to do with it.

Besides the military and naval terms, the French were insistent that a clause referring to reparations should be inserted in the armistice. Clemenceau raised the topic at the conference of November 1. It met the opposition of Lloyd George, who regarded reparations as a condition of

[29] Terrail, *op. cit.*, p. 264.

peace; he was willing however to insert a clause covering merely restitution of property. House and Sonnino felt that the subject was so large it might hold up the armistice indefinitely. On the next afternoon Clemenceau returned to his demand. " It would not be understood in France," he said, " if we omitted such a clause. All I am asking is simply the addition of the words, ' reparation for damages,' without other commentary." Bonar Law objected that it was useless to insert in the armistice a clause which could not be immediately carried out, and that special mention of it was to be made in the note to be sent Wilson. But Clemenceau's insistence carried the point: " You must not forget that the French people are among those who have suffered most; they would not understand our failure to allude to this matter. . . . I beg the Council to comprehend the feeling of the French people." " Yes, and of the Belgian," interjected Hymans. "And the Serbs," said Vesnitch. " Italians also," added Sonnino. Thus the reparations clause came to be inserted.[30]

More serious in its ultimate consequences was an apparently innocuous amendment introduced by the French Minister of Finance, Klotz. " It would be prudent," he urged, " to put at the head of the financial section a clause reserving future claims of the Allies and I propose the following text: ' With the reservation that any future claims or demands on the part of the Allies remain unaffected.' " The clause was accepted without arousing any difference of opinion. Doubtless it was regarded, as Mr. Keynes suggests, as a " casual protective phrase." [31] But it was later to plague

[30] Minutes of Conversation, November 1, 1918, Y.H.C.
[31] John M. Keynes, *Economic Consequences of the Peace*, p. 114.

the Peace Conference. Upon it the French financial representatives were to base their contention that they were not
bound by any pre-armistice agreement as regards reparations,
and were free to insert in the peace treaty any terms that
seemed advisable to the Peace Conference.[32]

By the evening of November 4, the terms of the armistice
were thus agreed upon. There had been some discussion as
to how they should be notified to Germany. Clemenceau,
at the conference of October 29, had taken it for granted
that since Wilson had conducted the conversations with Germany the terms would be sent him and transmitted by him
to Germany. Lloyd George objected that this process would
permit of no give and take. The Germans would have to
accept or refuse outright. There might be points of no particular importance to the Allies which the Germans would
regard as humiliating. But if the terms were published,
opinion would not permit the Allies to make any concession.

House then proposed that the terms should be passed on
first to Wilson for his endorsement, and that if he approved
he should inform the Germans that their request for an
armistice would be granted. The terms in detail however
would be given without publication directly to Germany by
the Allies. Clemenceau objected. " It will be necessary for
Marshal Foch to send a parliamentary to go to the German
lines with a white flag to ask for an armistice. Marshal Foch
would never do this and I would never permit him to do it."
" No," replied Lloyd George, " we could merely ask President Wilson to ask the Germans to send a parliamentary

with a white flag to ask for an armistice." Thus it was decided, and on November 5 Wilson informed Germany that Marshal Foch had been authorized to receive properly accredited representatives of the German Government and to communicate to them the terms of an armistice.[33]

4

In the meantime events in Germany were rapidly drawing the nation into capitulation. Further resistance was futile. Ludendorff had initiated a movement that could not be stopped; Wilson's manipulation of the appeal for an armistice stimulated the popular demand for peace. More and more the American President was looked upon as a possible saviour who must be placated.[34] In this feeling is to be found the explanation of the charges of betrayal levelled at him following the Versailles Treaty.

President Wilson, whether consciously or otherwise, strengthened the belief that a rapid democratization of Germany would lead to milder terms. Prince Max, although irritated by what he regarded as interference with domestic German problems, hastened to develop a parliamentary régime, so that he could assure the President that the arbitrary power capable of disturbing the peace of the world no longer existed. Still Wilson was not satisfied. In his note of October 23, after stating that the request for the armistice had been sent to the Allies, he came back to the question of the control of Germany:

---

[33] Text of note, Lansing to Swiss Minister, November 5, 1918, *F.R., 1918, Suppl. 1,* I, 468-469.

[34] Cf. Prince Hohenlohe-Langenburg to Prince Max, October 25, 1918, Prince Max of Baden, *Memoirs,* II, 211-214.

" It may be that future wars have been brought under the control of the German people, but the present war has not been; and it is with the present war that we are dealing. It is evident that the German people have no means of commanding the acquiescence of the military authorities of the empire in the popular will; that the power of the King of Prussia to control the policy of the Empire is unimpaired; that the determining initiative still remains with those who have hitherto been the masters of Germany."

The United States was waiting to deal with the German people. " If it must deal with the military masters and the monarchical autocrats, . . . it must demand, not peace negotiations, but surrender." [35]

There was in this note a decided implication that a democratic revolution in Germany would mean more lenient peace terms. What else could be the distinction implied between " peace negotiations " and " surrender "? There was an equally strong implication that the clearest proof of the democratization of Germany would be the elimination of the Kaiser. He was even mentioned specifically in the note, as though his " unimpaired control " of policy evidenced the failure to meet Wilson's demands. Whether the elimination of the Kaiser was actually in Wilson's mind as a prime objective when he wrote the note is, even now, uncertain. None of his associates in the administration have thrown any light upon the question.[36] But in Germany it was believed

[35] Note of October 23, Lansing to Swiss Chargé, October 23, 1918, *F.R., 1918, Suppl. 1*, I, 383.

[36] Colonel House was on his way to Europe at the time the note of October 23 was written. In none of his earlier conversations with House had the President regarded the elimination of the Kaiser as important or especially desirable, although he always emphasized the desirability of a limited monarchy in Germany.

that the note was aimed directly at the Kaiser and the imperial régime.

Its effect in military circles was to stiffen resistance to Wilson's conditions. The political leaders, as Ludendorff insists, " could not grasp what the Emperor meant to the army." The Supreme Army Council urged the rejection of humiliating demands. The army was still on enemy soil and undefeated. The peace movement was growing strong in the enemy countries.[37] On the 28th, after the resignation of Ludendorff, General von Gallwitz was still opposed to yielding to Wilson's demands and urged measures that would make possible a desperate defense. He demanded that negotiations be ruptured and a *levée en masse* proclaimed.

But in political circles the feeling grew that if the Kaiser were really an obstacle to peace it was necessary to offer him up as a propitiatory sacrifice to Wilson. As early as the 15th of October the German Minister in Brussels telegraphed that he had it on good authority that Wilson aimed at the abdication of the Emperor and Crown Prince.[38] The word trickled in from other quarters. Doubtless young and irresponsible American attachés in neutral countries were free in their explanation of the President's policy. On October 25, the Prime Minister of Bavaria and his Minister of War expressed the belief that Wilson's third note was an indirect demand for the Kaiser's abdication; they urged that the Kaiser be informed that no acceptable peace could be secured without this personal sacrifice on his part. The Social Democrats of Munich were openly insisting upon it.[39]

[37] Ludendorff, *Ludendorff's Own Story*, II, 423.
[38] *P.H.A.*, No. 59, p. 102.
[39] *P.H.A.*, No. 77, p. 115; No. 97, p. 134.

24

Even more discouraging were the reports from Switzerland, a vast whispering gallery, where the Germans picked up information or misinformation of opinion in the Allied countries. The German Minister at Berne, Romberg, transmitted a statement from a source " to be taken with the utmost consideration, both on account of his standing and connections," that the demand of public opinion at home compelled Wilson to ask for the Kaiser's abdication. Such a step would facilitate the President's peace programme in America, where the Senate was more interested in the overthrow of Germany than in a reasonable peace. The old German régime in the eyes of Americans was embodied in the person of the Kaiser. " Only the elimination of this personality would have a convincing effect and would indicate for the President a success which would once again put it in his power to oppose influentially the extreme chauvinists in his own country and those of the Entente." [40]

The German Imperial Ministers reached the same conclusion. Solf expressed the belief that Wilson needed the prestige of the Kaiser's abdication for his programme; that armed with this success he could overcome the demand of Roosevelt and the Allies that Germany be destroyed, and successfully push forward his own efforts to secure a just peace. Scheidemann, who was the only republican in the Government, records that in the last days of October not a single member of the Government spoke in favor of the Kaiser. Prince Max evidently hoped that the Kaiser would abdicate without pressure. The latter did not, according to Max, realize the situation, and the Chancellor was naturally

[40] *P.H.A.,* No. 78, p. 116; No. 95, p. 132.

unwilling to be the one to open his eyes.[41] At the front in France, and among the sailors in Kiel, the cry for the abdication of the Kaiser became audible. If victory had come, as Scheidemann points out, the Kaiser would have been a demi-god. " It turned out otherwise, a scapegoat must be found, and there was the Emperor." [42]

On November 8 the Chancellor finally sent the Minister of the Interior to inform the Kaiser of the opinion openly expressed in the newspapers. " Drews, in short, well nigh suggested to me," writes Wilhelm in his memoirs, " that I myself should decide to abdicate, in order that it might not appear that the Government had exerted pressure upon me." He indignantly refused. The Chancellor himself, writing as a relative, then told him that the Government favored his abdication and requested it immediately in order to avoid bloodshed. The Kaiser agreed to abdicate the Imperial throne but not the Kingship of Prussia. " I would remain, as such, with my troops, for the military leaders had declared that if I abdicated completely the officers would leave in crowds, and the army would then pour back, without leaders, into the Fatherland, damage it and place it in peril." But when he sent this word to the Government he received the reply that it was too late. In the hope of preventing the spread of radical revolutionary movements the Chancellor

[41] Scheidemann, *Der Zusammenbruch,* pp. 199, 203-204; Prince Max of Baden, *Memoirs,* II, 225-231; Nowak, *Collapse of Central Europe,* p. 284. So serious an historian as Valentin, *Aussenpolitik,* p. 397, believes that Wilson demanded the abdication in the hope of influencing the Congressional elections of November 5, a manœuvre totally outside the range of possibility for one of Wilson's political character.

[42] Scheidemann, *op. cit.,* pp. 192-193.

had already published the announcement of the Kaiser's abdication and the renunciation by the Crown Prince of the Imperial office and the throne of Prussia. On November 9 the Kaiser hastily crossed the Dutch frontier.[43]

These events completely shattered the moral qualities of the German army. The rank and file, tired and to some extent disaffected, had nevertheless been held in control by the officers. But to the latter, who knew nothing of inner political circumstances, the flight of the Kaiser seemed like a desertion. The symbol of their loyalty had disappeared. The soul of the army was destroyed.

The physical fate of the army as distinguished from its moral quality had been sealed by the surrender of Austria. Even the most determined of the German generals, such as Gallwitz and Mudra, admitted that if the Allies could attack Germany from the south she would be defenceless. " If Austria capitulates unconditionally and puts herself on the side of the enemy," said Mudra on October 28, " our cause is lost." [44] The day previous, the Emperor Karl had warned Germany that " my people are neither in condition nor are they willing to continue the war any further . . . useless bloodshed would be a crime, which My conscience forbids." But he promised that he would never permit the Allies to use Austrian territories for an attack on Germany. If the Italians made it a condition of peace that they be allowed to use the railroads of the Tyrol and Carinthia for the transportation of troops attacking Germany, " I will place myself at the head of my German-Austrians and pre-

[43] Wilhelm, II, *My Memoirs,* pp. 274 ff.; Prince Max of Baden, *op. cit.,* II, 314, 352-353.
[44] *P.H.A.,* No. 86, p. 127.

vent their passage by force of arms." [45] But when it came
to actual negotiations with the Allies, the Austrian Government merely " expressed its hope that the Entente would not
make use of Bohemia for its advance against the German
Empire." [46]

The Entente Powers were determined to use not merely
Bohemia but any other strategic positions that might be of
value, in case it proved necessary to continue the war. On
the morning of November 2 Lloyd George raised with the
Prime Ministers the relative merits of an advance by Bavaria
or Bohemia as well as the possibility of utilizing the forces
of the friendly Czechoslovaks. Beneš, representing the latter
in Paris, was called in to discuss the matter with the generals.
Foch proposed a concentric attack against Munich by three
Allied armies, one advancing from the south (the Inn Val-
ley) and two from the east (Salzburg-Linz). They would
be under the immediate command of an Italian but the
operations as a whole would be directed by Foch. In fact
it was upon this occasion that for the first time Foch was
given the supreme command of all the allied armies. The
concentration of the main force would take from thirty to
thirty-five days. Orlando pointed out that the Italian army
was wearied by the battle it had just fought and by pursuit
of the enemy. But Foch brushed aside the objection. " Victory is winged," he said, " and abolishes weariness." [47]

The Prime Ministers also authorized the generals to study
the possibility of sending an army including Czechoslovak

[45] *P.H.A.,* No. 83, p. 119-120; No. 88, p. 129.
[46] *P.H.A.,* No. 90, p. 129.
[47] Minutes of Conversation, November 2, 4, 1918, Y.H.C.

forces to Bohemia and Galicia, and to establish its coöperation with Franchet d'Esperey, advancing from Bulgaria, and to establish aerodromes for the purpose of bombing Germany. The last proposal drew from the French Prime Minister the interjection that he was "delighted with this suggestion."

Germany could not avoid complete defeat. The armistice signed by Austria made possible all these plans, for Austria agreed that the Allied armies " shall occupy such strategic points in Austria-Hungary . . . as they may deem necessary to enable them to conduct military operations." [48] The publication of these conditions, as General Bliss pointed out, showed Germany that such a plan of operations was on the cards as would oblige her " to accept any conditions that might have been proposed in the armistice." [49]

The German delegates left Berlin on the afternoon of November 6 and arrived within the French lines on the evening of the 7th. They were taken to the train of Marshal Foch on Friday the 8th, and received by him and Sir Rosslyn Wemyss, who represented the Allied navies. Foch did not facilitate their opening remarks, for he was determined to make plain that Germany was on her knees for peace. He asked the delegates the purpose of their visit, received the obvious reply, and responded that he had no proposition to make. After Erzberger had read Wilson's note stating that Foch was authorized to make known the conditions of the armistice, the Marshal stated he was so authorized if the

[48] Armistice of November 3, 1918, *Official U. S. Bulletin*, November 4, 1919, *War Aims and Peace Proposals*, 446-455.

[49] Bliss, " The Armistices," *American Journal of International Law*, XVI, 510.

German delegates asked for the armistice. " Do you ask for
the armistice? If you ask for it, I can make known the conditions under which it may be obtained." Erzberger and
Oberndorff then declared that they asked for it.[50]

As to the main conditions the German delegates raised no
serious protest. They made no observation regarding the
bridgeheads or the fleet. " They asked," wrote Clemenceau,
" what we were going to do with the left bank of the Rhine.
Foch answered that he didn't know and that it was not his
business." They asked that more time be given them for
the evacuation and above all for food. " Their line is to say
that they will be overwhelmed by Bolshevism if we do not
help them resist it, and that afterwards we shall be invaded
by the same plague. . . . They are much depressed. From
time to time a sob escaped the throat of Winterfeldt. In
these circumstances I do not think there is any doubt about
their signing. . . ." [51]

The Germans requested an immediate cessation of hostilities during the progress of negotiations. This Foch refused abruptly. " I too am indeed anxious to reach a conclusion and I will help you so far as possible. But hostilities
cannot cease before the signing of the armistice." They also
asked in vain for an extension of time for consideration. The
German Army command telegraphed the urgent need of
securing alleviations in the terms, specifying the most important. But the telegram concluded: " If it is not possible
to gain these points it would nevertheless be advisable to
conclude the agreement." Various concessions were made

[50] Memorandum of Conversation, Foch to Clemenceau, November
8, 1918, *I.P.*, IV, 137-138.
[51] Clemenceau to House, November 9, 1918, *I.P.*, IV, 139.

by Foch: reduction in the number of machine guns, planes, and wagons to be surrendered; the neutral zone on the right bank of the Rhine was reduced to 10 kilometres. A clause was added : " The Allies and the United States contemplate the provisioning of Germany during the armistice as shall be found necessary." [52]

On November 10 the German delegates were authorized to sign, although the telegram of authorization protested that " the execution of certain points of these conditions will plunge the population of the unoccupied parts of Germany into the misery of starvation." The telegram bore the signature " Reichskanzler." Actually it was sent by the Supreme Army Command on its own responsibility, for Berlin was in a state of political chaos.[53]

5

President Wilson took no direct part in the drafting of the armistice terms. Colonel House, as his representative, followed the advice of the military and naval leaders, accepting the military terms put forward by Foch and the naval terms of the British. But the entire process of drafting the armistice was none the less dominated by the President's policy as laid down in his notes to Germany. By his early development of the negotiations he had given the Allies a chance of victory quite as complete as they could have gained through fighting for it. The military and the naval advisers

---

[52] Foch, Memorandum of Conversation with German Delegates, November 8, 1918, *I.P.*, IV, 138; Foch, *Memoirs*, pp. 465-488; Erzberger, *Erlebnisse*, pp. 326-334; 336-337; Mordacq, *Le ministère Clemenceau*, II, p. 341.

[53] *P.H.A.*, No. 108, pp. 149-150; Erzberger, *op. cit.*, p. 338.

took his definition of the sort of terms that must be imposed, the continued superiority of Allied military forces, as the standard of reference. To it they appealed in their debates. It was the pervading influence of Wilson upon the German people that made it impossible for the Berlin Government to break off the negotiations, once they had been started. It was above all because of demands that Wilson was believed to have made, that the movement for the abdication of the Kaiser developed and the last moral prop of the army disappeared.

Wilson's share of responsibility for the sudden surrender of Germany was thus very large; but on the other hand he secured for the German people a moral and a legal position which would have been lacking if he had not conducted the negotiations. The surrender was to be complete in a military sense, but it was not unconditional in the political. It was based upon the understanding that the ultimate peace should be founded on Wilson's own principles as expressed in the Fourteen Points and in later speeches. The Allies also entered into this understanding, as a result of the diplomatic pressure exercised by Colonel House, and their acceptance marks one of the greatest triumphs of American diplomacy.

Chapter X

THE PRE-ARMISTICE AGREEMENT

1

The conflict between the international aims of President Wilson and those of the European statesmen has frequently been over-dramatized. It was a conflict resulting from basic differences in geographical position, historical background, and economic experience, and not, as some writers have insisted, a struggle between the forces of good and of evil.[1] It was none the less a conflict which had to be fought out or compromised. Europe was not yet ready to accept, without reservation, the principle of universal concert characteristic of Wilson's new world policy. More particularly the territorial aspirations of the Allied Powers, as expressed in the secret treaties, were inconsistent with the Fourteen Points.[2]

Upon Colonel House, as Wilson's representative in the armistice conferences, fell the responsibility of persuading the Allies that they must modify their policy so as to approve the principles enunciated by Wilson and already accepted by the Germans as the basis of the settlement. He fulfilled the task with success but only with the greatest difficulty. "When the armistice conferences started," wrote Sir William Wiseman, "it seemed for a time as if it would be

[1] R. S. Baker, *Woodrow Wilson and the World Settlement*, I, 98.
[2] Cf. Harold G. Nicolson, *Peacemaking*, pp. 82-84.

366

utterly impossible to get the Allies to agree to an armistice based on the Fourteen Points." [3] Sir Henry Wilson's diary gives a vivid impression of the attitude of British leaders at this time. He had been called into a luncheon conference, on October 14 including Lloyd George, Balfour, Milner, Churchill:

" We discussed: (1) What we were now to say to President Wilson; (2) What we were to say to the Press. As regards Wilson, we agreed that we would wire to say that he must make it clear to the Boches that his 14 points (with which we do not agree) were not a basis for an armistice, which is what the Boches pretend they are. As regards the Press, we agreed that they should be told that Wilson is acting on his own, that the War is *not* over, that the 14 points are *not* an armistice, and that an armistice is *not* a peace. It was a very interesting afternoon. Everyone angry and contemptuous of Wilson.[4]

The heads of the Allied Governments were naturally disturbed by the increasing popular prestige of the American President and feared lest the control of the peace process should fall completely into the hands of a statesman about whom they really knew very little, who was certainly an idealist in the extreme and who might be a visionary. House reported immediately after his arrival in Paris:

" General opinion of all American correspondents in Paris is that the one definite policy of the Allies at this time is to take the control of the peace negotiations out of the [hands] of President Wilson.[5]

[3] Wiseman to C. S., *I.P.,* IV, 149 n.

[4] Callwell, *Field Marshal Sir Henry Wilson,* II, 136.

[5] House to Lansing, October 29, 1918, *F.R., 1918, Supp. 1,* Vol. I, 413. In December, Clemenceau was to speak, not without

It was not that the Allies were deliberately planning to wreck the programme of the Fourteen Points. They had not bothered in the stress of war to study them. What they wished to avoid at this stage was a commitment to any programme. They were quite willing, and without cynicism, to endorse Wilson's principles in the matter of the rights of small nations, a " just and permanent settlement," perhaps even the idea of an international league to preserve the peace. But the details of the settlement must be left to later negotiation. There were always the obligations of the secret treaties, which they were not inclined to scrap at the suggestion of an American who probably knew little about European politics or history.[6]

On the whole the British were less unsympathetic with the Wilson programme than the French and Italians. They had no territorial aspirations comparable to those of the continental nations, and they had much interest in seeing that Germany was not permanently incapacitated in either a political or an economic sense. But they were intensely disturbed by the second of Wilson's points, " absolute freedom of navigation upon the seas." They feared the abolition of the right of blockade, their chief offensive weapon in time of war. Lloyd George told House that " he did not wish to discuss the Freedom of the Seas with Germany and if the Freedom of the Seas was made a condition of peace Great

---

a trace of satire, of the " elevated simplicity " (*noble candeur*) of President Wilson, Speech in Chamber of Deputies, December 29, 1918, *Le Temps,* Paris, December 30, 1918.

[6] " Wilson was a noble figure," said Clemenceau some years later, " but he did not appreciate the facts or the significance of European history," Clemenceau to C. S., July 16, 1925.

Britain could not agree to it." From Sir William Wiseman House learned that the British " Cabinet have been having some stormy sessions over the President's peace terms. They rebel against the Freedom of the Seas." At the same time House received clear warning of French and Italian unwillingness to bind themselves in any way to Wilson's programme. " Clemenceau and Sonnino," he cabled the President, " are not at all in sympathy with the idea of a league of nations. Sonnino will probably submit many objections to the Fourteen Points." [7]

For Wilson, the definite acceptance of the main portion of the Fourteen Points programme as a basis of the peace was absolutely vital. It was upon this basis that the Germans had made and transmitted to the Allies their appeal for an armistice. Furthermore, Wilson was now approaching the point which would determine whether the lofty expressions of service to the world accompanying American entrance into the war had been mere rhetoric. It was easy enough to declare the war a crusade for a new international organization; now that the victory was at hand it was going to be more difficult to make the sacrifice of old interests. But it was vital. If the European statesmen distrusted Wilson and feared his ideal-

[7] House Diary, October 28, 1918, House to Wilson, October 29, 1918, *I.P.,* IV, 160-161. Comment by Lord Lothian, October 27, 1933: " I remember going through the Fourteen Points with Lloyd George before he entered the conference in Paris referred to in Chapter 10. His view then was ' The Fourteen, five, and other points are not very definite. They leave a large margin for interpretation. They are satisfactory as a basis for peace except for the one relating to the Freedom of the Seas. We refuse to discuss this question with Germany at all. We shall have later to discuss it with the U. S. A.' "

ism, he on his side did not regard them as capable by themselves of creating a peaceable and just world organization. They were too close to the struggle, too much affected by prejudices and selfish ambitions which would disturb their judgment.

Nor did Wilson regard the European Governments as really representative of popular desires in Europe. A few weeks later, while on the way to the Peace Conference, he insisted that *" we would be the only disinterested people* at the Peace Conference, and that *the men whom we were about to deal with did not represent their own people."* It was going to be the Americans' business at the Peace Conference, he added, to fight for a new order, *" agreeably if we can, disagreeably if necessary."* He was distrustful of Allied interpretation of justice; their leaders reminded him of the silversmiths of Philippolis who for about the space of two hours cried *" Great is Diana of the Ephesians "*—to which, with a chuckle, the President added, *" in the interest of the silversmiths."* [8]

Not merely the welfare of the world, Wilson believed, but the special interests of the United States demanded the fulfilment of his peace policy. America had a right to insist upon international tranquillity. She had entered the war at a critical moment, when Allied strength was weakening. She had furnished necessary and vital assistance; huge credits, food, raw materials. Her troops had appeared in unexpectedly large numbers and without them, on the testimony

[8] Bowman Memorandum on Conference with President Wilson, December 10, 1918, *I.P.,* IV, 280, 282-3. Italics as in the original document.

of Marshal Foch, the danger of a German victory was imminent. The United States was certainly in a position to demand that the political conditions which had brought the war to Europe and ultimately to America should be eliminated.

Wilson's determination was not weakened by the rising tide of chauvinist sentiment in the United States. Both in political circles and the press, influential voices were raised in protest against the President's " softness " and the peril of permitting Germany to escape due vengeance. Roosevelt, known throughout Europe, frankly encouraged the Allies to pay no attention to the President and to divide the spoils. " Mr. Wilson," he said, " and his fourteen points and his four supplementary points and his five complementary points and all his utterances every which way have ceased to have any shadow of right to be accepted as expressive of the will of the American people. . . . Let them [the Allies] impose their common will on the nations responsible for the hideous disaster which has almost wrecked mankind." [9] In America as in Allied countries the cry *Vae victis* began to sound.

Even more acutely than Wilson, because of his closer contact with European conditions, Colonel House realized the importance of winning Allied approval of the Fourteen Points before the armistice was signed. If the Allies entered the Peace Conference with free hands it was certain that they would capitalize the helplessness of Germany to the advantage of purely European purposes and Wilson would be almost powerless to restrain them.

[9] *Kansas City Star*, November 26, 1918.

"As the Allies succeed," wrote House to the President, " your influence will diminish. This is inevitable. By the time of the Peace Conference you will be nearing the end of your second term and this too will be something of a challenge to those, both at home and abroad, who have the will to oppose you. Therefore I believe that you should commit the Allies now to as much of your programme as possible." [10]

At the moment however, and before Germany had surrendered, they would make large sacrifices in order to retain the full coöperation of America. Thus for House the drafting of the military and naval clauses of the armistice was a comparatively minor matter that could be left to the military and naval experts. The only matter of real moment was Allied endorsement of the Fourteen Points.[11]

In preparation for the debate with the Allies, which he recognized as imminent, Colonel House ordered the drafting of a document which came to have historical as well as political importance. This was nothing less than a gloss upon, or an interpretation of, President Wilson's Fourteen Points. It was designed first of all to meet the criticism that the Fourteen Points, whether or not impracticable in their nature, were too general in form to provide a workable programme. It was prepared under the supervision of Colonel House by Frank Cobb, editor of the New York *World,* a clear-thinking liberal devoted to Wilsonian principles, and Walter Lippmann, who had served as secretary of the Inquiry. The interpretation was telegraphed to Wilson

[10] House to Wilson, September 3, 1918, *I.P.,* IV, 64.

[11] Comment by Sir William Wiseman, May 23, 1933: " In all armistice negotiations House guided the discussion to the conclusion that unless the Allies accepted the Fourteen Points, they must forego the coöperation of America, and that without that coöperation there could be no permanent settlement."

in extenso for his correction and comment. This the President gave, so far as the general points were concerned: the document, he cabled, is a " satisfactory interpretation of principles involved." The details of application contained in the document he felt should be regarded as merely illustrative suggestions.[12]

President Wilson's sanction of this document made of it something reasonably close to an official American programme. On two important issues, mandates and reparations, it laid down the lines that were consistently followed by the United States during the Peace Conference.[13] During the conferences with the European Prime Ministers it provided a clear and reasonably detailed statement of the American position and pointed definitely to the issues that must be settled.[14]

2

The expected conflict with the Allied leaders developed at the first conference of October 29, when Colonel House met with Clemenceau, Pichon, Lloyd George, Balfour, and

[12] Wilson to House, October 30, 1918, *F.R., 1918, Suppl. 1,* I, 421. Text of the interpretation, *ibid.,* 405-413.

[13] It has been asserted that Wilson received the idea of mandates as a means of settling the colonial problem from General Smuts. But the principle of mandates is clearly set forth in a report of Professor George Louis Beer, of January, 1918, a year before the publication of the Smuts pamphlet, and is taken over in the Cobb-Lippmann interpretation. See *I.P.,* IV, 192-200, and James T. Shotwell, " The Paris Peace Conference," in *George Louis Beer,* p. 86.

[14] Colonel House later commented: " These interpretations were on the table day after day when we sat in conference. . . . Many times they asked the meaning of this or that point and I would read from the accepted interpretation," *I.P.,* IV, 154.

Sonnino. The British were the first to point out that in view of the terms of the correspondence between Wilson and the Germans, Allied approval of an armistice carried implicit approval of the Wilsonian programme:

" Germany has asked for an armistice," said Lloyd George, " on condition of President Wilson's Fourteen Points being the terms of peace. If we send terms across, it would appear that we accept those terms. . . . The question is: Do we or do we not accept the whole of President Wilson's Fourteen Points? I am going to put quite clearly the points which I do not accept. Should we not make it clear to the German Government that we are not going in on the Fourteen Points of peace? " [15]

Clemenceau was apparently taken by surprise and was by no means ready to commit himself. " Have you ever been asked by President Wilson," he said to Lloyd George, " whether you accept the Fourteen Points? I have never been asked." " I have not been asked either," replied Lloyd George. The French Foreign Minister, Pichon, then suggested that the Fourteen Points could for the moment be pushed to one side. " We can say to Germany that we are only stating terms of an armistice, not terms of peace." But the British did not believe that the issue could be so easily evaded. The German appeal for an armistice was conditioned upon the Fourteen Points being made the basis of peace. " We cannot say that we are interested merely in the terms of an armistice," insisted Mr. Balfour. " For the

[15] This and the following paragraphs are based upon Minutes of Conversation, October 29, 1918, Y.H.C. Excerpts have been published in *I.P.*, IV, 162 ff. A brief account of the conference is given in House to Lansing, October 30, 1918, *F.R., 1918, Suppl. 1*, I, 421-423.

moment, unquestionably we are not bound by President Wilson's terms; but if we assent to an armistice without making our position clear, we shall certainly be so bound." "Then," said Clemenceau, "I want to hear the Fourteen Points." "Yes," added Sonnino, with a touch of sarcasm, for he did not like the Wilsonian programme, "and the five more and the others."

The first point, regarding "open covenants of peace openly arrived at," was passed without great difficulty after Clemenceau had made it plain that he was not ready to agree "never to make a private or secret diplomatic agreement of any kind." House showed, with the help of the commentary, that the intent was not to throw all conferences into the open, but merely to assure publicity of results. He was supported by Balfour.

The second point, the Freedom of the Seas, immediately drew Lloyd George's attack:

"This point," he insisted, "we cannot accept under any conditions; it means that the power of blockade goes; Germany has been broken almost as much by the blockade as by military methods; if this power is to be handed over to the League of Nations and Great Britain were fighting for her life, no league of nations could prevent her from defending herself. This power has prevented Germany from getting rubber, cotton, and food through Holland and the Scandinavian countries. Therefore my view is that I should like to see this League of Nations established first before I let this power go."

The French and Sonnino supported him. "I cannot understand the meaning of the doctrine Freedom of the Seas" said Clemenceau. "War would not be war if there was freedom of the seas." Sonnino also felt that the use of her naval power by Great Britain to control neutral trade was natural and justified. " Nations like animals had different weapons; one animal had teeth, another tusks, another claws, and so it was with nations." He suggested that all that could be done at the moment was to settle the naval and military terms of the armistice; the bases of the peace must be kept until later.

But postponement of the issue was exactly what Colonel House was bound to prevent. The Germans had made their appeal on the basis of the Fourteen Points and an answer must be given them. Furthermore, postponement would weaken Wilson's position. Reassured by the surrender of Germany and less dependent upon American assistance as time passed, the Allies would certainly raise even stronger objection to the American programme.

Up to this moment Colonel House had not taken an active part in the discussion. But now, very quietly, he suggested that if the Allies persisted in their refusal to accept the Fourteen Points, upon which the German request for an armistice was based, there could be only one result: the negotiations with Germany would have to be wiped off the slate; President Wilson would be compelled to inform Germany that his terms were not acceptable to the Allies; the question would then arise whether America would not have to take those matters up directly with Germany and Austria. " That would amount," said Clemenceau, " to a separate peace between the United States and the Central Powers? " " It might," was the reply of Colonel House.

Such intimation of the possibility of a virtual rupture between America and the Allies produced a sobering effect. The atmosphere changed. For a moment Lloyd George still persisted. " If the United States made a separate peace we would be sorry, but we could not give up the blockade; the power which enabled us to live." But when House, seconded by Balfour, suggested that the first step was to see how serious would be the proposed limitation of the Fourteen Points, he became conciliatory. Balfour felt that with few exceptions the Allies could accept the Wilsonian programme. On the points at issue a compromise might be arranged. Lloyd George then proposed that each Power make a draft of its reservations on the Fourteen Points and " see tomorrow whether we cannot agree upon a common draft." The suggestion was adopted, with some disappointment apparent on the part of both Clemenceau and Sonnino, who evidently wished to enter the Peace Conference with completely free hands.

Despite the attitude taken by the French and Italian leaders, so unfriendly to the Wilson programme, Colonel House was convinced that the American position was one of diplomatic strength and could be successfully capitalized. Not merely did the Allies need the full economic and financial support of the United States, but Wilson's prestige in England, France, and Italy was so high that they would not dare openly to repudiate his principles. " The last thing they want," cabled House to Wilson, " is publicity and they do not wish it to appear that there is any cause for difference between the Allies. Unless we deal with these people with a firm hand everything we have been fighting for will be lost." [16] House was determined that if they did not yield he would warn them frankly that Wilson

[16] House to Lansing, October 30, 1918, *F.R., 1918, Suppl. 1,* I, 423.

would lay the whole question of what America was fighting for before Congress and " ask the advice of Congress whether the United States should make peace with Germany now that she has accepted the American terms, or whether we should go on fighting until Germany had accepted the terms of France, England, and Italy, whatever they might be." [17]

Fortunately, during the night the British attitude became much more conciliatory. Lloyd George was perhaps disturbed by the suggestion of publicity, for Wilson was very strong at the moment in British Liberal and Labour circles. An open dispute with him would precipitate an angry debate over war aims. Furthermore, on consideration, the only serious point at issue between British and Americans was the question of the Freedom of the Seas. Lloyd George foresaw serious differences with the French at the Peace Conference and it would certainly be convenient to count upon American support. The draft memorandum he prepared differed therefore both in temper and in substance from the debate of the previous afternoon.

This draft accepted the Fourteen Points as the basis of peace, merely reserving complete liberty of interpreting the meaning of the Freedom of the Seas, and specifying more definitely Allied understanding of the meaning of the President's reference to restoration of invaded territories. The draft memorandum was almost literally the same as that ultimately embodied in the final note to the Germans.

A meeting had been arranged between the French and British Prime Ministers and House at Clemenceau's room in the War Office, for the morning of the 30th. Just before going in, Lloyd George showed his draft to House with the intimation that if the reservation on the Freedom of the Seas could be accepted by Wilson, the British would be glad to coöperate enthusiastically on the rest of the American programme. House replied to the British Prime Minister, as he reported to Wilson, that he was afraid Lloyd George's " attitude at yesterday's meeting had opened the floodgates and that Clemenceau and Sonnino would have elaborate memoranda to submit containing their objections to the President's Fourteen Points, and that I doubted whether Clemenceau would accept the answer as drafted by the British, which was in marked contrast to the position taken by George yesterday."

So it turned out. As soon as the conversation opened, Clemenceau produced a bundle of voluminous documents and prepared to draft lengthy reservations. House then intervened. The Italians would doubtless have just as many objections. Extended and developed reservations to the Fourteen Points would have all the effect of complete rejection of the American programme. If the Allies felt constrained to such a course, " it would doubtless be necessary for the President to go to Congress and to place before that body exactly what Italy, France, and Great Britain were fighting for and to place the responsibility upon Congress for the further continuation of the war by the United States in behalf of the aims of the Allies. . . ." [18]

[18] House to Wilson, October 30, 1918, *I.P.,* IV, 171; *F.R., 1918, Suppl. 1,* I, 425; Minutes of Conversation, October 30, 1918, Y.H.C.

The reiterated threat had an immediate effect upon Clemenceau, who turned to the British draft for study. With very little delay he agreed that if they could settle upon it immediately, he was willing to accept it. Sonnino was less complaisant. After Lloyd George had read his draft Sonnino at once objected. " I have also prepared a draft on the subject of the ninth clause of President Wilson's Fourteen Points [Italian frontiers]." He received no support from the British or French. Lloyd George pointed out that Point IX affected Austrian frontiers, whereas the memorandum in question was related to the armistice with Germany. " It has nothing to do with Austria." " Yes," said Sonnino, very much to the point, " but if we state our concurrence in the Fourteen Points, subject to the observations of Mr. Lloyd George, it will be assumed that the whole of the remainder are accepted and the case of an armistice will be prejudiced."

The Italian reservation was then read. It was not based upon the secret treaty of London, to which no reference was made, but upon a variety of factors, national, historical, geographical, strategic, which the Italians believed justified expansion beyond Wilson's standard of " recognizable lines of nationality." Clemenceau was opposed to its insertion in any note applying to Germany. " It would be just as relevant to put into the note referring to Austria-Hungary some observation about Alsace-Lorraine." Lloyd George suggested that its insertion in a note to Austria could be later considered, " although he himself hoped it would not be inserted." Having found a basis of compromise with the Americans, the British and French were anxious to settle

the matter. Paying no attention to Sonnino's continued protests, Clemenceau ended the debate abruptly with: "Are we
agreed regarding the reply to Germany? I accept, Lloyd
George accepts. [To Orlando:] Do you accept?" "Yes,"
said the Italian Premier, evidently reserving the right to
raise the question later before the full council.

3

The acceptance of the Fourteen Points by Clemenceau and
Lloyd George, with the two reservations indicated, and the
wavering opposition of the Italians, promised all that the
Americans could reasonably expect. House looked upon the
British draft of acceptance as a satisfactory basis for a reply
to the Germans. If it "is adopted by the Allies as their
answer to your communication," he cabled to Wilson, "I
would strongly advise your accepting it without alteration." [19] The Fourteen Points had still to run the gauntlet of
the full Supreme War Council. But House felt that the
battle had been won. His position was the stronger in that
the President had cabled full power to use threats of publicity, should opposition to the Freedom of the Seas or a league
of nations develop.

"I feel it my solemn duty," telegraphed Wilson, "to
authorize you to say that I cannot consent to take part in the
negotiation of a peace which does not include freedom of
the seas because we are pledged to fight not only to do away
with Prussian militarism but with militarism everywhere.
Neither could I participate in a settlement which does not
include league of nations because peace would be without

[19] House to Wilson, October 30, 1918, *I.P.*, IV, 172; *F.R., 1918,
Suppl. 1*, I, 427.

any guarantee except universal armament which would be intolerable. I hope I shall not be obliged to make this decision public." [20]

House felt that there was no longer any necessity for threats. " Everything is changing for the better since yesterday," he cabled on October 31, " and I hope you will not insist upon my using your cable except as I may think best. . . . It is exceedingly important that nothing be said or done at this time which may in any way halt the Armistice which will save so many thousands of lives." [21] With this the President agreed, and he apparently appreciated the extent of Colonel House's success, for he cabled to him, " I am proud of the way you are handling the situation." [22]

President Wilson, however, was not yet ready to give complete approval to the British draft, until he understood the exact significance of the reservation on the Freedom of the Seas. Did this reservation imply a definite objection to the principle or was it designed merely to reserve the right to discuss later the implications of the principle? During the following two days Colonel House labored incessantly to clarify the issue. He would have preferred to commit the British explicitly to an acceptance of the principle. He must at least win from them a promise not to oppose it flatly and to discuss it at the approaching Peace Conference. " The difficulty," wrote Sir William Wiseman,

" was to phrase so vague and yet so far-reaching and vital a principle. The British leaders were in general agreement

[20] Wilson to House, October 30, 1918, *F.R., 1918, Suppl. 1,* I, 423.

[21] House to Wilson, October 31, 1918, *I.P.,* IV, 174.

[22] Wilson to House, October 31, 1918, Y.H.C.

with House, but the sailors arrived at the conference breathing fire. The British feared that they might be committing themselves too far, and that the country would reject anything that appeared to be giving up their sea power. This is easy enough to understand if we realize that the British Empire had experienced a war in which they would have been at the mercy of the enemy at any moment if their naval power had not protected them. . . . House believed a policy could be developed so as to afford the protection to the British Empire which they quite naturally demanded, and at the same time meet the principle that Wilson was trying to evolve." [23]

House's line of argument was double: first, that the British would be quite as safe under the operation of the doctrine of the Freedom of the Seas, and, second, that it was essential to Anglo-American friendship and a necessary pre-requisite of naval disarmament. " The benefits which would accrue to Great Britain through the Freedom of the Seas," he wrote later, developing this theme, a favorite one with him, " would be free communication with her Dominions, and the certainty that her food supply and raw materials could never be interrupted. Such a policy would eliminate the terrors of submarine warfare, for submarines could be used only against battleships and craft of war." [24]

[23] Wiseman to C. S., February 17, 1928, *I.P.,* IV, 179.

[24] *Contemporary Review,* April, 1928, 421. Cf. Kenworthy and Young: " The whole position of both countries in respect of sea power in war has now changed in almost every conceivable circumstance; . . . their future interests lie not in efforts to claim or compete for a command of the seas in war but in the opposite policy of combining in Command of the Seas to secure a new Freedom of the Seas as complete in war as in peace," *Freedom of the Seas,* p. 25.

Even British opinion has come to appreciate the possible advantages of the Freedom of the Seas. " We should aim at such a change in belligerent rights at sea," said Viscount Cecil, " as will enable us to feed our people in war-time without risk of hostile capture." [25]

" If then the British now frankly and fully accepted the application of the Wilsonian principle," writes Commander Kenworthy, " how would they stand? They would lose the arbitrary power they have enjoyed of initiating and imposing an economic blockade for slowly starving and strangling their enemy. . . . But this power they have in fact already lost. . . . It only became really effective when exercised in conjunction with America after its entry into war. The future exercise of it except in association with America or with American approval, will be impossible." [26]

Such arguments could not be successfully brought forward at the armistice conferences. The British naval experts were not in a mood to listen to them. By the extension of the blockade against Germany, which was not so much a blockade as a supervising control of all trade on the high seas, the Allies believed they had proved the value of this weapon of war against a continental foe, and the British were not minded to give it up. But House could and did emphasize the fact that unless some understanding were reached between Great Britain and the United States on sea rights, there was no chance of permanent friendship between the two countries. With the growth of American overseas trade, it was inevitable that there should come a demand for a navy capable of protecting it; if the guarantee of safety were not provided by international law the United States would

[25] *The Sunday Times,* London, November 27, 1927.
[26] Kenworthy and Young, *op. cit.,* p. 255.

certainly feel free to build as far as circumstances warranted. President Wilson saw this fact so clearly that he authorized House to tell the British that if they would not accept the Freedom of the Seas, they could " count on the certainty of our using our present equipment to build up the strongest navy that our resources permit and as our people have long desired." [27]

On November 1 House explained to Wiseman the necessity of impressing the British leaders with the seriousness of the issue.

" I told him that unless Lloyd George would make some reasonable concessions in his attitude upon the ' Freedom of the Seas,' all hope of Anglo-Saxon unity would be at an end; the United States went to war with England in 1812 on the question of her rights at sea, and that she had gone to war with Germany in 1917 upon the same question. . . . Our people would not consent to allow the British Government or any other Government to determine upon what terms our ships should sail the seas, either in time of peace or time of war."

The following day he worked at the problem for two hours with Lord Reading, " but got nowhere." The same result followed conferences with Lloyd George, who declared that

" Great Britain would spend her last guinea to keep a navy superior to that of the United States or any other Power, and that no Cabinet official could continue in the Government in England who took a different position. I countered this by telling him that it was not our purpose to go into a naval building rivalry with Great Britain, but it was our purpose to have our rights at sea adequately safeguarded, and that we did not intend to have our commerce regulated by Great Britain whenever she was at war." [28]

[27] Wilson to House, November 4, 1918, Y.H.C.
[28] House Diary, November 1, 2, 4, 1918, *I.P.,* IV, 180-181.

Lloyd George thus came to the meeting of November 3 in House's apartment without having approached any agreement with the latter. House felt it was essential to send to Wilson that day the clarification of British purpose which he asked. " Clemenceau and Orlando," he cabled Wilson, " will accept anything that the English will agree to. . . . I have spent almost every minute outside my conferences discussing this article with the British. I am insisting that they must recognize the principle that it is a subject for discussion at the Peace Conference or before, and I am having the greatest difficulty in getting them to admit even that much. I have contended that they might as well refuse to accept the principle that laws governing war upon land formed a subject for discussion. . . ." [29] He laid before the Prime Ministers a paraphrase of the President's cable of October 31, commenting upon the draft memorandum:

" The President says that he freely and sympathetically recognizes the necessities of the British and their strong position with regard to the seas, both at home and throughout the Empire. Freedom of the Seas he recognizes is a question upon which there should be the freest discussion and the most liberal exchange of views. The President is not sure, however, that the Allies have definitely accepted the principle of the Freedom of the Seas and that they are reserving only the limitations and free discussions of the subject. The President insists that the terms 1, 2, 3 and 14 are essentially American terms in the program and he cannot recede from them. The question of the Freedom of the Seas need not be discussed with the German Government provided we have agreed amongst ourselves beforehand. Blockade is one of the questions which has been altered by the developments in

[29] House to Wilson, November 3, 1918, *I.P.*, IV, 175-176; *F.R., 1918, Suppl. 1*, I, 448.

this war and the law governing it will certainly have to be altered. There is no danger, however, that it will be abolished."

The original cable concluded with a reiterated suggestion of throwing the dispute into the open. Wilson stated in his cable that if Freedom of the Seas were not accepted he might be compelled to lay the matter before Congress, " who will have no sympathy or wish that American life and property shall be sacrificed for British naval control." This sentence House did not read to the Prime Ministers. It could be kept in reserve for use if no concessions were made.[30]

One difficulty lay in the fact that when the President spoke of preserving the principle of the blockade he meant the blockade of enemy ports; the doctrine of the Freedom of the Seas was not directed against the traditional formal blockade recognized by international law but against the so-called pseudo-blockade established by the Reprisals Order in 1915, with all its extensions. But in the British mind the two had become confused. Lloyd George was pleasant but unyielding. Clemenceau, who above everything at this time desired agreement, pressed him. " I do not see any reason for not accepting the principle. We accept. You do also, do you not? " [31]

" No," said Lloyd George. " I could not accept the principle of the Freedom of the Seas. It has got associated in the public mind with the blockade. It's no good saying I

[30] The original cable, with omission of the threat, is printed in *F.R., 1918, Suppl. 1,* I, 427-428.

[31] This and the following paragraphs are based upon the Minutes of Conversation held November 3, 1918, Y.H.C., and upon House to Wilson, November 3, 1918, *F.R., 1918, Suppl. 1,* I, 455-456.

accept the principle. It would only mean that in a week's time a new Prime Minister would be here who would say that he could not accept this principle. The English people will not look at it. On this point the nation is absolutely solid. It's no use for me to say that I can accept when I know that I am not speaking for the British nation."

House then went directly to the heart of the matter. Did the reservation contained in the draft imply a peremptory challenge of the doctrine of the Freedom of the Seas? Or were the British, although at the moment unable to accept the principle, willing to agree that it was open to discussion in later debates when circumstances of time were not so pressing?

Lloyd George grasped eagerly at the compromise. " This formula," he said, " does not in the least challenge the position of the United States. All we say is that we reserve the freedom to discuss the point when we go to the Peace Conference. I don't despair of coming to an agreement." " I wish you would write something I could send the President," said House. " Will he like something of this kind ? " replied Lloyd George: ' We are quite willing to discuss the Freedom of the Seas and its application.' "

With such a compromise the matter was left for the Peace Conference. Lloyd George confirmed his statement by a brief note repeating British willingness to discuss the Freedom of the Seas in " the light of the new conditions which have arisen in the course of the present war." He had talked the matter over with Balfour, who quite agreed. " In our judgment this most important subject can only be dealt with satisfactorily through the freest debate and the most liberal exchange of views." [32] Wilson accepted the British explanation as sufficient guarantee of future opportunity to secure a new code of maritime rules; if the British did not yield in the end, he promised a big American navy.[33] Curiously enough, he never attempted to capitalize the opportunity.

4

In the meantime the draft memorandum accepting the Fourteen Points was brought before the formal meetings of the Supreme War Council on October 31 and November 1. Orlando again raised the question of the Italian reservation and Hymans, speaking for Belgium, desired further clarification of Points III and V, referring to equality of trade conditions and colonial problems. At the suggestion of House it was decided to take up possible reservations at a meeting of the Prime Ministers with Hymans. Obviously, the less discussion in a semi-public meeting the better, in order to avoid any impression of lack of unity of purpose among the Allies.[34]

The Belgian objections were not serious. Hymans feared lest the application of Point III, which called for a " levelling of trade barriers," might permit Germany to dump cheap products and swamp the Belgian markets. House rejoined that " we have got to remember that Germany must

[32] Lloyd George to House, November 3, 1918, *I.P.*, IV, 184; House to Lansing, November 3, 1918, *F.R., 1918, Suppl. 1*, I, 456.

[33] Wilson to House, November 4, 1918, Y.H.C.

[34] The essential portions of the *procès-verbaux* of November 1 and November 2 are printed in Terrail, *Les Negociations Secrètes et les Quatres Armistices*, pp. 226 ff.

necessarily pay out thousands of millions and that she must be in a condition to pay them. If we prevent her from making a living she will not be able to pay." Clemenceau suggested that there was really no need of a reservation since Wilson's phrase already included the words, " so far as possible." Lloyd George, who had supported Hymans, agreed that the qualifying phrase was sufficient to protect the interests of Allied nations and the proposed reservation was dropped. Hymans was assured that Point V was not in any sense directed against Belgian colonies, but was concerned purely with the conquered German colonies.[35]

Hymans then raised the question of reparations, and suggested the need of a more ample phrase than merely " damages to the civilian population." " It is then for indirect compensation that you ask? " said Lloyd George. " I do not ask for it now," replied Hymans, " but I should like to have a phrase referring to it." But Lloyd George insisted: " I think it will be a mistake to put into the Armistice terms anything that will lead Germany to suppose that we want a war indemnity." The others agreed and no change was made in the British draft reference to reparations. The brief interchange between Hymans and Lloyd George is of the first historical importance. In the following spring the Americans insisted that the draft memorandum in its reference to " damages to the civilian population " estopped the Allies from adding indirect compensation, such as payment for war costs and pensions, to the categories of reparation. The French and the British argued for the introduction of

---

[35] This and the succeeding paragraphs are based upon Minutes of Conversation, November 3, 1918, Y.H.C.

indirect costs. The record shows that the intent of those who drafted the memorandum was to exclude indirect compensation.[36]

Orlando made another unsuccessful effort to introduce the Italian reservation on Point IX. The armistice terms had already been sent to Austria, directly and not through the interposition of President Wilson. There had been no opportunity of apprising him formally of Italy's desire to make a reservation. Neither Lloyd George nor Clemenceau would admit the relevancy of the Italian reservation in a memorandum concerning Germany. House suggested that it would be inadvisable to increase the number of exceptions; and Clemenceau, in quite a different spirit from that in which he had first approached the question, agreed: " It

[36] Comment by Lord Lothian, October 27, 1933: " I remember very distinctly discussing with Lloyd George the interpretation to be put upon the question of ' restoration ' or reparations. His view was ' We must make it clear that we cannot charge Germany with the costs of the war. (The popular demand at the time.) She could not possibly pay it. But she must pay ample compensation for damage and that compensation must be equitably distributed among the Allies and not given entirely to France and Belgium. Devastated areas is only one item in war loss. Great Britain has probably spent more money on the war and incurred greater indirect losses, for instance in shipping and trade, than has France. She must have her fair share of the compensation.'

" He instructed me to prepare a form of words interpretative of Wilson's point on these lines. I did so and he took it into the Conference in the Rue de l'Université. The original form referred, if my memory serves me, to ' damage done to the Allies by the armed forces of Germany ' or some similar phrase. I remember thinking, after the draft had been taken by Lloyd George, that this did not cover adequately the point that compensation was due to all the Allies and not merely to those whose countries had been devastated. I therefore revised it to read ' damage to the

is desirable," he said, " to suggest as few changes or reservations as possible to the Fourteen Points." Orlando did not press his reservation and no more was heard of it until the following spring at the Peace Conference. There was, and is, some doubt as to whether the reservation could be regarded as valid. It had been read to the Prime Ministers but never approved by them or by the Supreme War Council, nor was it ever formally notified to Wilson. The President himself did not later attempt to raise a point of *chicane,* and readily admitted the intent of the Italians as equal to a formal reservation.[37]

---

civilian population of the Allies by the aggression of Germany by land, air and sea ', gave this amended form to L. G., who obtained the consent of the conference to it.

" This sentence, about which so much controversy has since raged, was thus definitely intended to rule out the total cost of the war, but to put in a general claim for reparations on account of damage, the details of which were to be settled at the Peace Conference, but damage of a character which would give compensation to the Allies and not to France and Belgium only.

" It is not usually realized that it was the difficulty of finding a basis upon which reparation payments could be fairly distributed among the Allies, which led to the inclusion of the item war pensions in the reparations claim against Germany. Liability for war pensions were just as much a war cost as the cost of restoring destroyed farm houses or towns. They were included in the account made up between the Allies themselves as being the best basis, indeed the only basis upon which they could agree, on which reparation payments were to be distributed among themselves."

[37] If Wilson had been more adroit at the Peace Conference, he might have capitalized the fact that the Italian reservation was not based upon the Treaty of London. It might have been argued that by introducing into the debate the variety of national, geographical and historical factors listed in the reservation and by making no reference to the Treaty, they had tacitly surrendered the legal position which the Treaty, if valid, would give them. For the text of the Italian reservation, see *I.P.,* IV, 173.

On November 4 the Supreme War Council finally approved the British draft. Thus the Allies, like the Germans, agreed to accept the Fourteen Points as the basis of the peace, with a single reservation and a single elucidation:

" The freedom of the seas, is open to various interpretations, some of which they could not accept. They must therefore reserve to themselves complete freedom on this subject when they enter the peace conference. . . . The President declared that invaded territories must be restored as well as evacuated and freed; the Allied Government feel that no doubt ought to be allowed to exist as to what this provision implies. By it they understand that compensation will be made by Germany for all damage done to the civilian population of the Allies and their property by the aggression of Germany by land, by sea, and from the air." [38]

This memorandum, sent to the President on the evening of the 4th, was forwarded by him to the Germans on the following day, together with his note informing them that terms could be received from Marshal Foch. Wilson's note of November 5 including the memorandum, implicitly accepted by the Germans, forms the pre-Armistice agreement:

" It constitutes the formal and written offer of the Allied and Associated States to conclude with Germany (a) an armistice convention, and (b) a treaty of peace. This offer, it is conceived, was accepted by Germany by the act of sending representatives through military channels, to meet Marshal Foch for the purpose of arranging an armistice. By the acceptance of the offer a solemn Agreement was reached

[38] House to Lansing, November 4, 1918, *F.R., 1918, Suppl. 1,* I, 461. The only change from the original British draft was the substitution of " by the aggression of Germany " for " by the forces of Germany."

which served, both morally and legally, as the basis of the armistice convention and the treaty of peace." [39]

Both sides accepted the pre-Armistice agreement as binding. To it the Germans appealed in their protests against the Versailles Treaty, and although denying the relevance of German protests the Allied and Associated Governments expressed their complete accord with Germany in recognizing the validity of the agreement.[40]

The most important and the most difficult of the diplomatic problems faced by America and the Allies was thus brought to successful solution. Colonel House had forced the acceptance of Wilson's principles by the Allied leaders, in the face of a hostile and influential group in the United States and the distinctly unsympathetic personnel constituting the Allied Governments.[41] According to the New York Herald correspondent, by no means friendly to Wilson's policy, the European statesmen had looked upon the Fourteen Points merely " as a good solvent upon Germany." That they should actually accept his plan for the peace constituted at once a surprise and an " immense diplomatic success of the United States." [42] Similar appreciation came from an observer quite as competent and more friendly: " Frankly, I did not believe it was humanly feasible, under

[39] Harold W. Temperley, A History of the Peace Conference, I, 382. Text of note in Lansing to the Swiss Minister, November 5, 1918, F.R., 1918, Suppl. 1, I, 468-469.

[40] Reply of the Allied and Associated Powers to the Observations of the German Delegation on the Conditions of Peace, I.P., IV, 188 n.

[41] House to Wilson, November 5, 1918, I.P., IV, 188.

[42] New York Herald, November 26, 1918.

conditions as they seemed to be in Europe," wrote Mr.
Walter Lippmann to Colonel House, " to win so glorious a
victory. This is the climax of a course that has been as
wise as it was brilliant, and as shrewd as it was prophetic.
The President and you have more than justified the faith
of those who insisted that your leadership was a turning
point in modern history." [43]

5

On November 10, the eve of the signing of the armistice,
Colonel House cabled Wilson in reference to his approaching address to Congress: " You have a right to assume that
the two great features of the armistice are the defeat of
German military imperialism and the acceptance by the
Allied Powers of the kind of peace the world has longed
for." [44]

Wilson had, it appeared, attained the double purpose
which he had outlined at the moment when the United States
had entered the war. The defeat of Germany was an essential preparatory step to the creation of a new international order. In this way only could the " military
masters " of Germany be disposed of; their elimination must
precede the acceptance of a new Germany into the society
of nations that would be dedicated to the rights of peoples,
great or small, and the organization of the peace. Wilson
did not reach this conviction until the final declaration of
the unrestricted submarine warfare in January, 1917, but he
never thereafter wavered from it. As leader of the country

[43] Lippmann to House, November 7, 1918, *I.P.,* IV, 188-189.
[44] House to Wilson, November 10, 1918, *I.P.,* IV, 142.

at war, he furthered every step that facilitated the transformation of the country into an effective belligerent machine, held up the hands of the military and industrial experts, threw the whole weight of his influence into forcing effective coördination between American and Allied resources, marshalled the whole force of his denunciatory rhetoric in the attack upon German morale.

But it was the creative rather than the destructive, the pacific rather than the belligerent purpose of the war that really interested Wilson. The defeat of Germany would be worse than waste effort if it did not lead to a new and better international system, one that would guarantee justice to the small nations and peace to all. To this creative purpose Wilson committed the United States. It was a committal of a much higher degree of importance than the decision to embark upon the war against Germany, since it involved not merely a single temporary effort but a complete break with American tradition and entrance upon revolutionary paths.

To the furtherance of this revolutionary policy President Wilson was brought by gradual steps and in the process his own development was dictated largely by adventitious circumstances. It was not first evolved in his own brain as the result of logical reasoning, but was forced upon him by events. Contrary to the probabilities of historical tradition and to his own original expectations, the nation was brought to intervene actively in a war which he at first believed to be none of our business; it was brought further to the advocacy of a world policy totally new to American ideas, and to participation in a world revolution. Wilson did not dictate circumstances, but was governed by them. As we survey these four years there is something reminiscent of a Greek tragedy in the obvious omnipotence of Fate.

At the beginning of the war the President was a determined isolationist. He believed that the war did not touch us in its origins and need not touch us in its course or conclusion. He was convinced that the United States must maintain a rigid neutrality and must at all cost avoid being caught in the European madness. The peace of America should be the ultimate and sacred purpose of American policy.

But from this position he was forcibly driven by the events of the war. It proved to him that the peace of America was not an independent abstraction but a state of affairs dependent upon conditions active outside of America. Belligerent Europe would not permit us to maintain an isolated neutrality. Our rights and interests were violently attacked by the one side and the other, by the commercial regulations enforced through Allied mastery of the seas, and by the German submarines that sank merchant vessels without warning. Hence Wilson's plans of an American mediation that might end the war, which, as Count von Bernstorff perceived and still asserts, offered the only alternative to American participation in the war. For if the war continued, sooner or later the submarine would force us in.

American plans of mediation, although they failed of their immediate purpose, were of the first importance in the evolution of Wilson's ultimate policy. As he studied the essentials of a peace settlement, he came to accept Grey's thesis that only through an organization of the states of the world with guaranteed protection for the smaller nations, could compensation be found for the waste of the war; he further accepted Grey's corollary that only with the full participation of the United States could that organization be made permanent. The idea became for him the major war aim of the United States. To its fulfillment all the details of the peace must be made contributory. It ran through all his speeches from May 27, 1916, January 22, 1917, the speech of the Fourteen Points, down to the Metropolitan Opera House speech of September 27, 1918.

This idea, revolutionary for Europe and even more so for America, was accepted by the people of the United States. Surprising though the fact may seem to the historian, in view of the election of 1920 and the events of the succeeding decade, it is attested clearly by almost universal newspaper comment from the time of the speech of the Fourteen Points until the end of the war. The idea was hailed by liberals and working classes in Europe as the doctrine of salvation. It was accepted by the defeated Central Powers as the condition of surrender. Finally the diplomatic skill of Colonel House brought even the official Governments of Great Britain, France, and Italy to approve it. All that was necessary was for the Peace Conference to translate the principle into the actual terms of the peace settlement.

6

As so often happens in the construction of a play, the last act of the Wilsonian drama proved an anticlimax. Thousands of pages have been written to explain it. Delays in calling the Peace Conference, due to the exigencies of democracy, gave to the forces of reaction an opportunity of redressing their strength. Wilson's insistence upon conducting the negotiations in person weakened his prestige and finally led to the whittling down of his own purpose by his own hand.[45] Even so, the Peace Conference achieved the great dream of the President by the creation of the League of Nations in the form he had conceived it. The real tragedy came only when, overwhelmed by illness and

---

[45] Comment by Colonel House, May 3, 1933: " You fail to emphasize the mistake President Wilson made in going to Europe in person and sitting in the Peace Conference. Just what caused him to do this I never knew, since I was not in Washington but in Paris representing the United States in the making of the Armistice.

" I do not believe he realized his commanding position. He was the *God on the Mountain,* and his decisions regarding international matters were practically final. When he came to Europe and sat in conference with the Prime Ministers and representatives of other states, he gradually lost his place as first citizen of the world.

" His decision to go to Paris showed modesty on his part, for had he realized the pedestal he was on he would never have consented to place himself, more or less, on a level with the other delegates at the Peace Conference.

" Had he not suffered his stroke, I believe he would have accepted the Senate reservations to the Treaty and the United States would have entered the League of Nations with practically the entire Nation approving. The whole question was later thrown into the political arena by his Jackson Day letter, with the result we know.

" I wish again to express my admiration for Woodrow Wilson as a statesman and patriot, and to reiterate my belief that had his program gone through as planned the disastrous crisis we are now experiencing might not have occurred. Unhappily he was stricken at a time when he needed all his powers most, and he developed many of the unyielding vagaries of a sick man. Even then, in my opinion, he was right and his opponents wrong, but they had the strength to crush him and they used it mercilessly to the ultimate undoing of our international well being."

partisan conflict, Wilson saw his League rejected by the Senate of the United States. Less than a year previous, complete success had seemed to be in his grasp.

Whatever the apparent failure, Wilson's greatness remains. It lies not in the control of circumstances, for he was the plaything of events, but in the attempt to mould evil circumstances so as to bring forth good. He set himself to maintain the neutrality of the United States, and he failed. Using war as a means to establish permanent peace, he fought for a new international order. Again he failed, at least for the moment. Perhaps the story is not yet told. Historians of the future may yet cite Wilson as the classic example of Browning's thesis of success through failure. Whatever the future may bring forth he waked the world to a great vision.

BIBLIOGRAPHICAL NOTE

American foreign policy during the war, so far as the larger issues were concerned, rested in the complete control of President Wilson. Several of the more important negotiations were conducted through agencies other than the Department of State, and there is hardly a hint of them in the published state papers. His policy was essentially a personal one, although, as he believed, directly responsive to popular will. For my interpretation of that policy I have, therefore, relied chiefly upon the numerous letters which he wrote to his intimate friend and adviser, Colonel House, and which are now deposited in the Edward M. House Collection in the Sterling Memorial Library of Yale University. The President's literary executors have not permitted the publication of this voluminous and frank correspondence, but it may be examined by qualified students. Almost all of these letters were written by the President himself on his own typewriter, without the intermediary of a secretary and without any carbon copy being taken. They are fresh, frequently hurried, uncorrected. " I am rushing this through on my typewriter (and through my mind too, for that matter)," he writes, " and may not have expressed my conclusions very happily, but I am in no doubt as to their substance." Such letters reveal far better than studied state papers the process by which Wilson's ideas developed.

Hardly of less importance are the letters which House received from Grey, Balfour, Northcliffe, Reading, Bernstorff, and the American ambassadors in European capitals. These letters, very frank because very personal, were passed on to the President and are valuable not merely as giving a record of the diplomatic situation abroad but as an indication of the picture of Europe seen by Wilson in the White House. Many of these letters and portions of the diary of Colonel House, already printed in my edition of *The Intimate Papers of Colonel House,* are reprinted by special permission of and arrangement with Houghton Mifflin Company, authorized publishers.

Of published documentary sources the most important is the collection of papers relating to American foreign affairs issued by the Department of State in the World War supplements. The volumes cover the period from the outbreak of war until the signing of the armistice. Although they throw little light on some of the more intimate negotiations, they form the main stuff of the material which the student of American diplomatic history in this period must use. They are supplemented, in the study of particular episodes, by the documents published by the German Reichstag investigating committee, which have been made available in convenient editions by the Carnegie Endowment for International Peace. The correspondence of Ambassador von Bernstorff with Berlin and that exchanged between the military and civil chiefs of the German Government previous to the armistice, thus put at our disposal, are essential to an understanding of American intervention in 1917 and of the German surrender to Wilson's Fourteen Points in 1918.

Personal letters, diaries, and memoirs have been published in abundance and are often of the utmost value in the interpretation of official papers. In many biographies primary materials of this kind are to be found, and such works have been classified accordingly. The amount of secondary material that bears directly or indirectly upon the subject is enormous. The list that follows has been severely restricted to those works that may be regarded as absolutely indispensable to the student of American war-time diplomacy. Whenever authoritative English translations are available they have been listed. Available American editions are cited.

SELECTED BIBLIOGRAPHY OF PRINTED MATERIAL

I. OFFICIAL DOCUMENTS

Baker, Ray Stannard, *and* Dodd, William Edward, *eds*. *The Public Papers of Woodrow Wilson*. New York: Harper, 1925-1927. 6 v.

Brest-Litovsk. *Proceedings of the Brest-Litovsk Peace Conference. The Peace Negotiations between Russia and the Central Powers, 21 November, 1917–3 March, 1918*. Washington: Government Printing Office, 1918.

Carnegie Endowment for International Peace, Division of International Law.
  Official German Documents relating to the World War. New York: Oxford University Press, 1923. 2 v.
  Official Statements of War Aims and Peace Proposals, December 1916 to November 1919. Edited by James Brown Scott. Washington: The Endowment, 1921.
  Preliminary History of the Armistice. Official Documents published by the German National Chancellery by order of the Ministry of State. Edited by James Brown Scott. New York: Oxford University Press, 1925.

Foreign Policy Association. *Russian-American Relations, 1917-1920; Documents and Papers*. Edited by C. K. Cumming and Walter W. Pettit. New York: Harcourt, 1920.

Mermeix, *pseud*. (Gabriel Terrail). *Les Négociations Secrètes et les Quatres Armistices*. Paris: Ollendorff, 1919.

Die Ursachen des Deutschen Zusammenbruchs im Jahre 1918. [Das Werk des Untersuchungsausschusses der Deutschen Verfassunggebenden Nationalversammlung und des Deutschen Reichstages 1919-1926. Vierte Reihe. Dritter Band.] Berlin: Deutsche Verlagsgesellschaft für Politik und Geschichte, 1925.

U. S. Department of State.

European War no. 3: Diplomatic correspondence with belligerent governments relating to neutral rights and duties. Washington: Government Printing Office, 1916.

Papers relating to the foreign relations of the United States. Supplements. *The World War: 1914, 1915, 1916, 1917, 1918. Russia: 1918.* Edited by Tyler Dennett and Joseph V. Fuller. Washington: Government Printing Office, 1928-1933. 12 v.

II. LETTERS, DIARIES, MEMOIRS

Bernstorff, *Count* Johann Heinrich, *My Three Years in America.* New York: Scribner, 1920.

Bethmann-Hollweg, Theobald von, *Reflections on the World War.* Translated by George Young. London: Butterworth, 1920.

Bliss, Tasker H.,
" The Unified Command," in *Foreign Affairs,* December, 1922, I, 1-30.
" The Armistices," in *The American Journal of International Law,* October, 1922, XVI, 509-522.

Bryan, William Jennings, *and* Bryan, Mary Baird, *The Memoirs of William Jennings Bryan.* Philadelphia: Winston, 1925.

Churchill, Winston Spencer, *The World Crisis, 1911-18.* New York: Scribner, 1923-1927. 4 v.

Clemenceau, Georges, *Grandeur and Misery of Victory.* Translated by F. M. Atkinson. New York: Harcourt, 1930.

Conwell-Evans, Thomas P., *Foreign Policy from a Back Bench 1904-1908.* London: Oxford University Press, 1932.

Czernin, *Count* Ottokar, *In the World War.* New York: Harper, 1920.

Dumba, Constantin, *Memoirs of a Diplomat.* Translated by Ian F. D. Morrow. Boston: Little, Brown, 1932.

Erzberger, Matthias, *Erlebnisse im Weltkrieg.* Stuttgart and Berlin: Deutsche Verlags-Anstalt, 1920.

Falkenhayn, Erich Georg Anton Sebastian von, *The German General Staff and its Decisions. 1914-1918.* New York: Dodd, 1920.

Foch, Ferdinand, *Memoirs.* Translated by Col. T. Bentley Mott. New York: Doubleday, Doran, 1931.

Gerard, James Watson, *My Four Years in Germany.* New York: Doran, 1917.

Grey, Edward Grey, *1st Viscount* of Fallodon, *Twenty-Five Years, 1892-1916.* New York: Stokes, 1925. 2 v.

Gwynn, Stephen, *ed., The Letters and Friendships of Sir Cecil Spring Rice.* Boston: Houghton Mifflin, 1929. 2 v.

Helfferich, Karl, *Der Weltkrieg.* Berlin: Ullstein, 1919.

Hindenburg, *Marshal* Paul von, *Out of My Life.* Translated by F. A. Holt. London: Cassell, 1920. (New York edition, Harper, 1921. 2 v.)

Houston, David Franklin, *Eight Years with Wilson's Cabinet, 1913-1920.* New York: Doubleday, Page, 1926. 2 v.

Jusserand, Jean Jules, *Le Sentiment Américain pendant la Guerre.* Paris: Payot, 1931.

Lloyd George, David, *War Memoirs of David Lloyd George. 1914-1915, 1915-1916.* Boston: Little, Brown, 1933. 2 v.

Ludendorff, Erich,
   The General Staff and Its Problems. Translated by Frederic Appleby Holt. London: Hutchinson, 1920. 2 v.
   Ludendorff's Own Story, August 1914–November 1918. New York: Harper, 1920. 2 v.

Maximilian, *Prince of Baden, Memoirs.* Translated by W. M. Calder and C. W. H. Sutton. New York: Scribner, 1928. 2 v.

Mordacq, Jean Jules Henri, *Le Ministère Clemenceau.* Paris: Plon, 1930-1931. 4 v.

Nicolson, Harold, *Peacemaking 1919.* Boston: Houghton Mifflin, 1933.

Painlevé, Paul, *Comment j'ai nommé Foch et Pétain.* Paris: Alcan, 1923.

Payer, Friedrich, *Von Bethmann-Hollweg bis Ebert: Erinnerungen und Bilder.* Frankfurt am Main: Frankfurter Societäts-Druckerei, 1923.

27

Poincaré, Raymond, *Au service de la France*. Paris: Plon, 1930-1932. Vols. VI-IX.

Redfield, William C., *With Congress and Cabinet*. New York: Doubleday, Page, 1924.

Scheidemann, Philipp, *Der Zusammenbruch*. Berlin: Verlag für Sozialwissenschaft, 1921.

Steed, Henry Wickham, *Through Thirty Years*. New York: Doubleday, Page, 1924. 2 v.

Tardieu, André,
  France and America. Boston: Houghton Mifflin, 1927.
  The Truth About the Treaty. Indianapolis: Bobbs-Merrill, 1921.

Tirpitz, *Grand-Admiral* Alfred von, *My Memoirs*. London: Hurst and Blackett, 1919. 2 v.

Tumulty, Joseph P., *Woodrow Wilson as I know him*. New York: Doubleday, Page, 1921.

Wilhelm II, *The Kaiser's Memoirs, 1888-1918*. New York: Harper, 1922.

III. BIOGRAPHIES, HISTORIES, SPECIAL STUDIES, ARTICLES

Baker, Ray Stannard, *Woodrow Wilson and World Settlement*. New York: Doubleday, Page, 1922. 3 v.

Baruch, Bernard, *The Making of the Reparation and Economic Sections of the Treaty*. New York: Harper, 1920.

Bemis, Samuel Flagg, ed., *The American Secretaries of State and their Diplomacy*, vol. X: *William Jennings Bryan*, anonymous; *Robert Lansing*, by Julius W. Pratt. New York: Knopf, 1929.

Bishop, Joseph Bucklin, *Theodore Roosevelt and his Time*. New York: Scribner, 1920. 2 v.

Bolling, John Randolph, *and* Pennington, Mary V., *Chronology of Woodrow Wilson*. New York: Stokes, 1927.

Bourget, Jean Marie, *Gouvernement et Commandement*. Paris: Payot, 1930.

Brooks, Sydney, "America at the Cross-Roads," in *The English Review*, June, 1915, XX, 356-366.

Buchan, John, *A History of the Great War*. New York: Nelson, 1921-1922. 4 v.

Callwell, Sir Charles Edward, *Field Marshal Sir Henry Wilson.* New York· Scribner, 1927. 2 v.

Consett, Montagu William Warcop Peter, *and* Daniel, Octavius Harold, *The Triumph of Unarmed Forces, 1914-1918.* New York: Brentano, 1923.

Dickinson, Goldsworthy Lowes, *The Choice before Us.* London: Allen and Unwin, 1917.

Garner, James Wilford, *International Law and the World War.* New York: Longmans, Green, 1920. 2 v.

" The Genesis of the Fourteen Commandments," in *The North American Review,* February, 1919, CCIX, 145-152.

Guichard, Louis, *The Naval Blockade 1914-1918.* Translated and edited by Christopher R. Turner. London: Philip Allan, 1930.

Hendrick, Burton J., *Life and Letters of Walter H. Page.* New York: Doubleday, Page, 1922, 1925. 3 v.

House, Edward M., " The Freedom of the Seas," in *The Contemporary Review,* April, 1928, CXXXIII, 416-421.

Kenworthy, Joseph Montague, *and* Young, George, *Freedom of the Seas.* New York: Liveright, 1929.

Keynes, John Maynard, *The Economic Consequences of the Peace.* New York: Harcourt, 1920.

Laurens, Adolphe, *Histoire de la Guerre Sous-Marine Allemande.* Paris: Société d'Éditions Géographiques, 1930.

Lawrence, David, *The True Story of Woodrow Wilson.* New York: Doran, 1924.

Michelsen, Andreas Heinrich, *Der U-Bootskrieg.* Leipzig: Koehler, 1925.

Nevins, Allan, *Henry White.* New York: Harper, 1930.

Nowak, Karl Friedrich, *The Collapse of Central Europe.* New York: Dutton, 1924.

Parmelee, Maurice, *Blockade and Sea Power.* New York: Crowell, 1924.

Pratt, Julius W., " The British Blockade and American Precedent," in *United States Naval Institute Proceedings,* XLVI, 1789-1802.

Roosevelt, Theodore, " The World War: Its Tragedies and Its Lessons," in *The Outlook,* New York, September 23, 1914, CVIII, 169-178.

Salter, Sir Arthur, *Allied Shipping Control: An Experiment in International Administration.* Oxford: Clarendon Press, 1921.

Seymour, Charles,
  The Intimate Papers of Colonel House. Boston: Houghton
    Mifflin, 1926, 1928. 4 v.
  Woodrow Wilson and the World War. New Haven: Yale Uni-
    versity Press, 1921.
Spender, John Alfred, *and* Asquith, Cyril, *Life of Herbert Henry
    Asquith, Lord Oxford and Asquith.* London: Hutchinson,
    1932. 2 v.
Temperley, Harold William Vazielle, *ed., A History of the Peace
    Conference of Paris.* London: Frowde, 1920-1924. 6 v.
Thimme, Hans, *Weltkrieg ohne Waffen.* Stuttgart: J. G. Gotta'sche
    Buchhandlung Nachfolger, 1932.
Valentin, Veit, *Deutschlands Aussenpolitik von Bismarcks Abgang
    big zum Ende des Weltkrieges.* Berlin: Deutsche Verlagsgesell-
    schaft für Politik und Geschichte, 1921.

INDEX

Ackerman, Carl W., reports on conditions in Germany, 292.

Algeciras Conference, 1906, American influence at, 2.

Algonquin, submarine attack upon, 206.

Alsace-Lorraine, included in Point VIII of Fourteen Points, 286; evacuation of, provided in armistice proposals, 333, 334.

American War Mission, 230-244.

Ancona, submarine attack upon, 107.

Arabic, sinking of, by submarine, 14, 70, 100-105, 106.

Archibald, J. F., newspaper correspondent, arrest of by British, 107.

Armed merchantmen negotiations, 111-116, 118.

Armistice:
  Austrian, 341-342, 362.
  German: Drafting of, 341, 342; military terms, 345-348, 351; naval terms, 343, 344, 348-352; proposed Italian reservation, 380, 389, 391, 392; reparations clause, 352-354, 390; reservation on Freedom of the Seas and restoration of invaded territory, 378, 379, 393; signing of, 364.
  Turkish, 341, 342.

Article X, League of Nations, origin, 258.

Asquith, H. H., British Prime Minister, on Allied blockade, 28, 40; discusses American mediation, 150; resignation, 187.

Balfour, Arthur J., British First Lord of the Admiralty, later Secretary of State for Foreign Affairs, on armed merchantmen, 112; discusses American mediation, 150;

mission of 1917 to United States, 217-219; on Allied financial danger, 221; on Treaty of London, 267; at armistice conferences, 340, 343, 373, 374, 377.

Beer, G. L., historian, suggests mandates plan, 373n.

Beneš, Eduard, Czecho-Slovak Minister for Foreign Affairs, at armistice conferences, 361.

Benson, Admiral W. S., member of American War Mission, 233; at armistice conferences, 331, 337, 339; advocates destruction of German navy, 350.

Berlin, German mine-sower, 36.

Bernstorff, Count Johann von, German Ambassador to the United States, on Allied blockade, 70, 180-181; House's attitude toward, 121; on submarine warfare, 83, 94-95, 98, 99, 101-103, 105, 114, 116, 120-124, 127, 181, 185n., 193, 198; on United States mediation, 127-128, 132, 144, 184n., 185n., 193, 397; on United States neutrality, 9, 11, 13, 193; on Wilson's attitude toward Germany, 209.

Bethmann-Hollweg, Theodor von, German Chancellor, on peace terms, 146; approves German submarine warfare, 197; resigns, 274.

Blacklisting, 44, 76.

Bliss, General Tasker H., member of American War Mission, 233; on unified military command and Supreme War Council, 245-246; military adviser to Supreme War Council, 249; at armistice conferences, 327, 328-329, 331, 335-337, 362.

409

ALBERT SHAW LECTURES ON
DIPLOMATIC HISTORY